THE
GENEALOGIST'S
computer
▪ COMPANION ▪

RHONDA R. McCLURE

BETTERWAY BOOKS
CINCINNATI, OHIO

www.familytreemagazine.com

About the Author

Rhonda R. McClure has been involved in online genealogy for more than thirteen years. She has written more than two hundred genealogical columns, including a five-day-a-week e-mail newsletter, Family Tree Finders. She is author of a number of other books, including the award-winning *Complete Idiot's Guide to Online Genealogy*. She is a nationally known speaker on family history research methodology and computer genealogy.

The Genealogist's Computer Companion. © 2002 by Rhonda R. McClure. Manufactured in the United States of America. All rights reserved. No part of this book may be reproduced in any form or by any electronic or mechanical means including information storage and retrieval systems without permission in writing from the publisher, except by a reviewer, who may quote brief passages in a review. Published by Writer's Digest Books, an imprint of F&W Publications, Inc., 1507 Dana Avenue, Cincinnati, Ohio 45207. (800) 289-0963. First edition.

Other fine Betterway books are available from your local bookstore or on our Web site at www.familytreemagazine.com. To subscribe to Family Tree Magazine Update, a free e-mail newsletter with helpful tips and resources for genealogists, go to http://newsletters.fwpublications.com.

06   05   04   03   02   5   4   3   2   1

Library of Congress Cataloging-in-Publication Data

McClure, Rhonda R.
   The genealogist's computer companion / Rhonda R. McClure.—1st ed.
      p.   cm.
   Includes index.
   ISBN 1-55870-591-0 (alk. paper)
   1. Genealogy—Computer network resources—Handbooks, manuals, etc. 2. Genealogy—Databases—Handbooks, manuals, etc. I. Title.

CS14.M345   2001
929'.2'0285—dc21   2001043535
                                                                         CIP

Editor: Sharon DeBartolo Carmack, CG
Production editor: Brad Crawford
Production coordinator: Emily Gross
Cover designer: Andrea Short
Interior designer: Sandy Conopeotis Kent
A portion of the cover collage contains an image by John Still © Photonica

For Rhody, a fellow computer genealogy enthusiast and partner in crime

Acknowledgments

A book is never the work of a single individual. From conception to finished product, many hands and heads, some far less emotionally involved than the author, help to ensure the best work possible. To that end, there are some people I owe much thanks.

First, Myra Vanderpool Gormley, my mentor and my friend. She has guided me in writing and been there whenever I needed her, just a phone call or e-mail away. I am sure the telephone company appreciates our constant phone calls.

Second, Sharon DeBartolo Carmack. She is not just my editor. With her thoughtful guidance and comments, I have grown as a writer and as a genealogist. She has been there from the beginning to answer any questions and calm my butterflies. Her friendship has been the icing on the cake and the part of our relationship I hold most dear.

Above all, Amy Johnson Crow, my friend, who dropped everything when I needed help. She read the manuscript. She contributed insightful comments, and she shared some of her knowledge, which she allowed me to include in the book. She kept me sane when I thought that was an impossible task. She is a diamond, and I look forward to watching as others discover her many talents.

Finally, to my husband, Michael, for his unwavering support as I tackle each new project. To my children, Marie, Ben, Elizabeth, and Jessica, who give me hugs when I need them, even when I don't realize I need them. Without their love, I couldn't do any of this.

Abbreviations Used in This Book

AGBI   *American Genealogical-Biographical Index*
CG   Certified Genealogist
FHL   Family History Library
FHLC   Family History Library Catalog
IGI   *International Genealogical Index*
PERSI *Periodical Source Index*

Icons Used in This Book

 Case Study
Examples of this book's advice at work

 Citing Sources
Reminders and methods for documenting information

$\di'fin\ vb$ **Definitions**
Terminology and jargon explained

 For More Info
Where to turn for more in-depth coverage

 Idea Generator
Techniques and prods for further thinking

 Important
Information and tips you can't overlook

 Internet Source
Where on the Web to find what you need

 Library/Archive Source
Repositories that might have the information you need

 Notes
Thoughts, ideas, and related insights

 Printed Source
Directories, books, pamphlets, and other paper archives

 Reminder
"Don't-Forget" items to keep in mind

 Research Tip
Ways to make research more efficient

 Step By Step
Walkthroughs of important procedures

 Supplies
Advice on day-to-day office tools

 Timesaver
Shaving minutes and hours off the clock

 Tip
Ways to make research more efficient

 Warning
Stop before you make a mistake

Table of Contents
At a Glance

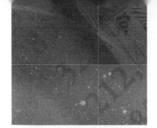

Table of Contents

road when it comes to research. Just because no more information can be found online does not mean no further information exists. Enter the world of books and microfilm, and see what is waiting for you at various repositories.

ONE

Computers and Genealogy: Where We've Been

G enealogical research is a paper generator by nature. Visit any genealogist's house, and you will discover that he or she has piles of paper, bulging file cabinets and binders full of family group sheets and pedigree charts. Genealogists have been known to twitch when they get close to other researchers' papers. The problem with all those papers is that genealogists often spend more time pushing through the papers or duplicating them in one form or another than they do researching.

Of course, in the past no one complained. That was just the way things were. Many genealogists were thrilled simply to have preformatted family group sheets and pedigree charts. In fact, some of the research I have inherited includes hand-drawn charts of all sizes.

NO MORE DUPLICATION

The first thing that computers did for genealogists was to make duplicating information easier. In all those papers, there were family group sheets. Each family group sheet records the information on a family unit. This includes the father, mother, and individual children. The duplication comes when one of those children has children. You then have to record the same information for that child as a parent on a new form.

Genealogists swear by basic information on the family group sheets and pedigree charts. This information consists of

- name of the individual (maiden name for all females)
- date of birth or christening
- place of birth or christening
- date of marriage
- place of marriage
- date of death
- place of death

Notes

Family Group Sheet

Husband's Full Name ROBERT McCLAIN   **Chart No.**

Husband's Data	Day Month Year	City, Town or Place	County or Province, etc.	State or Country	Add. Info. on Husband
Birth	14 DEC 1780			PENNSYLVANIA	
Chr'nd					
Marr.	abt 1813				
Death	1864		ORANGE CO.	INDIANA	
Burial					

Places of Residence

Occupation   Church Affiliation   Military Rec.

Other wives, if any No. (1) (2) etc.
Make separate sheet for each marr.

His Father   DANIEL McCLAIN   Mother's Maiden Name   NANCY

Wife's Full Maiden Name ELIZABETH VAN ZANT

Wife's Data	Day Month Year	City, Town or Place	County or Province, etc.	State or Country	Add. Info. on Wife
Birth	abt 1796			KENTUCKY	
Chr'nd					
Death					
Burial					

Places of Residence

Occupation   Church Affiliation   Military Rec.

Other husbands, if any No. (1) (2) etc.
Make separate sheet for each marr.

Her Father   Mother's Maiden Name

Form A100, Family Group Sheet by The Everton Publishers, P.O. Box 368, Logan, UT 84321. Publishers of The Genealogical Helper. Send for a free catalogue with list and full descriptions of many genealogical aids.

Sex	Children's Names in Full (Arrange in order of birth)	Children's Data	Day Month Year	City, Town or Place	County or Province, etc.	State or Country	Add. info. on Children
M	1 WILLIAM McCLAIN	Birth	1814			KENTUCKY	
		Marr.	10 MAR 1834		ORANGE CO.	INDIANA	
	Full Name of Spouse	Death	1 SEP 1870		ORANGE CO.	INDIANA	
	MARTHA IRVINE	Burial					
M	2 JOHN McCLAIN	Birth	1818			INDIANA	
		Marr.	bef 1845				
	Full Name of Spouse	Death					
	CHARLOTTE J.	Burial					
F	3 JANE McCLAIN	Birth	18 JUL 1820		ORANGE CO.	INDIANA	
		Marr.	12 NOV 1840		ORANGE CO.	INDIANA	
	Full Name of Spouse	Death	14 FEB 1879	SULLIVAN	MOULTRIE CO.	ILLINOIS	
	JESSE LOCKE	Burial					
F	4 MARGARET McCLAIN	Birth	1825			INDIANA	
		Marr.	18 AUG 1848		ORANGE CO.	INDIANA	
	Full Name of Spouse	Death	27 JUL 1894		ORANGE CO.	INDIANA	
	WILLIAM G. BAKER	Burial					
F	5 ELIZA McCLAIN	Birth	1828			INDIANA	
		Marr.					
	Full Name of Spouse	Death					
		Burial					
F	6 EMILY McCLAIN	Birth	25 SEP 1830			INDIANA	
		Marr.	4 JAN 1849		ORANGE CO.	INDIANA	
	Full Name of Spouse	Death	8 JUN 1860		ORANGE CO.	INDIANA	
	WILLIAM CHISHAM	Burial					
F	7 SARAH ANN McCLAIN	Birth	abt 1833			INDIANA	
		Marr.	23 OCT 1851		ORANGE CO.	INDIANA	
	Full Name of Spouse	Death					
	WALTER MOODY	Burial					
M	8 ISAIAH McCLAIN	Birth	25 FEB 1839			INDIANA	
		Marr.					
	Full Name of Spouse	Death	17 NOV 1875		ORANGE CO.	INDIANA	
		Burial					

Compiler   Notes:

Address

City, State, Zip

Date

Husband's Full Name

Figure 1.1

In the past it was necessary to handwrite all of the forms, like this one from Everton Publishers (see http://www.everton.com), in recording our ancestry. To share with a cousin, we either photocopied these forms or filled out new ones.

- date of burial
- place of burial

You may be one of those lucky individuals whose ancestors all lived in a place with a short name. I was not so lucky. My maternal line loved places like Manchester, Hillsborough County, New Hampshire, and Haverhill, Essex County, Massachusetts. You can imagine how quickly those can become tedious to write.

Now multiply that by three. For each person on the pedigree chart, you will need to write out that place at least three times, and that assumes only one life event took place there. You must write it out on the pedigree chart, on the family group sheet where the individual is a child, and again on another family group sheet where the individual is a parent. That's a lot of writing, and that doesn't even count sharing your research with others and sending them copies of these forms.

When it came to researching my family tree, I can honestly say that, before computers, I spent more time writing on forms than I did doing almost anything else. I was quite a sight as I would troop into my public library to the genealogy department. There I was, with a large legal-size binder full of family group sheets and pedigree charts. Even then I wanted to take everything with me.

ENTER THE COMPUTER

About sixteen years ago, when I had been involved in genealogy for a couple of years, my husband happened to attend a computer conference. He had a personal computer long before they were cool. His ran off cassettes, which were much like audiotapes today. Now he was itching to get a new one. Personal computers were just becoming reasonably priced. As luck would have it, that happened to be the year that the Church of Jesus Christ of Latter-day Saints released Personal Ancestral File (PAF). I had seen information about the requirements for this new genealogy program and was putting the pressure on him too.

That was my foray into computers, and I suspect that as my husband looks back now, he may regret that choice. A few computers and a number of must-have gadgets later, I am still as obsessed as ever with my genealogy and computers. The most intriguing aspect of this whole computerized-genealogy movement was the possibility of recording information once and then reusing it. Instead of writing the information on three different forms, I now had to type it in only once. I could then tell the computer to print out a pedigree chart, a family group sheet with that person as a child, or another family group sheet with that individual as a parent. No more writer's cramp.

That's not to say this ended all my duplication. While I no longer had to write those long town names three times for each person, I did have to type them in each time. The earliest genealogy programs were pretty basic in what they could do and how they could do it. I would even venture that in some ways they weren't any faster: certainly not in the data entry phase. Come to think of it, at that point we weren't even calling it "data entry." Few of us were so high tech as to be spouting off such terms.

In looking back now, I confess that I had it easy. My husband, eager for any excuse to sit at this new marvel in our living room, willingly typed in names, dates, and places for me as I began the laborious task of transcribing all the research I had already accomplished. Of course, I was one of the lucky ones. I hadn't been researching for very long when these newfangled gadgets came out. I hadn't yet accumulated twenty years of research.

TECHNOLOGY IMPROVES

As I mentioned, the early genealogy programs were slow. They eliminated some of the duplication, but not all of it. I have already confessed to typing and retyping long place names as my ancestors continued to have life events in the same localities. That first version of PAF, while a big step forward, did have some major problems in the speed department. Fortunately for me, my husband, a computer programmer by profession, began to tinker with the program and managed to speed it up a little for me. This is not to say that I wasn't on the sidelines wringing my hands in dread that he was killing all my hard work.

As computer technology in general was improving, so too were the computers and software that genealogists were using. The first improvement we saw was the release of different programs, all coming from small businesses. Genealogy was still very much a closet operation, and this was more true of the programs than anything else. You see, some genealogists hadn't yet jumped on the computer genealogy wagon.

In addition to PAF, there were a few other programs; one of the best-known and well-liked programs was ROOTS, produced by COMMSOFT. Dubbed "the Cadillac of genealogy programs," it came with a sticker price to match. But it was one of the first programs to help eliminate the need to retype place names. It also offered more reports than just the standard pedigree chart and family group sheet.

For the first time, you could print out your genealogy in a narrative-style report that resembled those found in periodicals such as the *New England Historical and Genealogical Register* and the *National Genealogical Society Quarterly*. In fact, it was this ability that made me decide to save my pennies and purchase the ROOTS program. At the time it was the most expensive genealogy program available, retailing at about $295, but the benefits seemed to justify the cost.

Timesaver

GOING ONLINE

Genealogists soon found that they could contact fellow researchers without even leaving their houses. **Online communication began to build communities of genealogists that spanned the country instead of the town.** Evenings found the phones at the homes of genealogists busy for hours as they chatted online with fellow researchers and shared their latest finds.

WHAT IS A BULLETIN BOARD SERVICE?

While many researchers today know only of electronic bulletin boards, there was a time, back in the dark ages of the 1980s, when many genealogists didn't understand them. I have always likened them to a bulletin board found in the lobby of the public library. You could put up your "Boat for Sale" notice or your "Puppies to Good Home" flyer. Others would come along at their leisure to read these notices.

The difference with the electronic bulletin boards is that they generally had a focus, in this case genealogy. Also the message might take awhile to make it to your side of the country. Unlike the instant posting we see today on the Internet, these messages were relayed from one computer to another, generally in the late-evening or early-morning hours when calls were less expensive.

Like the corkboard in the public library, you could visit the bulletin board when it was convenient for you and read the messages. This assumes you were able to connect. These early bulletin boards were found on single personal computers, usually with one or two phone lines connected at the most.

Online communication at this time was slow. This was the mid 1980s, and everything was done in text. Those of us who were involved at this early stage got adept at creating pictures using the characters on the keyboard to enhance the text; some were better at it than others. Our efforts were geared to sharing the most information in the least number of lines of text.

At this time, there were "bulletin boards" that genealogists could dial up with their modems. Many of these bulletin boards were long-distance phone calls, and it was easy to get sticker shock when the phone bill came. Even though there were many bulletin boards around the country and eventually around the world, sometimes the closest bulletin board offering genealogy messages required a long-distance phone call. The bulletin boards worked on a sort of relay system. A message came into one bulletin board, and somewhere in the wee hours of the morning, when the phone charges were cheapest, the Sysop (systems operator) for that bulletin board would then call one of the other bulletin boards and pass along the messages. This process was repeated up and down the line as new messages posted to different bulletin boards were shared with all the others. This was FidoNet, a free online communication tool, and genealogy bulletin boards were popping up all over the place. Eventually they connected genealogists around the world.

About this time, large companies were beginning to rely more heavily on computers in their day-to-day operations. Companies such as General Electric offered communications networks to large companies with offices across the country so that they could communicate effectively. Once the day's work was done, these machines sat idle. General Electric discovered that it could sell this time to home computer users, thus making the machinery pay for itself around the clock. Commercial services, such as GEnie, were born.

The commercial services contracted with individuals who were knowledgeable in a variety of fields, such as genealogy, writing, photography, space exploration, and so on. These people were known as Sysops. It was their job to keep the area, sometimes known as a forum or roundtable, on the subject at hand as well as to grow their area by adding files that the customers could download, host chats where everyone could get together, and in general manage the area.

The benefit of these commercial services was that, unlike the bulletin boards, they offered local phone connections to many of their at-home customers. However, whereas the bulletin boards were free except for phone charges, the commercial services usually charged a monthly fee and sometimes an additional fee for using parts of the service. Some charged just a monthly fee; others charged by the hour. As more commercial services appeared, the competition to keep clients got stiffer, and prices generally fell. Genealogists flocked to these online services.

It was not yet possible to easily communicate with researchers on different services. For instance, if I used GEnie, I could not send a message to someone using CompuServe. As a result, many genealogists found themselves paying for more than one service. If they had to limit their spending to a single service, they shopped around and went with the one that supplied them with the items that were most important to them. For genealogists, this often meant choosing the commercial service that offered what they felt was the best genealogical area.

GENEALOGISTS UNITE

As genealogists began to settle on one or another of these services, they created online genealogical communities. Across the country, researchers conversed with each other on a regular basis. Instead of having to wait days or weeks for an answer to a letter mailed through the post office, you could get a response in a day or even quicker. Researchers volunteered to do lookups for those who were not in the area, and paybacks were often, although perhaps not reciprocal. I would look in my resources for an answer to your question, and then a week or so later you might be able to help someone with your resources.

Chat rooms would fill weekly with researchers sharing their trials and tribulations. In fact, I can still vividly remember my first night on such a chat room; it was actually my first night on a commercial service. I had just signed up, specifically to visit the genealogy area and join others in the chat room. However, this was a form of communication I had never seen before. It took a little getting used to. There were conversations flying back and forth among about thirty genealogists. At first it was hard to tell when someone was talking directly to me, but then I began to see the rhyme and reason in what had looked like pandemonium.

At first I would hesitate to type in my message and press the Return key for fear of interrupting another conversation. Eventually, though, I saw that there were always multiple conversations going and I could join as many or few as I chose.

I think that was when I learned to type fast. For an hour or sometimes more, I would sit glued to my computer, tying up the phone line, but getting the chance to talk with other genealogists. Like most other genealogists, I have a spouse who tolerates my search for the family tree. He will freely admit that he doesn't understand the fascination or how I do what I do, so it was wonderful to share with these people my thoughts and finds and get a response that was akin to the same excitement or frustration that I was feeling.

THE FACELESS MASSES

The one downside to communicating online was that you had no face to go with the individual you were sharing with. You could only imagine what they might look like. Once in a while, as I have met them over the years, I have been pretty close. More often than not, though, I have been totally off base.

As the National Genealogical Society's and Federation of Genealogical Societies's annual conferences rolled around, those of us who conversed online and were going to the conference made plans to meet face to face. I believe that participation in these online communities encouraged individuals who might not otherwise have gone to attend these conferences. Instead of going without knowing anyone, they had some friends. Granted they had no idea what these people looked like, but that was soon a nonissue.

The positive side to the faceless masses was the general lack of prejudice or preconceived notions by those sharing online. Conversations didn't touch on such things. About the only time you knew about someone's background was when they posted in one of the ethnic subject areas or pointed out that they were researching slaves or Native Americans.

Somehow that didn't color the way in which they were helped. The common bond among genealogists seemed to transcend any other barriers that might have taken precedence had they met first in person.

BACK TO THE PROGRAMS

While genealogists were spending more and more time tying up their phone lines and communicating with each other online, the developers of genealogy software were getting busy too. Genealogists were using their computers more, and they were beginning to voice their opinions about what they felt worked or didn't. They wanted a program that did more than just record information about their ancestors.

I already mentioned how ROOTS could print out narrative-style reports. Other genealogy programs began to offer such reports and more. Then as the computers began to run Windows, genealogy software developers found they could do even more.

As new programs were released and older ones were updated, big business began to take note. They saw that genealogists were many and spent money.

Over the last five years many changes have occurred in the genealogy software industry. Gone is the cottage industry with its friendly banter among competitors. Now big businesses invest in these programs. Developments and upgrades are kept under wraps until they are ready for release.

For the consumer this competition is a benefit. Remember, back in its heyday, the ROOTS program cost about three hundred dollars. Today, most genealogy programs are available for under one hundred dollars. In the past you had to know where to purchase these programs, primarily through mail order. Now you can find genealogy software on the shelves of computer stores and even in discount stores such as Wal-Mart and Target.

Because of this and the Internet, genealogists have been flocking together for some time now. In genealogy there is strength in numbers. You need to be able to share and converse with other researchers. Some people are brought into the hobby of genealogy simply because they saw the software on the shelf at the store and became intrigued.

ENTER THE INTERNET

Colleges and the military knew about the Internet long before those of us with home computers did. Of course, back then it wasn't the monster it has become. For many back before the 1990s, it was similar to the commercial services: text and commands. It certainly has come a long way.

We are now enthralled by what the Internet can do. We converse with people around the world in seconds. This instant access has made us an even more impatient group than we were before. I have even had some people get a little testy when I did not answer their e-mails immediately. I will always maintain that genealogists have never been a very patient people, but with e-mail and instantly available Web pages, we have become even more impatient.

Notes

The Internet is similar to the commercial services in that you have to connect to the service. However, the Internet differs from those commercial services because it makes the world available at your fingertips. Each commercial service was limited by the information available on that service. With the Internet, access to information is not limited by a user's Internet service provider or geographic location. With the click of a mouse, a U.S. resident can view pages that were designed and uploaded in Switzerland or Germany.

For genealogists this is nothing short of a miracle. While a lot of work still must be done through viewing microfilm or visiting courthouses or other repositories, being able to contact someone from another country and get guidance on foreign research is a dream come true.

THE ONLY WAY IS UP

I have always found it interesting that while genealogists look to the past to find their ancestors, their focus for tools that will help them accomplish this is on the future. Even those who did not grow up with computers have grabbed

HOW MY RESEARCH HAS CHANGED WITH COMPUTERS AND ONLINE RESEARCH

Things I probably never would have found without being online:

- Letters my great-grandparents wrote to my great-grandmother's Kentucky family in the 1880s and 1890s describing how great a speller and reader my grandfather was; the names of two of their children (and who they were named for) who died between 1883 and 1900 and for whom no family or civil records exist.

- The scanned image of the genealogy information from the 1800 Bible of my ancestors who married that year. It provides the names of the fathers of the bride and bridegroom and lists all their children and their spouses and their marriage dates.

- The dozens of delightful cousins with whom I've exchanged volumes of genealogical tidbits, treasures, and photographs on numerous ancestral lines.

- The Illinois federal land grant online that finally enabled me to find the missing links in the family tree for the couple who disappeared somewhere between Indiana and Missouri in the 1835 to 1850 time frame.

- The online Texas census and marriage records of a county in which I'd never thought to search. They solved a frustrating research problem.

- Photographs of the tombstones of ancestors in a locality I never had the opportunity to visit. I accessed them just a year before vandals destroyed the stones.

- The joy of e-mail and keeping in fast and frequent touch with colleagues, friends, and family who share my passion for genealogy.

—Myra Vanderpool Gormley, CG

the beast by the horns and tried to master at least the basics so they can come along for the ride.

And what a ride it has been and continues to be. Genealogy is more popular than ever, and the technology makes some of that research easier than ever. For instance, while most of us were thrilled to have access to microfilms of the census records, these records are now being made available online. Companies are digitizing these census pages, usually from the microfilm, and creating computer images that can be viewed online. They are even going one step further: they are enhancing those hard to read pages. This could mean a chance to find one of your lost families on a page that before was unreadable.

In the past professional genealogists saved for microfilm readers. If they were lucky or rich, they might have even purchased one that could make copies. Today companies offer machines that connect to your computer and allow you to create your own digitized image of a census record or other microfilm.

We truly live in marvelous times. Now let's look at how you can get the most out of all this technology.

TWO

Understanding Your Computer

I have lectured around the country on computerizing genealogy. Each time I mention that the genealogist is really in charge of the computer, attendees greet me with gales of laughter because for many that statement is the biggest untruth of them all. They find their computers to be nothing but a frustration. Some are sure that their computers laugh at them when they are not looking.

I confess that at one time I too considered the computer a little intimidating. It tended to beep in strange places, causing me to jump. This is a story that my fourteen-year-old son loves to bring up and laugh at. Nevertheless, I suspect that some others know what I was feeling and may still feel that way. What few people seem to think about while they stare, intimidated, at their computer as it beeps is that a learning process must take place.

I have heard all the excuses as to why that learning should not take place. I know that computers are in general a new technology. I know that many people did not grow up on them as my children have. I also know that many cannot program their VCR, so they think they should not have to understand their computer.

To all of these genealogists, I ask one question: Were you born knowing how to research your family history?

ALLOW ME TO PRESENT YOUR COMPUTER

When we began the task of researching our family trees, we did not mind that we had things to learn. We eagerly read books. We asked questions of fellow genealogists. Many of us have joined societies over the years to learn more about the places where our ancestors settled or passed through. Yet when dealing with the computer, some of us throw up our hands and offer excuses as to why we do not master it.

With that in mind, it's time to introduce you to your computer. This chapter

Tip

will familiarize you with the terms that may be hindering your progress with the computer. Remember, every hobby or interest has words that are significant to that hobby or interest. **Once you master the lingo, mastering the whole thing will be a lot easier.**

This chapter groups these terms into three areas:

- the computer
- the software
- the Internet

While all three of these are computer oriented, each has terms and issues unique to that aspect of the world of computers, and thus computer genealogy.

THE COMPUTER

When most of us think of the word *computer*, we think of the entire package. We do not think of all the parts that make up a computer, also known to some as their nightmare.

The computer is actually a compilation of electronics that, when in sync with each other, can help you in ways unimaginable with the research of your family tree. I am sure that you have figured out the magic words in that sentence—*in sync*. If the components of your computer do not work together, then you truly do have a nightmare. If you do not know what different parts make up the computer, then there is no way for you to begin to diagnose what might be wrong. To that end, this is a short list of some of the important components of your computer.

Your computer is made up of the monitor, the keyboard, a pointing device, and the main box that we often think of as the computer. In addition to these, you may have a printer, a scanner, or other peripherals. As you connect each new piece of equipment, you add to the list of what you must examine to make a diagnosis.

The computer box, or central processing unit, holds a number of circuit boards. Some items that attach to the computer may come with a board that must first be inserted in the computer. When those who are not comfortable with their computer purchase such a device, they usually arrange to have a professional insert the board.

The board into which these various smaller boards connect is known as the motherboard. The motherboard runs your computer much like a mother runs a household. When the mother is ill or away, the household doesn't seem to run as well. The same thing happens with the computer. If the motherboard is having problems, then the computer will not run well.

The motherboard also controls the processing speed of your computer. When you look at advertisements for computers, you will often see a number such as 600 MHz. *MHz* is the abbreviation for *megahertz*. The number of megahertz tells you how fast the computer will be. Generally, the higher the number, the faster the computer is supposed to run.

Another number that is important to your computer is the RAM, random-

GLOSSARY OF COMPUTER TERMS

byte: A byte is one character of information. A character is any keystroke, such as a space, letter, number, special character, etc.

CD-R drive: CD-Recordable. A type of disk drive that can record or write to a CD once using special software. The CD-ROM drive creates CD-ROMs and can read them as well. Many computers today offer such recordable CD-ROM drives. CD's created using this technology are usable on a standard CD player.

CD-ROM: A small disc (usually about 5" [13cm] in diameter) that is created much like albums were in the past. A master is made, and from this the compact discs (CDs) are created. The attachment of the *ROM* in the name indicates that the information on the disc can be accessed and copied, but it cannot be changed on the disc.

CD-RW: CD-Rewritable. With this technology you can record multiple times using a CD-RW drive. Similar to recording on a videotape or saving data to a floppy disk, you can save your information to a CD-RW disc, then write over it at a later date.

floppy disk: A magnetic disk that stores computer data. It got its name because if you were to wave a 5¼" (13cm) disk, it would flop back and forth. The 3½" (9cm) disks, developed later, are encased in hard plastic. These disks are portable, allowing you to save information and take it with you. Today you will mostly find 3½" (9cm) disks for sale; each one can hold 1.4 megabytes of information.

gigabyte: A gigabyte is equal to about 1.1 billion bytes. Yes, I said *billion*! The newest and fanciest computer systems are now being shipped with eight- and nine-gigabyte hard drives. And yes, it is easy to fill up a hard disk of this size.

hard disk: A magnetic disk that stores data. Differentiated from a floppy disk, a hard disk is designed to remain inside the computer; the disk is not easily removed and transported. Information is written to it through the various software programs loaded onto the computer. Hard disks offer much more storage capacity—in the gigabyte range—than floppy disks.

Jaz drive: A removable disk drive that uses a cartridge. Each cartridge can hold up to two gigabytes of information. This drive was developed by Iomega Corporation.

laser, ink-jet: Types of printers. The laser printer works like a copier, heating the paper to allow toner to adhere to the page. The ink-jet printer sprays heated ink onto the page.

megabyte: One megabyte is equal to about one million bytes. You may still find a few systems, such as notebooks, whose hard drive capacities are listed in megabytes. For example, the hard drive size may be listed as 850MB, meaning about 850 megabytes (million bytes).

continued

megahertz (MHz): This lets you know how fast your computer will run. The higher the number, the faster your computer is supposed to go.

modem: Acronym for **mo**dulator-**dem**odulator. The modem was designed to convert digital information from a computer into an analog (audio) wave and transmit it over a phone line. The modem then converted data returning to the computer from audio back to digital. While digital options now exist for online communication, the term *modem* for the transmission device remains.

monitor: The display screen that allows you to see the commands entered into the computer through pictures and text on the screen. As you view the display screen, you select these pictures to launch or close programs.

motherboard: The motherboard runs the entire computer, much as a mother is responsible for keeping her family and home going. The various peripherals attach to the motherboard. The central processing unit (CPU) chip installed on the motherboard governs its speed. Many current systems may have an Intel Pentium CPU installed.

mouse: This mouse is nothing to fear! It is a small device with a rolling ball inside that allows you to move the cursor you see on the screen. As you glide the mouse around on a hard surface, the computer translates this movement and changes the position of the cursor accordingly. (See also "trackball, track pad.")

RAM: Acronym for **r**andom-**a**ccess **m**emory. Your computer puts information into RAM for easier and quicker access. This area can be written and rewritten to many times during a single session on the computer. RAM is your computer's work space.

ROM: Acronym for **r**ead-**o**nly **m**emory. This type of memory stores basic operating system files. Current systems come with a standard 640 kilobytes (640K) of ROM. Data stored in this type of memory can only be read or copied; you cannot change it.

scanners: Scanners work along the concept of a copier, but instead of transferring the image to a piece of paper, the scanner displays the image on the monitor. The scanned image can be saved to disk. This allows you to import an image into a variety of programs and use one image in many different ways.

sound card: An expansion board—that is, a physical piece of the computer—that when inserted allows the computer to manipulate and put forth sound. These are so common that computers today are not sold without one.

tape backup: Copying to a tape all the information stored on your hard drive. This works like a tape recorder when you talk and the tape records. In this case, your computer "talks" and the tape records.

trackball, track pad: Alternatives to a mouse for moving the cursor and selecting items. With the trackball, the computer translates the motion of a ball within a cup to move the cursor on the screen. With a track pad, the computer translates your finger movement across a pad to move the cursor. Both require much less space than a conventional mouse.

video adapter: Inserted on the motherboard of a computer, a board that allows the computer to have display capabilities. These displays are then sent through the adapter to the monitor, allowing you to interface with the computer. This is a standard board that comes in all computers; however video adapters with enhanced graphic capabilities can be purchased separately.

Zip disk: A high-capacity floppy disk. The Zip disk and Zip drive were developed by Iomega Corporation. While a conventional floppy disk will hold about 1.4MB of data, each Zip disk will hold 100MB or 250MB of data.

access memory. A computer puts information in RAM for easier and quicker access. This area can be written and rewritten to many times during a single session on the computer. You could think of this as your computer's work space. Just as you have files and photocopies within easy reach, your computer does the same thing.

The final item you need to be aware of in the computer is the hard drive. When you install a program, it is placed on the hard drive. When you are working in your genealogy software program, the information you add, such as names or source citations, gets saved on your hard drive. Many people confuse RAM and the hard drive. If your computer gives you an error message that states you are out of memory, this refers to the RAM, not to the hard drive space you have left.

In addition to these hardware items, you may have a modem of some sort for your system. The modem allows you to dial out and connect to commercial services such as America Online (AOL) or CompuServe or access the Internet through an Internet Service Provider. Commercial services offer proprietary sections in addition to a way to connect to the Internet. Internet Service Providers exist solely as a means for connecting to the Internet. (More about the Internet is found later in this chapter.) In order to use the Internet, you must have a modem.

Modems come in many speeds and varieties. They may be internal—the modem fits inside your computer and a phone line is connected to your computer—or external.

An external modem is a box you connect to your computer. You then connect the phone lines to the box. When your computer connects either to a commercial service or Internet service provider, lights on the front of the modem begin to blink. These lights let you know if the modem is connected and if information is being passed back and forth between your computer and the Internet or the commercial service. These idiot lights, as I call them, do not actually tell me much, but I feel better when I see them flashing. Many people prefer external modems because of the "idiot lights." Internal modems do not have this feature. However, those who run Windows 95 or higher will see a small icon in the lower right corner tray of icons that looks like two monitors connected with a thread. This will tell you more about what is going on. If you double click on it, a window will open and display the number of bytes received, the number of bytes sent, and the connection speed. You can also move the cursor over this icon to have similar information displayed in a pop-up box.

While the modem is important when dealing with online issues, it seldom affects your choices when it comes to selecting software. It is important to keep in mind the speed of your computer, the capacity of your hard disk, and the amount of RAM. You will need to recall these numbers when selecting software.

CAN I REALLY RUN THIS?

When you purchase software, you need to keep some things in mind. Most of the information relates to the capabilities of your computer. We looked at the terms and numbers in the computer section because you will find them on each software package.

Important

When you shop for software, pay close attention to the minimum system requirements. The developers include these on the package to help consumers determine whether the program will run on their computers. I emphasize that these are the program's *minimum* system requirements. If you want the program to run amazingly fast, then your computer system needs to be a faster and better system than that described on the package.

Understand that most computer stores will not give refunds on software programs that have been opened. If you discover only after installing the software that your computer is not up to the challenge, you may be out of luck. That is why it is so important to be familiar with your computer and its speed, RAM, and disk space. Some software companies provide a money-back offer for software returned in the first thirty to ninety days.

Notes

When you are deciding on new software, pay close attention to all of the system requirements. **It may be helpful to first write down what your computer has.** In addition to the RAM and the speed of your computer, you may need to pay attention to the CD-ROM drive, the video board, and the sound card. Many of the newer software programs rely on movies and other animated files that may not run on older machines or system components.

You can find all of this information about your computer in Microsoft Windows by accessing the System icon found in the Control Panel. To get to the Control Panel, click on the Start button found in the lower-left corner of your screen. Move the cursor to Settings, and a submenu will appear. Click on Control Panel, and the Control Panel window will open. You may need to use the scroll bar at the right to see all the icons, which are usually arranged alphabetically. Look for and double click on the System icon. When the System window opens, you will see what your system is using. Here you can find the speed of the computer and the amount of RAM. To find out about your CD-ROM drive, video card, and audio card, you may need to look at the paperwork or manuals that came with your computer. If you had your system configured by a professional, you may want to call that person; he should have that information in his records.

FASTEN YOUR SEAT BELT

Now that you better understand your computer and the components it relies on most heavily to run your programs, it is time for a look at the Internet. You need to consider some required hardware and software when going online.

As mentioned earlier, a modem is necessary. Modems can be internal or external, and while you need to make that choice based on your own comfort in how you interact with your computer, the most important aspect of a modem is its speed.

If you are a relatively new computer user, you are likely to have no slower than a 56K modem. This number is the maximum transfer rate of bytes going back and forth. A byte is a character of information. The number of bytes that go back and forth through the modem is directly related to what is sent or received. For instance, a page with lots of text may take fewer bytes than one that has one sentence and three images. These images online cause people to need faster modems for accessing the Internet. Even if you access through a commercial service, you will still find that all the graphics and photographs take a while to download. If you use an older computer, you will find that accessing with a 14.4K modem is intolerable. Even 28.8K seems pretty slow.

In fact, in today's fast-paced world, there are faster modem connections available. One is the integrated services digital network (ISDN) modem. It requires some hardware from your phone company: a special phone line. An ISDN modem doesn't have to convert the digital data to noise, so you won't hear modem noises when an ISDN modem connects like you do with a 56K modem. The 56K modem works with your regular phone line.

Regular phone lines can only carry noise. After all, they were designed to transmit voices. So modems convert digital information from the computer into noise and send the noise over the phone line. If you have ever picked up a phone while a computer was online, you no doubt heard some strange static sounds emanating from the handset. That was the computer talking on the phone. ISDN connections don't make that noise, because the information remains in its digital format.

Another new option is digital subscriber line (DSL). This requires a special modem and remains connected all the time. You never actually dial to make a connection. A similar option that has become available is a cable modem. This uses the cable that comes into your house for cable TV to send your computer data. The difference here is that a cable modem shares cable with others in your neighborhood. If everyone logs on at the same time and is watching something like the Olympics, you could notice a slowdown because of all the traffic on that cable. However, when compared with analog modems—which change your data to an audible tone—a cable modem is still much faster.

Understand that you may never be completely satisfied with the access rates you get when going online. A friend of mine refers to this as the "greed for speed." I recall first going online back when there were no pictures; I am amazed at how much has changed. I am also the first to admit that I get a little frustrated when I try to access something online quickly and it does not display as quickly as I think it should.

SURFING THE WEB

In addition to the modem, you must have a way to connect to the Internet. This usually means signing up with an Internet service provider, or ISP. These companies make the Internet available to home computer users. They generally charge a monthly fee for providing a local phone number to dial and either a set number of hours a month or unlimited time on the Internet. Usually you also get an e-mail address through these providers.

Commercial services such as CompuServe and AOL also offer a gateway to the Internet, so if you are a member of these services you have access to the Internet. Gateway access is different from that provided through an ISP. The gateway is like a doorway; the more people trying to get through the slower the response, and this can be frustrating.

Important

Besides a way to access the Internet, you must also have software that will allow you to view the pages you find on the Internet. This software is known as a browser. The two most popular browsers are Microsoft Internet Explorer and Netscape Navigator. The browser converts the computer codes written by the Web page author into text and pictures. The codes determine the font and color of the text and the placement of the pictures.

Browser software is not a program that you usually purchase separately. You probably already have a browser on your system. Microsoft Internet Explorer has long come installed on computers that run the Microsoft Windows operating system. Your ISP may also send you its preferred browser software to install when you sign up with the provider.

Through your browser software you can click on links, the means to get from one Web page to another. You can also type in an address, known as a uniform resource locator (URL), that will take you directly to the front page

COUNTRY CODES	
Australia	au
Canada	ca
France	fr
Germany	de
Japan	jp
Mexico	mx
Russia	ru
Switzerland	ch
United Kingdom	uk
United States	us

UNDERSTANDING A URL

Web addresses or Uniform Resource Locators are the address that you use to find a Web site. Just as you must know an address of a store or office if you hope to drive to it, so too must you use the address of a Web site if you hope to arrive at the correct Web site.

Many people think URLs are confusing, but they do make some sense if you look at the separate pieces to the address. Just as an address on a letter has a name, a street address, a city, a state and a zip code, the URL has parts that when put together make up the address to take you to the Web site you want.

The address <http://www.rootsweb.com/~websites/index.html> is separated as follows:

http: This stands for *hypertext transfer protocol*. This is the part of the address that tells you that the file (in this case a Web page) is found on the World Wide Web. It helps your browser differentiate this from a file that can be downloaded (such a URL would begin with ftp://).

www: While this does stand for World Wide Web, not all URLs will include this in the address. This is the conventional part of the address, but it does not indicate that this page is indeed a Web page.

rootsweb.com: This is the domain name. This is the part of the address that lets you know who owns the site. Usually it relates to the company or individual that owns the domain.

~websites/index.html: This is the path to the specific file on that Web site that you want to view. This is telling your browser to look in the Web sites folder for a file named index.html.

Files on Web sites will usually end in either html or htm. The only difference is that some operating systems (you remember—Windows is an operating system) can't handle an extension beyond the period of more than three characters.

of a Web site. Some examples of URLs are <http://www.rootsweb.com>, the RootsWeb site address, and <http://www.familysearch.org>, the address of the FamilySearch Web site.

RootsWeb and FamilySearch are Web sites. A Web site is made up of different Web pages, some of which have links you can click on to take you to a Web page on a different Web site, even one from a different country.

Web sites often consist of many different Web pages. A good Web site will show you an easy-to-read front page once you access the site via its URL. This front page, or home page, will have links to the site's more detailed and involved pages.

To surf the Web, simply click on a link shown on a Web page. The browser will display the link in a different color than the rest of the text, with an underline or both. When you move the cursor over a link, the cursor will change from the regular pointer, generally an arrow, to a pointing hand. This lets you

---

I SELDOM SEE THE UNITED STATES
COUNTRY CODE IN A URL—WHY?

You will seldom see the .us code included in URLs for sites that originate in the United States. This stems from the history of the Internet. In its infancy, the Internet was a method for those working in military establishments and educational facilities to communicate with those working at similar places across the United States. The Internet was reserved for those in these specialized services. At this time, the extensions .mil (military organizations) and .edu (educational institutions) were the main extensions found in domain names. Soon after though the government would also have access, and its extension would be .gov (governmental organizations). It would be some time before the .com (commercial organizations), .net (network organizations) and .org (organizations—such as non-profit groups) extensions we use most frequently would make an appearance.

Because of this early history in the United States, it is the one country that does not have to include a country code in the URL. Therefore, using our examples, you can tell that both <http://www.rootsweb.com> and <http://www.family search.org> originate in the United States.

---

know that you are pointing to a link. Clicking on the link will take you to another Web page or a different Web site.

Sometimes, when you click on a link, your browser will display a plain white screen with a message that you can't access the page. URLs can change, and links on other Web pages may not get updated accordingly, especially when the page in question is found on another person's site.

Sometimes the problem isn't with the link but with the Internet. The Internet is not a direct connection. When you click on a link, you are not instantly whisked directly to that Web page. You actually hop from system to system until you get there. Think of it as getting on an airplane and having to make three or four stops at other airports before you get to the one where you will deplane. Even if you do not have to get off the airplane at the other airports, the plane still stops.

Reminder

Sometimes the problem lies at one of these stops. The power may be out, or unusually high traffic may be going through that same hop as you get there. Your browser gets tired of waiting and tells you that the page cannot be found. Going back to the airport analogy, this is similar to landing at an airport only to have a major thunderstorm delay your takeoff. Unlike an airplane, which will eventually take off after a delay, your computer will not wait for long. If the browser can't get to a page in a given amount of time, it assumes that the page does not exist.

If you experience such an error, go on to other things for a while and then try again. Consider trying the link on another day or check a search engine for an updated URL. After you have tried the link repeatedly over a period of days only to receive the error message, then you may want to contact the owner of that Web page so she can see about updating or removing the link.

RETURNING TO THE SCENE

How to Organize and Work With Bookmarks

The Scenario: You've been surfing the Web for a few hours. You are bordering on disappointment for the night. It is midnight, and you haven't been able to find anything you consider useful. And suddenly, there it is. You discover a site devoted to your Sickafus line. This is the line you have been working on for the last ten years, largely without success. You want to spend the rest of the night scouring the site for information. But it is late, and you decide to turn in instead.

The next evening, you get back online, intent on returning to that site. But you didn't create a bookmark for it, and worse yet, you don't remember exactly how you got there.

You may think that this would never happen to you. Unfortunately, it happens all too often. We see a site and promise ourselves we'll get back to it. Somehow we are never able to find it again. And then we spend our time looking forlorn and wondering why we didn't bookmark it before logging off that night.

Organize Bookmarks in Your Browser: As you spread your wings and visit more and more Web sites, you will quickly discover that you cannot remember all of their addresses. After all, how many URLs can you type in from memory?

Most genealogists dump these URLs into the Favorites or Bookmarks section of their browser. Some of you may not realize that you can create subfolders for these URLs (and that you can rename the Web pages you find). Some subfolders to keep in mind include

- surnames

- localities

- history

- societies

- miscellaneous

Each of these subfolders will have its own additional subfolders. I suggest the following

- **surnames**

  — one folder for each surname you are presently researching

- **localities**

  — one folder for each state or other division you are researching

  — additional subfolders for counties or shires you are researching

- **history**

  — one folder for each historical event that is of interest to you

- **societies**

  — one folder for societies for each locality that is of interest to you.

- **miscellaneous**

  — a folder for odds and ends such as RootsWeb and Ancestry

Decide what you want to be able to find, then tailor your browser's Bookmarks or Favorites to suit you. That way you can easily return to Web sites that are of use to you in researching your family.

A SEA OF BOOKMARKS

As you begin to surf the Internet, you will discover some sites that you find especially useful. A Web site may have information about a particular ancestor or family line. Another site may supply you with information on a county that your ancestors lived in. Another site may offer you guidance in using the Web.

When you find such a site, it is natural to want to remember it so that you can return to it. We have already looked at URLs, and it's OK to admit that you couldn't remember them. They can be massive. I confess that many of them roll off my fingertips when I get near a computer, but I spend a lot of time accessing these particular sites. There are many other sites that I find useful, but cannot remember their URLs. Fortunately my computer can save me the trouble.

Regardless of which browser software you use, **you can save these URLs in an understandable format.** You can tell your browser software that you want to keep a particular site for future reference. This is called creating a bookmark; some browser programs refer to it as adding to your favorites.

When you create a bookmark or add a favorite, you tell your browser software to remember the URL for you. You can then click on the Favorites or Browser option in the program and select the specific Web site from the list that appears. We will look at this in more detail in chapter four, "Heading Onto the Internet." The steps for creating folders are on page 23. In chapter four you will find steps on how to add the link to a favorite site to one of the browsers.

Timesaver

TALK THE TALK, WALK THE WALK

We have looked at some of the terms that are directly associated with your computer. They are no longer hard-to-understand technical words. Now that you can talk the talk, let's walk the walk. Your computer is one of the most powerful machines that you will use, especially in your genealogy. Now it is time to put you in charge and harness all that power so that you can spend more time researching your family tree.

Step By Step

HOW DO YOU CREATE NEW FOLDERS?

You have thought about what is important to you. As you surf the Web, you find a great site and want to add its URL to your bookmarks. Just how do you do that?

Microsoft Internet Explorer

1. Select the Favorites menu.

2. Select Add to Favorites.

3. In the window that opens, click the Create In button.

4. Click the New Folder button.

5. Name the folder.

6. The URL reference will be saved in this folder.

Netscape Navigator

1. Click the Bookmarks button that appears next to the URL field.

2. Select Add Bookmark.

3. Click the Bookmarks button again.

4. Select Edit Bookmarks.

5. Pull down the File menu.

6. Select New Folder.

7. Name the folder.

8. Highlight the title of the Web page you just added.

9. Pull down the Edit menu and select Cut.

10. Click on the newly created folder, pull down the Edit menu, and select Paste.

THREE

Put the Computer to Work for You, Part I

T he personal computer was supposed to solve all of our problems. It was supposed to transform us into a paperless society. I can speak only for myself, but my office seems to swim in more paper now than ever before. Despite the influx of paper, however, the computer does offer me many tools to help track my family tree and organize my work.

THE RECORDING PHASE

Genealogy is the record of the lineage of a given individual. More people actually do family history, enhancing the names, dates, and places for the blood lineage with family stories and anecdotes. Either way, the computer can play a key role in this aspect of your work.

Genealogy is a hobby for most of us, and it must be scheduled in between the other pressing areas of our life. Most of the time, we spend these hard-won hours searching out the important aspects of an ancestor's life. Before computers though, we spent more time committing our family histories to paper than we spent on anything else.

For each individual on a pedigree chart, we had to write that relative's information on three separate sheets of paper. The first piece of paper was the pedigree chart itself. The second piece of paper was the family group sheet where the ancestor was a spouse. The third piece of paper was the family group sheet where the ancestor was a child.

Each of these included the same information on our ancestor: name, date and place of birth, date and place of death, date and place of burial, date and place of marriage, and name of the spouse. Now, if all of your ancestors were named John Smith and they were born, were married, and died in Ai, Fulton, Ohio, this wouldn't seem like such a horrendous process. I was not that fortunate, and I suspect few people are.

Timesaver

Through the genealogy software technology, you can enter the information once and then use it where appropriate. I type in the name of the individual and the dates and places of the person's life events, and then as I find others related to that person I use the software to recall the individual. Besides eliminating the duplication, genealogy software programs offer ways to enhance your family tree.

MORE THAN BIRTH AND DEATH

I hope that your ancestors have all been nice to you by being easy to locate and having left paper trails showing their dates of birth and death. Mine were not so kind. While I can sometimes rely on things such as census records to estimate their dates of birth, at times I do not have an exact date of death. Thankfully, the better genealogy software programs keep this in mind, offering more than the basic life events or facts from which to choose.

You will find that many of the current releases of genealogy software offer a large array of life events. Such choices allow you to be as specific as you wish in recording the details of the life of an ancestor. Most of the genealogy software programs include not only events such as the writing of a will or the probating of an estate, but also the recording of the different religious events that signified the growth and maturity of an ancestor.

A few software packages still offer just the basic life events and no method for adding other events besides recording them in a general notes section. **Before purchasing any genealogy software package, be sure that if you want the ability to record other life events you select software that includes this feature.** I have listed in the table on page 26 a few of the packages to help you begin your search for the genealogy software that is right for you.

Tip

Even if you don't feel the need to record the date of a bar mitzvah or a first communion, you may want to consider taking the few extra moments to add this information. Remember that people you will share this information with may be interested in such items. These life events may bring back fond memories to those who read your family history.

These additional life events may also help you track your ancestors. For those of you who, like me, are on the trail of the hard-to-find, every life event you come across will help you identify and isolate your John Johnston in the sea of the many who share that name.

THE FOREST FOR THE TREES

Perhaps we develop tunnel vision when we research, and this hinders us when we try to differentiate our ancestor from other people. It is not unusual to discover more than one individual in a given locality and time period with the same name as our ancestor. Which events belong to our ancestor and which belong to the other person or persons are sometimes not clear to us.

Sometimes we don't notice the holes in our research theory until we sit down to enter information into our genealogy software. When we try to compile the

GENEALOGY DATABASE SOFTWARE			
Name	**Contact Information**	**Web Site Address**	**Operating System**
Ancestral Quest	The Hope Foundation 9547 S 700 E Sandy, UT 84070 (801) 816-1000	http://www.ancquest.com	Windows 3.1, Windows 95 or higher
Brother's Keeper	Brother's Keeper 6907 Childsdale Ave. Rockford, MI 49341 Fax (616) 866-3345	http://www.ourworld.compuserve.com/homepages/Brothers_Keepers/	Windows 3.1, Windows 95 or higher
Cumberland Family Tree	Cumberland Family Software 385 Idaho Springs Rd. Clarksville, TN 37043	http://www.cf-software.com	Windows 95 or higher
Family Matters	Matterware P.O. Box 2221 Valrico, FL 33495-2221 (904) 736-8030	http://hometown.aol.com/matterware/index.html	Windows 3.1, Windows 95 or higher
Family Origins	FormalSoft P.O. Box 495 Springville, UT 84663	http://www.formalsoft.com	Windows 95 or higher
Family Tree Maker	Genealogy.com 39500 Stevenson Place Suite 204 Fremont, CA 94539-3103	http://www.familytreemaker.com	Windows 95 or higher
The Master Genealogist	Wholly Genes, Inc. 5144 Flowertuft Court Columbia, MD 21044 (410) 715-2260	http://www.whollygenes.com	Windows 95, 98 and Windows NT
Generations	SierraHome 3060 139th Ave. SE, Suite 500 Bellevue, WA 98005 (425) 649-9800	http://www.sierra.com/sierrahome/familytree/	Windows 95 or higher
Legacy	Millennia Corporation P.O. Box 1800 Duvall, WA 98019 (425) 788-3774	http://www.legacyfamilytree.com	Windows 95 or higher
Reunion	Leister Productions P.O. Box 289 Mechanicsburg, PA 17055 (717) 697-1378	http://www.leisterpro.com	Macintosh
Parentèle	Parentèle.com 4650 Arrow Hwy. E-6 Montclair, CA 91763 (909) 624-2594	http://us.parentele.com	Windows 95 or higher
Personal Ancestral File	The Church of Jesus Christ of Latter-day Saints	http://www.familysearch.org	Windows 95 or higher

SOFTWARE WITH FEATURES TO PREVENT MISTAKES		
Name	**Web Site Address**	**Reliability Checks**
Ancestral Quest	http://www.ancquest.com	Built-in database check and repair. No immediate notification upon entry of unfeasible dates.
Cumberland Family Tree	http://www.cf-software.com/	Database verification option that can be run on the file and will point out any irregularities.
Family Origins	http://www.formalsoft.com	Offers a spell checker in all note windows.
Family Tree Maker	http://www.familytreemaker.com	Name errors and unlikely birth, marriage, and death dates error checking. Either or both can be turned on or off.
Generations	http://www.sierra.com/ sierrahome/familytree/	Date feasibility checks. All options can be turned on or off, as can specific feasibility checks.
Legacy	http://legacyfamilytree.com	Spell check in note windows. "Potential Problems" report can be run.
Personal Ancestral File	http://www.familysearch.org	Check & Repair function may be run. Verification of all new names (individual and place); this can be turned off. Date checks automatic when potentially incorrect date is entered.

information from the many different records into a single human time line, we begin to see its implausibility. We discover a child born when our ancestor was ten, or we have him witnessing a land deed three years after his death.

When we add information to our genealogy software, we are forced to focus our mind on the individual at hand, rather than the family or lineage on a large scale. Through this focus we often reevaluate our research. Seldom is this a conscious decision on our part; it usually happens as we look at the records in question while we update the information on that ancestor in our genealogy program.

While you may think that the forest is the entire family tree, try looking at the forest as the individual and his or her life. The trees are the events that made up that life. The magnitude of the records of these events sometimes clouds our view of the forest of the individual. We have overlooked what suddenly appears so obvious.

Of course, there are times when we do not catch an error, but the software package does. Many times the errors that are highlighted by the genealogy program are human errors, i.e., typos. While I consider myself proficient at the keyboard, I find that when dealing with a lot of numbers I am more apt to make mistakes. This is never truer than when I am working with dates. My eyes spend more time on the paper than they do on the screen and keyboard. As a result, I sometimes have a person dying before she was born.

There are times when an error is not my mistake, and having the computer point out a possible problem with dates is one of the things I like most about my genealogy software. Most of the packages available today can be set to warn of such discrepancies. The table above includes a list of software packages with notes as to whether they warn you and whether you can turn this option off.

The family tree as a whole is indeed another forest. You may find, especially when you research areas such as New England and the South, that many families intermarried and the tree limbs double back onto themselves. Your pedigree begins to overlap itself, and you find that you have duplications as you trace the generations further back.

The pedigree chart on page 29 is a perfect example of what happens. In most family trees, the common ancestral connection is more generations back. In this case, the couple that married were first cousins. William Ayer and Miriam Thornton were first cousins; they had the same maternal grandparents, Samuel Hicks and Thankful Bowen. William's mother, Elizabeth Hicks, and Miriam's mother, Mary Hicks, were sisters. The maternal line for both William and Miriam is duplicated from that point back.

UNRAVELING THE FAMILY TREE

One feature of genealogy software is the ability to keep track of familial relationships. You are responsible for entering the individuals correctly, but you can tell the software program to hand you a pedigree chart or descendant tree of a given line. In a matter of minutes, the computer will assemble and print the requested information. If you were to do this by hand, it would take you some time to compile the proper families, going back the necessary number of generations and then listing them in the proper order and with the proper method.

No number of generations seems to be too many for the computer. I would begin to choke if I had to display the information on more than four generations of an individual's descent. The computer, on the other hand, can handle this and more without breaking a sweat.

I'M MY OWN GRANDMA

Fortunately I am not my own grandmother, but there are some interesting relationships in my family tree. My grandfather's grandparents were first cousins. I confess this here and now, knowing that he found it funny when I made the discovery. Of course, a first cousin relationship is easy enough to chart and determine. What about eighth cousins twice removed?

One thing I do each week on the Internet is answer questions from fellow genealogists. I can truthfully say that a week doesn't go by where someone doesn't write a question about a degree of relationship or how to figure it out. Of course, when I answer such questions, I have to go through the lengthy chart process shown on page 30. While this is a good way to picture the true degree of relationship, sometimes the desired answer is just the degree of relationship, not the process of determining it.

Genealogy software can answer this question in a matter of seconds. **Most of the available software programs allow you to select two individuals in a given database and generate a display of how they are related.** Because the computer just hands over the result seventh cousins four times removed, you may not understand why that is the relationship, especially if you are new to genealogy. Instead of having to plot out the information yourself, however, you got the

Notes

Pedigree Chart

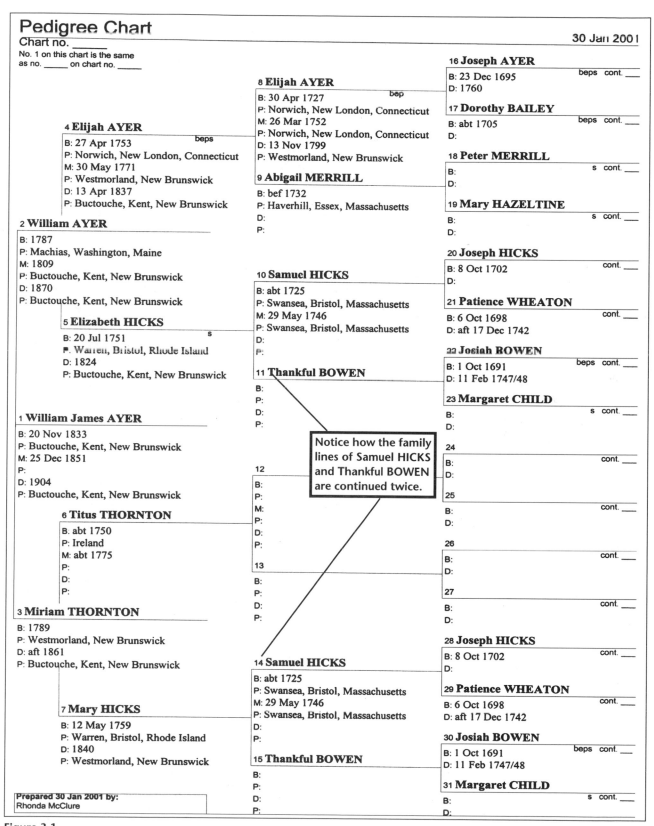

Chart no. _____

No. 1 on this chart is the same
as no. _____ on chart no. _____

30 Jan 2001

8 Elijah AYER
B: 30 Apr 1727
P: Norwich, New London, Connecticut
M: 26 Mar 1752
P: Norwich, New London, Connecticut
D: 13 Nov 1799
P: Westmorland, New Brunswick

4 Elijah AYER
B: 27 Apr 1753
P: Norwich, New London, Connecticut
M: 30 May 1771
P: Westmorland, New Brunswick
D: 13 Apr 1837
P: Buctouche, Kent, New Brunswick

9 Abigail MERRILL
B: bef 1732
P: Haverhill, Essex, Massachusetts
D:
P:

16 Joseph AYER
B: 23 Dec 1695   beps   cont. ___
D: 1760

17 Dorothy BAILEY
B: abt 1705   beps   cont. ___
D:

18 Peter MERRILL
B: s   cont. ___
D:

19 Mary HAZELTINE
B: s   cont. ___
D:

2 William AYER
B: 1787
P: Machias, Washington, Maine
M: 1809
P: Buctouche, Kent, New Brunswick
D: 1870
P: Buctouche, Kent, New Brunswick

5 Elizabeth HICKS
B: 20 Jul 1751
P: Warren, Bristol, Rhode Island
D: 1824
P: Buctouche, Kent, New Brunswick

10 Samuel HICKS
B: abt 1725
P: Swansea, Bristol, Massachusetts
M: 29 May 1746
P: Swansea, Bristol, Massachusetts
D:
P:

11 Thankful BOWEN
B:
P:
D:
P:

20 Joseph HICKS
B: 8 Oct 1702   cont. ___
D:

21 Patience WHEATON
B: 6 Oct 1698   cont. ___
D: aft 17 Dec 1742

22 Josiah BOWEN
B: 1 Oct 1691   beps   cont. ___
D: 11 Feb 1747/48

23 Margaret CHILD
B: s   cont. ___
D:

1 William James AYER
B: 20 Nov 1833
P: Buctouche, Kent, New Brunswick
M: 25 Dec 1851
P:
D: 1904
P: Buctouche, Kent, New Brunswick

6 Titus THORNTON
B: abt 1750
P: Ireland
M: abt 1775
P:
D:
P:

12
B:
P:
M:
P:
D:
P:

13
B:
P:
D:
P:

Notice how the family
lines of Samuel HICKS
and Thankful BOWEN
are continued twice.

24
B: cont. ___
D:

25
B: cont. ___
D:

26
B: cont. ___
D:

27
B: cont. ___
D:

3 Miriam THORNTON
B: 1789
P: Westmorland, New Brunswick
D: aft 1861
P: Buctouche, Kent, New Brunswick

7 Mary HICKS
B: 12 May 1759
P: Warren, Bristol, Rhode Island
D: 1840
P: Westmorland, New Brunswick

14 Samuel HICKS
B: abt 1725
P: Swansea, Bristol, Massachusetts
M: 29 May 1746
P: Swansea, Bristol, Massachusetts
D:
P:

15 Thankful BOWEN
B:
P:
D:
P:

28 Joseph HICKS
B: 8 Oct 1702   cont. ___
D:

29 Patience WHEATON
B: 6 Oct 1698   cont. ___
D: aft 17 Dec 1742

30 Josiah BOWEN
B: 1 Oct 1691   beps   cont. ___
D: 11 Feb 1747/48

31 Margaret CHILD
B: s   cont. ___
D:

Prepared 30 Jan 2001 by:
Rhonda McClure

Figure 3.1
This pedigree chart, created using Family Origins, displays cousins that have married. The computer automatically duplicates the necessary lines.

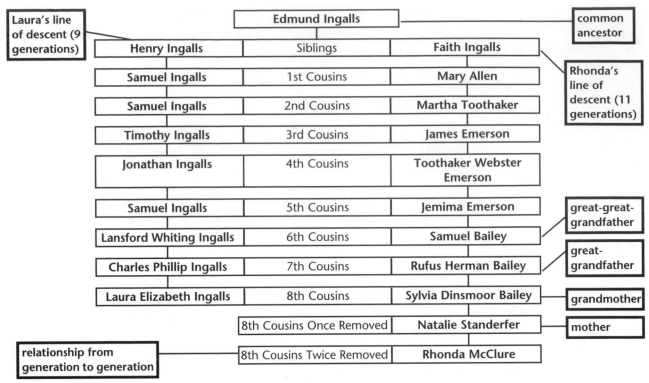

answer quickly. The two individuals are indeed related, and the Family Origins relationship calculator on page 31 shows how.

FIRST FAMILIES AND THE MAYFLOWER

Another aspect of relationship that many genealogists research involves direct descent from a given individual. Even if your surname is Alden, it is possible that your connection to the *Mayflower* does not come through a direct paternal lineage.

When I first got involved in researching my family history, I turned to my maternal grandmother. She had hired a researcher to trace her line so that she could join the Daughters of the American Revolution. This is just one of the societies that requires proof of a lineal descent from a given individual who fits the society's qualifications.

Recently I jumped with both feet into the possibility of having an ancestor recognized by the First Families of Ohio, an offshoot of the Ohio Genealogical Society. This group requires proof of blood descent from an individual who was in Ohio by 31 December 1820. They have restrictions on what resources are acceptable to prove the relationships you set forth. For me the problem was focusing on the lineage. It wasn't a straight paternal line; the surname changed five times.

I was able to focus my research on the direct individuals through the use of a report generated by my genealogy program. The direct drop chart on page 32 allowed me to specify the ancestor and the descendant, in this case myself, and then print a report showing the direct line from that ancestor down to me (on page 33).

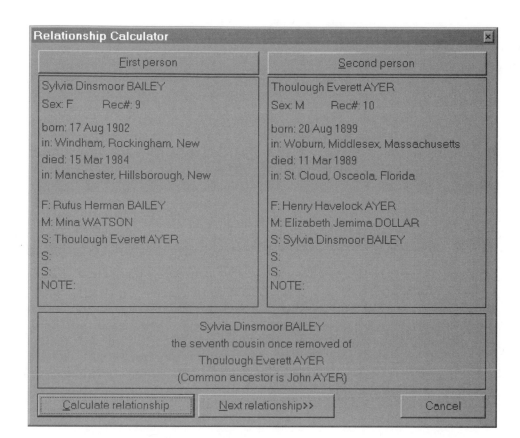

Figure 3.2
Many genealogy programs, like Family Origins, include a relationship calculator within the program to make it easier to figure out relationships between individuals in the database.

Because of this direct line, I wasn't lured to research other family lines. Instead, I concentrated on just a single family or individual in each generation. Such a report also makes it easier to fill out the required applications for these lineage societies. The applications often have spaces for the names of the individuals in the line, along with dates and places of birth, marriage, and death. Other state societies have similar pioneer or First Family programs. In fact, you may qualify for one of these and not know it yet.

PUBLISHING FOR THE FAMILY

As genealogists, we are consumed by a burning desire to learn more. We want to record more names, more dates, and more places. We want to add more stories. We want to add to the family tree, taking it back further and further. Of course, what spurs us and what will interest the nongenealogists in the family may be two different things. Fortunately, genealogy software programs offer a variety of methods for publishing the research we have compiled.

While we may prefer to work with pedigree charts and family group sheets, especially during the research phase, **the narrative-style reports will probably have greater appeal for our family members.** The narrative-style reports were the deciding factor when I changed genealogy software packages many years ago.

In the dark ages—about ten years ago—I was a staunch defender of a particular genealogy program. It was the first one I had ever used, and I had upgraded, purchasing the new version of the program, twice over the ensuing years. How-

Important

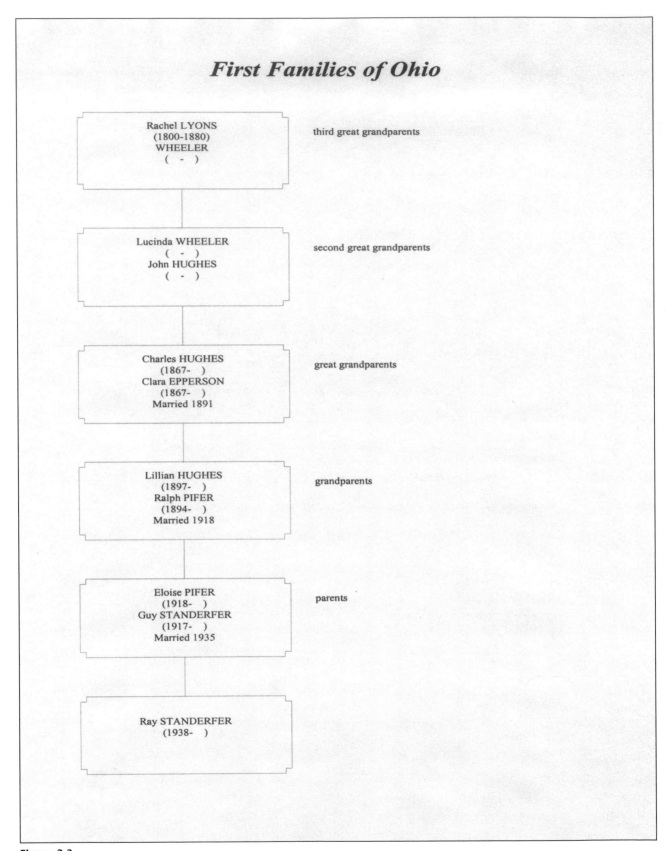

First Families of Ohio

Rachel LYONS (1800-1880) WHEELER (-)	third great grandparents
Lucinda WHEELER (-) John HUGHES (-)	second great grandparents
Charles HUGHES (1867-) Clara EPPERSON (1867-) Married 1891	great grandparents
Lillian HUGHES (1897-) Ralph PIFER (1894-) Married 1918	grandparents
Eloise PIFER (1918-) Guy STANDERFER (1917-) Married 1935	parents
Ray STANDERFER (1938-)	

Figure 3.3
A direct drop chart shows a line of descent from one person to another.

3. The said ___BAY EDWARD STANDERFER___ was the _____SON_____
Son or Daughter

of ___GUY EDWARD STANDERFER___

born on _12 JUL 1917_ at ___SULLIVAN, MOULTRIE, ILLINOIS___
City   County   State

died on _____ at _____
City   County   State

___ELOISE PIFER___ his wife

born on _26 APR 1918_ at ___SULLIVAN, MOULTRIE, ILLINOIS___
City   County   State

died on _24 MAY 1979_ at ___DECATUR, MACON, ILLINOIS___
City   County   State

married on _17 JUN 1935_ at ___DIXON, LEE, ILLINOIS___
City   County   State

4. The said ___ELOISE PIFER___ was the ___DAUGHTER___
Son or Daughter

of ___RALPH PIFER___

born on _28 OCT 1894_ at ___SULLIVAN, MOULTRIE, ILLINOIS___
City   County   State

died on _____ at _____
City   County   State

___LILLIAN VIOLET HUGHES___ his wife

born on ___MAR 1897___ at ___BELLE RIVE, JEFFERSON, ILLINOIS___
City   County   State

died on _bef. 1920_ at _____
City   County   State

married on _25 FEB 1918_ at ___SULLIVAN, MOULTRIE, ILLINOIS___
City   County   State

5. The said ___LILLIAN VIOLET HUGHES___ was the ___DAUGHTER___
Son or Daughter

of ___CHARLES HUGHES___

born on ___FEB 1867___ at _____OHIO_____
City   County   State

died on _____ at _____
City   County   State

___CLARA MARY EPPERSON___ his wife

born on _27 MAY 1866_ at ___MOORE'S PRAIRIE, JEFFERSON, ILLINOIS___
City   County   State

died on _4 APR 1930_ at ___DECATUR, MACON, ILLINOIS___
City   County   State

married on _13 MAY 1891_ at ___JEFFERSON CO., ILLINOIS___
City   County   State

6. The said ___CHARLES HUGHES___ was the ___SON___
Son or Daughter

of ___JOHN HUGHES___

born on ___1828___ at _____PENNSYLVANIA_____
City   County   State

died on _BEF 15 MAR 1879_ at ___JEFFERSON CO., ILLINOIS___
City   County   State

___LUCINDA WHEELER___ his wife

born on _16 MAY 1825_ at ___ATHENS CO., OHIO___
City   County   State

died on _12 MAR 1912_ at ___JEFFERSON CO., ILLINOIS___
City   County   State

Figure 3.4
Lineage societies require that you show your direct descent from the qualifying ancestor.

ever, a fellow researcher, who had hired me to do some research in New England for her, sent me a wonderful printout from her genealogy program. It was as if I had found that family published in the *New England Historical and Genealogical Register*. It impressed me so much that I finally made the leap and changed software programs.

The latest batch of software offers a vast array of pictorial reports and narrative-style reports that will appeal to our nongenealogists. These types of reports will help you obtain additional information at family gatherings. Folks will be intrigued by the photos and the way you have organized them. Then they will notice that you haven't put in the right date for Aunt Mary's death, or they will point out that Cousin John was buried in the Veterans Cemetery, not the Quaker Cemetery.

Suddenly the people who swore up and down that they didn't know anything about the family will supply you with more information than you can hope to remember. Be sure to take along pens so that your relatives can make notes on your report. Remember, you can always print a new one for the next gathering.

NO STONE TABLETS NEEDED

In the years before computers, publishing was something you did when you were done. I am sure you can see the problem here—when are you done? One reason I like genealogy so much is that it is a never-ending hobby. When I get stuck on one line, I can turn to another one. I may even find new resources or research aids that help me move past a brick wall that blocked my path down a line a couple of years ago.

If you look at published genealogies that were published from the late 1800s through the 1970s, you will find that they have something in common. Most of these volumes were typeset and published by professionals. For genealogists this meant two things: accuracy and expense.

People waited until they were as sure as they could be that they had truly found all the children and all the children's children for the five to eight generations they had compiled. They waited until they had amassed as many of the wills as they could. They waited until they had a chance to check "just one more record." Then they waited until they had the money. One has to wonder how these family histories were published at all. It makes the available ones all the more precious.

Most family histories that were published with a hard cover were done by one of the many vanity presses that exist. While I don't think that "vanity" really fits what they were doing, the process is the same. Vanity presses will publish your book, but it is up to you to get people to buy the book. Most of us think publishers do this work, but with a genealogy book, the genealogist does all of the marketing and selling.

The genealogist also had to find someone who would typeset the book. Usually this required hiring a professional, unless the genealogist was fortunate enough to have married someone with this skill, as a colleague of mine did. Typesetting is a time-consuming, detail-oriented job. Because of what was involved, most genealogists wanted to wait until they had the most complete family history possible before going through all of this. I can't help wondering how many genealogies didn't get published because researchers waited a little too long, and none of their children was willing to pick up the project when their parent died. How much research never saw the light of day?

At that time, publishing a family history was truly like etching it in stone. No changes could be made after it was published without republishing, and no one wanted to go through that. So instead of publishing some researchers waited.

YOUR PAPERLESS BOOK

With the advances in genealogy software, you can publish your narrative report not only on paper, using the format that once required the work of a typesetter, but also on the Internet. What a wonderful world we live in.

While I still hear from genealogists who want to wait until they are sure of everything they post, **I encourage you to publish your research on the Web now.** We will look at the mechanics of publishing information on the Web in more detail in chapter five. Posting a simple message at the front of your Web site pointing out that your genealogy is a work in progress will let those who are visiting know that you are aware there may be some omissions or unanswered questions.

Important

Even if you elect to publish in a paper form, you will find that the genealogy software does much of the organization and structural work for you. Conceiving and generating a published volume will not be difficult once you have done the hard part—finding your ancestors.

THE MULTIMEDIA BOOK

I have heard from genealogists in the last year who have described what I can best call a multimedia book. It has no pages, but instead is done on a CD-ROM. Actually it is similar to a Web page, but it is saved to a CD-ROM instead of online, and then it is sent to family members.

To do such a project, you need to have a recordable CD-ROM drive on your computer. These have come down in price. They can even be included on notebook computers now. They allow you to use a special type of CD-ROM that has nothing saved to it yet. You can then "burn" the information onto the CD-ROM, which runs just like any other CD-ROM you place in your computer.

Supplies

The benefit of such a published family history is the ability to include multimedia. *Multimedia* is the catchall term for pictures, motion pictures, and voice recordings. While you can include still pictures in a printed genealogy, the duplicated copies may not have the same impact as originals. When included on a Web site or on a CD-ROM, they have the vibrancy of the original scan.

Motion pictures and sound recordings cannot be translated into a paper book. When added to a Web site or put on a CD-ROM, however, they bring your family history to life. Imagine the great-great-grandchildren getting the

GENEALOGICAL STANDARDS AND GUIDELINES

Guidelines for Publishing Web Pages on the Internet

Recommended by the National Genealogical Society, May 2000

Appreciating that publishing information through Internet Web sites and Web pages shares many similarities with print publishing, considerate family historians—

- apply a single title to an entire Web site, as they would to a book, placing it both in the <TITLE> HTML tag that appears at the top of the Web browser window for each Web page to be viewed, and also in the body of the Web document, on the opening home, title, or index page.

- explain the purposes and objectives of their Web sites, placing the explanation near the top of the title page or including a link from that page to a special page about the reason for the site.

- display a footer at the bottom of each Web page which contains the Web site title, page title, author's name, author's contact information, date of last revision, and a copyright statement.

- provide complete contact information, including at a minimum a name and e-mail address, and preferably some means for long-term contact, like a postal address.

- assist visitors by providing on each page navigational links that lead visitors to other important pages on the Web site or return them to the home page.

- adhere to the **NGS "Standards for Sharing Information with Others"** regarding copyright, attribution, privacy, and the sharing of sensitive information.

- include unambiguous source citations for the research data provided on the site, and if not complete descriptions, offering full citations upon request.

- label photographic and scanned images within the graphic itself, with fuller explanation if required in text adjacent to the graphic.

- identify transcribed, extracted, or abstracted data as such, and provide appropriate source citations.

- include identifying dates and locations when providing information about specific surnames or individuals.

- respect the rights of others who do not wish information about themselves to be published, referenced, or linked on a Web site.

- provide Web site access to all potential visitors by avoiding enhanced technical capabilities that may not be available to all users, remembering that not all computers are created equal.

- avoid using features that distract from the productive use of the Web site, like ones that reduce legibility, strain the eyes, dazzle the vision, or otherwise detract from the visitor's ability to easily read, study, comprehend, or print the online publication.

- maintain their online publications at frequent intervals, changing the content to keep the information current, the links valid, and the Web site in good working order.

- preserve and archive for future researchers their online publications and communications that have lasting value, using both electronic and paper duplication.

chance to hear their great-great-grandmother's voice for the first time. Suddenly she is more than just an obscure name.

Multimedia presentations are great to share at family reunions. Also, they can solve the Web hysteria problem when saved to a CD-ROM and given out at the family reunion. You still get to share what you have found without upsetting family members by publishing their information on the Internet.

The downside to such multimedia books is that they may not be placed in a library collection. I do not know of any library that will accept electronic books. If you want to preserve your research for the years to come, I encourage you to produce one paper version of your research at some point. Donate that to the libraries you know are actively preserving family histories, and then save the multimedia productions for your family.

Warning

BACK TO THE INTERNET

We have looked at some of the ways the computer can work for you. While not specifically discussed over the next few chapters, your computer will continue to work hard, this time online. And first, we need to learn how to find things on the Internet. The Internet is no good to us if we cannot find anything on it.

FOUR

Head Onto the Internet

I n chapter three, I alluded to the ability to publish your family history on the Internet. This is just one of the many surprises waiting for you when you get onto the Internet. We have already discussed the software and hardware that you need to surf the Web. It is now time to discover what the Internet has to offer and how you can best take advantage of it in your research.

THE LIBRARY THAT NEVER CLOSES

Whenever I think about what the Internet offers in the way of resources and information in my family history research, I think of the Internet as a library. Think about it for a moment. When you go to a library, you avail yourself of the resources—mostly books and magazines—available at the library. Some books you may borrow and take home, while others require you to use them in the library.

The Internet is similar. I borrow the Web pages for a short time. I read what others have posted about their family histories. I may read an article by a genealogist who shares important how-to information. I may search a database. Regardless of what I do, the bottom line is that I am researching.

The biggest difference between this research and that which I conduct at a library building is the freedom. **When working on the Internet, I can do the research at a time that is convenient for me.** When I work in a library, even one that has extensive hours of operation, I am still forced to conclude my research for the day at closing time. Online, I can persevere in my research for as long as my eyes remain open and my brain continues to function. Best of all, I can also get comfortable in my pajamas and bunny slippers if I want.

Before we get into the types of records and resources you will use on the Internet, be forewarned that the Internet won't solve all of your genealogical nightmares. I would be misleading you if I were to claim it would. The Internet is a constantly changing entity. Each day that you venture out onto the Web,

Timesaver

you will discover sites that didn't exist before. You'll discover that some sites have changed considerably and that still others have disappeared altogether.

WHERE TO BEGIN

In order to discover these wonderful treasures, you must first understand how to use the "card catalog" to the Internet. Unlike the library, where you have a single card catalog, on paper or on computer, to all of the holdings, the Internet has many different ones. Among the tools, you will find that there are different methods for finding Web sites. The two that genealogists rely upon the most heavily are directories and search engines.

Now, before you get ready to offer excuses why you can't possibly manage to learn about these things, relax—you are probably already using them. If you have ventured onto the Internet at all, you have come in contact with either a directory or a search engine. Once you learn a little more about them, you will become more proficient with them, thus reducing the frustration you feel when you look for things on the Internet.

USING DIRECTORIES

A directory is compiled with human guidance. Someone organizes the URLs (remember these from chapter two) in some fashion. They may be arranged alphabetically in one giant list. Other directories are divided under subheadings, with the URLs grouped together through the common theme of the subheadings. **For genealogists, perhaps the best-known directory is Cyndi's List <http://www. cyndislist.com>**. At the time of this writing, this site had more than 98,000 links compiled into 150 categories.

Internet Source

When you visit Cyndi's List, you first see the list of headings from which to select. Once you decide which of the headings is most likely to contain the sites you need, you click on the link. A link on the Internet is a section of text or a graphic on which your cursor changes to a pointing hand. This lets you know that you can click on that text or graphic to go to another section of the Internet. Your browser software, unless you have changed the default settings, will also underline the links. Links are generally a different color from the rest of the text on a page to further highlight them and make them stand out.

On Cyndi's List, most of the pages are lists of links. That is the point of this Web site. Cyndi Howells has compiled these sites so that genealogists will know what is available on the Internet. Each link takes you to a page or site on the Internet where you should find information pertaining to the subject you sought.

Directories such as Cyndi's List offer you organized listings to look through. Directories differ from other types of search sites in that directories have that human intervention. The method by which the compiler of a directory has organized the links under the headings may be different from the way you would have listed them. Sometimes you may not find a link under the subheading you think it should be under. This may result from other angles that site could have.

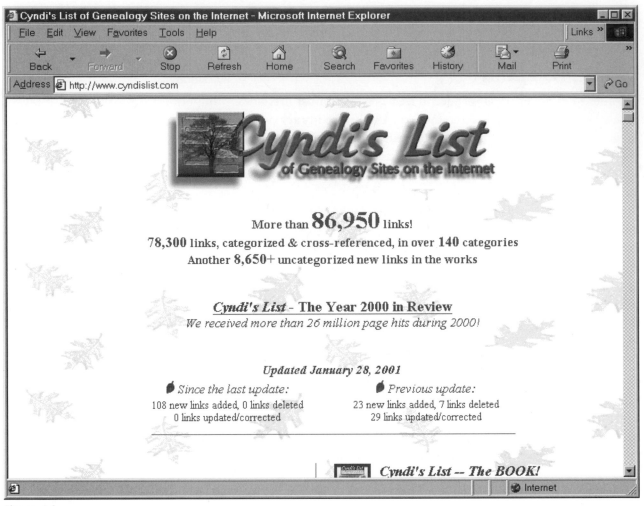

Figure 4.1
Cyndi's List is a well-known genealogy directory.

If it deals with death records and you do not find it under a "Death Records" subheading, perhaps it was placed under a "Vital Records" subheading.

The Site May Indeed Exist

Warning

There is an inherent problem with directories. Generally, directories are alphabetized by the title of the Web site. Unfortunately, many genealogists are not Web page designers. They do not understand the importance of giving their Web sites unique and informative titles. A look at the "Personal Home Pages" section of Cyndi's List for titles beginning with *M* reveals many links to Web pages titled "My Family" although the surnames covered do not begin with the letter *M*.

This means that you, through no fault of your own, may overlook some of the Web pages that would be the most useful in your research. Now that you are aware of this problem, however, I encourage you to check the sections for letters other than the initial letters of the surnames you are researching. The chart on page 42 includes some of the common titles for genealogy Web pages and the letters under which you will find them in an alphabetical directory.

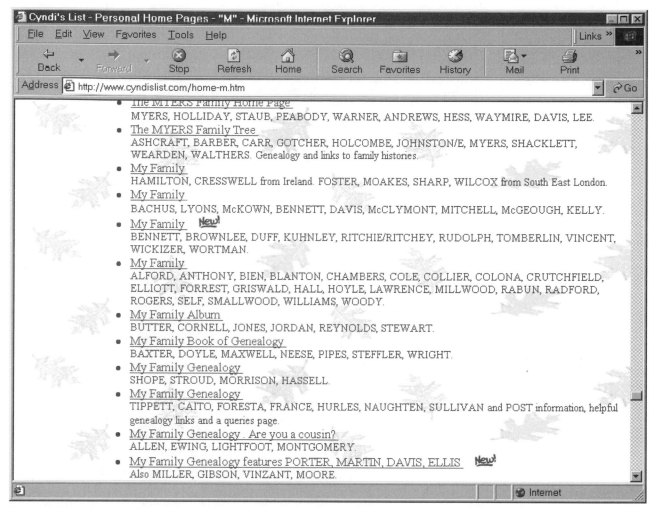

Figure 4.2
Unfortunately many different surname Web pages are listed in directory listings under *M* because the title of the Web page is "My Family."

USING SEARCH ENGINES

With a directory, you must work from a broad subject to a narrow subject to find a link that is of interest. With search engines, you work from a narrow subject or detail. **Search engines allow you to type in certain key words or phrases, which get compared to the database of links at the search engine site.** The search engine site then displays a list of possible matches.

Unlike a directory, where the compiler has grouped possible matches together using human evaluation, search engines supply the list of matches based solely on electronic computations. As long as the terms typed into the search engine form are included in the keywords or text of a given Web site, a link to that Web site will be included in the results list.

Because of this lack of human evaluation, you must first think like a computer and then decide how to outsmart the computer so that you get only those sites that are of interest to you. There are many different ways to control the results of a search engine. These include using phrases, using Boolean search terms or

\di'fin\ *vb*

Definitions

INEFFECTIVE SITE TITLES	
Name of Site	**Alphabetical Location**
Family Page	Sites with titles beginning with F
Genealogy	Sites with titles beginning with G
Home Page	Sites with titles beginning with H
My Family Tree	Sites with titles beginning with M
My Home Page	Sites with titles beginning with M
New Page	Sites with titles beginning with N

asking the computer to look for words within a certain distance of each other.

Boolean operators are named after mathematician George Boole, who applied algebra to computer searches. A computer search can be directly altered through the use of the words *and*, *or*, and *not*. The chart below lists each of the Boolean operators and the action taken by the search engine.

BOOLEAN OPERATORS	
AND	For a Web page to be considered a match, *all* search terms must be present on the page. Allows you to narrow the focus of your search.
OR	For a Web page to be considered a match, at least one of the search terms must be present on the page. Allows you to broaden the focus of your search.
NOT	For a Web page to be considered a match, it must include one search term but not the other search term. Allows you to exclude sites that do not pertain to your search. (For example, if you are researching the surname Duck, use "Duck NOT mallard" to exclude pages devoted to mallard ducks.)

As you can see, adding a Boolean operator to a string of search words will alter the way in which the computer performs the search. This will help you to eliminate some of the pages that have absolutely nothing to do with your genealogical pursuits. Working with Boolean operators is especially important when you are working with one of the mainstream search engines.

Mainstream search engines are those that allow anyone to search for anything on the Internet. They will show my children useful homework sites, my mother-in-law a gardening site, and me a genealogy site. They will also show in a genealogist's search results sites that do not apply to genealogy. Some of the major search engines, complete with URLs, are listed on page 43 to get you started.

Taking advantage of Boolean operators or required and prohibited search terms will help you narrow your search results, you hope to just those sites that interest you. This may take a little experimenting before you hit on the proper search formula.

There are no wrong answers when working with search engines. You simply need to experiment with the terms you include. The trick is to find the right balance between the semiobscure surnames you would really like to find and

SEARCH ENGINE SITES	
AltaVista	http://www.altavista.com
Excite	http://www.excite.com
Go.com	http://www.go.com
Google	http://www.google.com
Hotbot	http://www.hotbot.com
Lycos	http://www.lycos.com
Northern Light	http://www.northernlight.com
WebCrawler	http://www.webcrawler.com
Yahoo!	http://www.yahoo.com

the truly common surnames you would like to narrow down. That comes only with practice and an adventuresome spirit. Remember, if the first search doesn't work, try again. Even some of us who have been at this for a while must get a little creative when it comes to search engines.

Required and prohibited search terms act the same as the Boolean operators, but they use numerical symbols—the plus sign (+) and the minus sign (–)—instead of words. **The plus sign tells the computer to include both terms. The minus sign tells the computer to exclude the second term.** Using the Boolean terms AND, OR, or NOT, you would enter

Standerfer AND Illinois

No space is used after the required and prohibited symbols. The same search using the required symbol would be entered as

Standerfer +Illinois

There is a space after the first search term; the required symbol is followed immediately by the required word but no space.

Visit the search engines included in the chart above, and then spend time learning everything there is to know about how two of those search engines work. This will entail actually reading the online help files offered on the search engine sites. I can already hear the groans, but if you take the time to learn how the search engine wants you to search, then your searches will be more effective. In the end this is what we want—effective searches.

Working From the Obscure

You might think it is a good idea to begin a search using the most common word first and then adding the more unique words and Boolean operators later in the search string. **The search string, by the way, is the sentence you create with the terms you want the search engine to use.** By English standards it is far from a complete sentence, but to the computer, it is a directive. The order in which you type that directive will affect what is found as well as how fast it is found.

An example is a search for family history on the surname Standerfer. This

Notes

\di'fin\ *vb*

Definitions

WHERE DOES THE SEARCH ENGINE LOOK?

Probably the biggest misconception about search engines deals with what they search when you click that Search or Go button. Most researchers assume that whatever search engine they use will actually search the entire Internet on their behalf.

A search engine uses one of a variety of methods of ferreting out Web pages. One method is through the use of a "spider." Spider programs continually visit Web sites, amassing information from the title, text, and HTML code of each page. The spider's job is to look for Web sites, but it cannot find every Web page on the Internet. Therein lies the misconception.

Genealogists are used to library catalogs that include entries for everything housed in a library or repository. The Internet is too vast for this. No one search engine has managed to catalog the entire Internet. This is one reason we see so many search engines and directories. Each one uses a different search method. Some catalog just the home page of a Web site. Others dig more deeply into the site, therefore gathering more pages to help you find the information you seek.

I suggest that you use at least two different search engines. Get to know them; learn all there is to know about your search engines of choice. The best way to do this is to read the site's online help files. When searching though, remember that it may be necessary to visit another search engine from time to time to be sure that a site or subject matter you cannot find on the Internet is truly not there.

---

surname is not too common. Notice that in the example on page 45, I put the word *Standerfer* at the beginning of the search string, not at the end.

By inserting the plus sign (+) before *genealogy*, I tell the search engine to first concentrate on all Web sites and pages that include the word *Standerfer* and then list only those that also include the term *genealogy*.

While the final search results would be the same had I reversed the word order, the search is often faster when the less common word is placed first. The chart on page 46 shows the numbers for some single-term searches. This helps illustrate the difference in how many pages must be searched, which will affect the speed of the search depending on which search term is first.

Genealogists have a "greed for speed." You may not think you are in that category, but when you surf the Web, you might grow impatient when a Web site takes a minute to load or a search engine takes forever to give you search results. Never mind that the actual search took only forty-five seconds; it seemed a lot longer.

Changing the order of the search terms can affect the speed of the search, allowing the search engine to supply you with results in thirty seconds instead of fifty seconds. While those extra few seconds aren't as critical as milliseconds are in

Notes

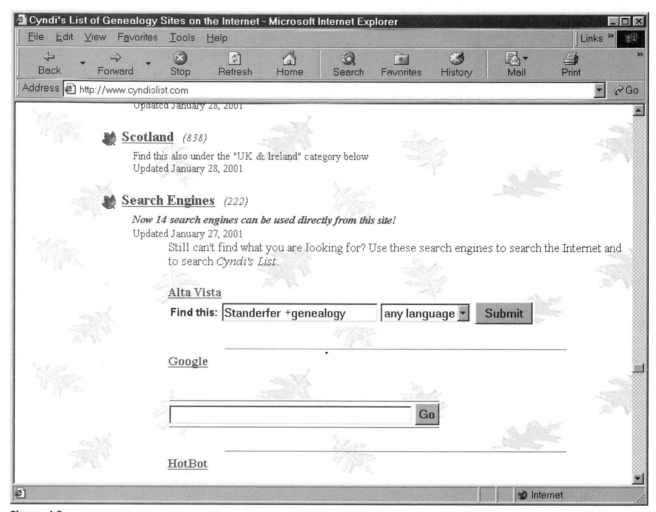

Figure 4.3
Including an uncommon surname first in a search string aids in guaranteeing the links you are most interested in will appear at the top of the search results.

an Olympic heat, the shorter waits will give you a more positive experience on the Internet and may be a determining factor as to whether or not you return.

Genealogy-Specific Search Engines

I am sure you guessed that there are some search engines configured just for genealogists. Some of them actually rely on the mainstream search engines when executing a search, while others search just their compiled list of genealogical sites. To learn which method a site uses, read what the Web site says and see what you get when you execute a search.

Some genealogy-specific search engines rely on the same software as the mainstream search engines, devices such as spiders, to search the Internet and gather information on sites that include keywords such as *genealogy*, *family history*, and *family tree*. These sites get added to the list of potential hits and may be included in the results of your next search.

The biggest difference between the mainstream and genealogy-specific search

SEARCH ENGINE SITES—SAMPLE RESULTS	
Genealogy	6,516,080 pages found
Family History	404,857 pages found
Family Tree	587,620 pages found
Bailey	566,365 pages found
Davis	1,772,635 pages found
Moon	1,116,515 pages found
Sickafus	173 pages found
Smith	3,688,425 pages found
Standerfer	741 pages found

engines is that the genealogy-specific search engines exclude mainstream, non-genealogical Web sites from their databases of potential sites. They do this through keywords or by relying on the developers of genealogy Web sites to register their sites at these search engines.

I am sure that you can see potential omissions with each of these methods. New developers of family history Web pages may not think to include the right keywords in the meta tags section of a page. Meta tags are hidden keywords that the spider programs use when seeking Web sites. Spider programs read and archive this list of words to compare later to the search terms that you or I submit to search engines.

As I did for the mainstream search engines, I am including a list of genealogy-specific search engines, on page 47. I encourage you to become familiar with at least a couple of them. Combined with the mainstream search engines, these will increase the probability that you will find sites in a timely fashion.

The Big Myth About Search Engines

Important

No one search engine on the Internet knows everything about every site on the Internet. **When you use a search engine, you are not searching the entire Internet.** You are searching the database of sites compiled by that search engine. Granted, this database may include millions of sites, but it doesn't include every site on the Internet. This is one of the hardest concepts for people to understand about the Internet and search engines.

While I encouraged you earlier to pick one or two each of the mainstream and genealogy-specific search engines and get to know them, I am now going to add to that. While it is important to have one or two search engines whose intricacies you know, you may need to extend your search capabilities. You can do this in one of two ways: You can visit each search engine, or you can put your computer and the Internet to work for you by doing metasearches, which will increase the power of your search.

\di'fin\ *vb*

Definitions

Metasearches

A **metasearch is a way of doing multiple searches at the same time.** There are a number of metasearch sites on the Internet; I have included a chart showing

GENEALOGY-SPECIFIC SEARCH ENGINE SITES	
Ancestor Search	http://www.searchforancestors.com/
FamilySearch	http://www.familysearch.com/
Family Tree Magazine	http://www.familytreemagazine.com/search/
GenSource I Found It!	http://www.gensource.com/ifoundit/index.htm
GenealogyPortal.com	http://www.genealogyportal.com
The Genealogy Register	http://www.genealogyregister.com/
Genlink.org	http://www.genlink.org/
GenSearcher.com	http://www.geocities.com/Heartland/Acres/8310/gensearcher.html
NedGen	http://www.nedgen.nl/
Surname Finder	http://www.surnamefinder.com/

just a few of them. A metasearch site applies your search terms to a number of different search engines. The number of search engines used in a metasearch will vary. Some metasearches search just the most common search engines, primarily those listed in the chart on page 43. Others search obscure search engines in conjunction with the more popular ones.

METASEARCH SITES	
Dogpile	http://www.dogpile.com/index.gsp
Find-It!	http://www.itools.com/find-it/
Mamma	http://www.mamma.com/
MetaCrawler	http://www.metacrawler.com/index.html
MetaGopher	http://www.metagopher.com/
One2Seek Metasearch	http://www.metasearch-engine.com/
ProFusion	http://www.profusion.com/
Search.com	http://www.search.com/
SpaceSonar	http://www.spacesonar.com/
Supercrawler.com	http://www.supercrawler.com/
Webtaxi.com	http://www.webtaxi.com/

For instance, I could search for sites relevant to my Standerfer genealogy by visiting AltaVista, Hotbot, Excite, and Lycos individually. Or I could type in "Standerfer + genealogy" at one of the metasearch sites and have it send that out to all four of these search engines and more.

The results of a metasearch look a little different. The results may be separated by search engine. They may be separated by probability and have which search engines brought back each site listed. The point is that you get all the information in one search instead of having to execute separate searches.

Many of the search engines, both stand-alone and metasearch sites, display the search results with a probability factor. This is often misleading. Researchers may think a site that has a probability of 95 percent will be more useful than a site that has a probability of only 65 percent. They may ignore the lower-probability site and be disappointed when the higher-probability site does not have the information they were looking for.

These probabilities confuse some people. I have done searches on *Standerfer* and had my own Standerfer home page come up with a probability of 70 percent. Roughly translated, a probability of 95 percent says that the search engine is 95 percent sure this site conforms to your search criteria. While this is a method of organizing the list of search results, you should never dismiss the lower-probability sites.

A Metasearch With a Memory

The downside to searches on the Internet is that if you want the same information later you must re-create the search in question. However, there is a software program that allows you to retain your searches along with the list of possible matching sites.

In fact, I have found this software program to be more efficient in the sites that it finds and the information I get from them. The software is Copernic 2000. You can learn more about it at <http://www.copernic.com>, where you

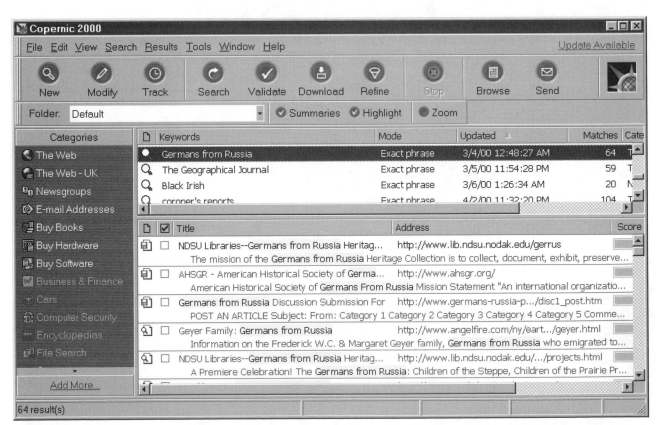

Figure 4.4
Copernic 2000 offers a metasearch system with a memory. Previous searches are stored so that they can be reused.

can take advantage of an offer for a free version, if you don't mind dealing with banner ads in the program. **Copernic 2000 (there is now a 2001 version available also) allows you to generate a search of hundreds of search engines and then receive a list of the most probable Web pages**. The list includes active links you can use to visit the sites found.

In addition to providing a strong search, it retains the search in a list for the next time you need to use that search. In genealogy the need to revisit a search is not a probability but a certainty. I will return to my Standerfer family research many times.

Before you object because new sites may have come online since the last

---

ADDING SITES TO YOUR FAVORITES FOLDERS IN MICROSOFT INTERNET EXPLORER

When you surf the Web, you will come across sites that you will want to visit again, so you create a bookmark or add it to your favorites. Unfortunately, after you've been online for a few weeks, months, or years, you will have so many favorites that your list is nearly as unwieldy as the Internet itself. Using folders will help organize your favorites, and adding your favorites to those folders is easy.

Microsoft Internet Explorer is fairly straightforward in how you can add favorites to the folders you have created. Once you find a site that you want to revisit,

1. Click on Favorites. A menu will appear.

2. Click on Add to Favorites. At this point, a window that allows you to add this site to your favorites, either by itself or in a folder, pops up.

3. Before you add this site, look at the name that appears in the Name field of this window. Does it make sense to you? If it is one of the thousands of sites titled "My Family," you should give it a more meaningful name that will distinguish it from other sites. If a site is about the Ramsey family in Adams County, Pennsylvania, call it something like "RAMSEY Adams Co, PA." Changing the names of the sites in your Favorites folders is perfectly acceptable; it's your list of favorites. To change the name of the site, click in the Name field and type in the name you want to use. (Remember that your favorites will appear in alphabetical order in your folders, so you may want to avoid beginning any names with *The*.)

4. Next, scroll through the list of folders. Click on the one you want this site to be in. If the folder you want is a subfolder, you will need to click on the plus sign (+) to the left of the main folder to reveal the subfolders.

5. Click on OK.

You have successfully added a favorite site to a folder.

search, know that the program keeps that in mind. Without having to alter my original search string, I can have Copernic 2000 regenerate the search.

Anything that saves me time gets high marks in my book. A program that remembers my search and allows me to either work from a list of previously found links or generate a new list is a must for my system.

REMEMBER TO RETURN TO THE SCENE

In chapter two, "Understanding Your Computer," you were introduced to the concept of saving links to your favorite Web sites. This allows you to return to them without having to regenerate a search or remember the steps through the links you took to get there the first time. The downside to this is that eventually you may have so many links that it will take you too long to weed through the list of favorites or bookmarks.

In chapter two, you learned how to create folders so that when you began to visit sites, after having run searches and visited directories, you would have someplace to store those favorite links in some sense of order. If you are new to computers, you may need to know how to save these in the folders.

"Adding Sites to Your Favorites Folders in Microsoft Internet Explorer" on page 49 walks you through the necessary steps to save a link in a folder and also points out that you can change the name of the site for display in your list of favorites.

When your browser software saves a link, it takes the name from the title supplied by the creator of the site. As we saw earlier in this chapter, many genealogy Web sites have noninformative titles. Such titles are of little use to you in your list of favorites. The point of organizing your links in folders is to be able to quickly locate a given site without the frustration of another search. If the title of the site is no clue as to why you like that site, then you need to give it a better title in your list of links.

WE CAN FIND, NOW LET'S USE

Now that you can search for sites on the Internet, let's examine the types of sites you are likely to find on the Internet. As with all aspects of genealogical research, there will be some caveats along the way.

FIVE

Tools of the Internet

I n chapter four, you were introduced to sites that help you find the real meat of the Internet—the Web sites with family histories and searchable databases. Now it is time to examine the different types of Web sites that you will encounter as you research your family history on the Internet.

While genealogists compiled some of the sites on a volunteer basis, other sites make available commercial databases. Some of the volunteer sites are of a higher caliber than some of the commercial sites. Each site was compiled with a goal in mind. Some may have been compiled to make money; others, to share genealogy. Unfortunately, some of them have been uploaded just so someone can take credit for the existence of a Web site.

Genealogical Web sites are a lot like the books we use in the library. We evaluate books as we work with them. If they cite sources, then we rank their validity on a higher scale than one that has no source citations. If the book has a bibliography, it has something to clue us in to where the compiler gathered the information and how they came to the conclusions they share in the book.

Reminder

For some reason when researchers find the same type of information on the Internet, they sometimes throw out this yardstick by which they measure all other resources. The Web is just another form of publishing. It is an easy form of publishing, so even those who are brand new to genealogy research are publishing online, sometimes before they should.

Let's look at some of the different types of Web sites. Each offers a different approach to research. Some allow you to perform searches; others limit you to simply reading through the site.

The basic genealogical sites include
- compiled family histories
- abstracts or transcriptions
- searchable databases
- discussion areas
- commercial sites

Each of these types of sites should supply you with information about the source of the data shared. It will be up to you to seek that information on some of the sites. Others will gladly state where they have gotten the information.

COMPILED FAMILY HISTORIES

It is fitting that this is one of the most prevalent varieties of genealogy Web sites. After all, if it weren't for all of the published family histories lining the shelves in the libraries, many of us would not have been able to overcome those brick walls.

Any seasoned genealogist will caution you to look out for undocumented works. View information from undocumented works with skepticism. Unless you can evaluate the information by comparing it with the sources cited, you cannot know the validity of a published work.

Somehow, genealogists do not always take this thinking to heart when they

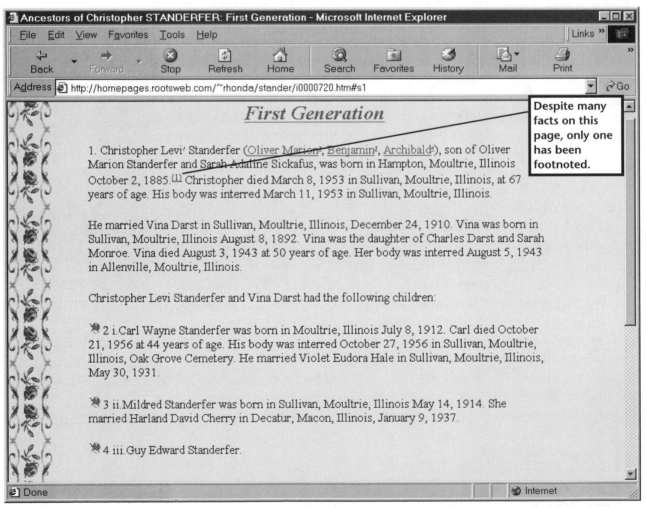

Figure 5.1
When online, genealogists use compiled family history Web pages the most. Not all of them include proper source citations.

venture onto the Internet. **Instead of questioning undocumented information, they swallow completely the family histories published on the Internet.**

Here is another little secret: The genealogy software programs that create those family history Web sites are designed to include source citations. They appear at the end of the Web site, and throughout the pages of the Web site you should find superscript numbers that are actually links to them. If you place your cursor over one of these links, you should see the familiar hand icon that lets you know you can click on the link. The link then takes you to the appropriate source citation for the number in question.

There is no excuse then for family history Web sites that do not include source citations. Yet many sites share information without any hint as to where the information came from.

Should you discover your family on such a site, go ahead and make a note of the information. You can even include it in your database if you wish, but be sure to make a thorough source citation. **Cite the Web site as your source.** A good reference is Elizabeth Shown Mills's *Evidence! Citation & Analysis for the Family Historian*. Also, take advantage of the notes features in your genealogy software. Note to yourself that this site contained no documents and that you need to follow up on the information found on the Web site.

You can be specific or vague, whatever works for you. I tend to record in notes the specific records that I want to check the next time I get to the appropriate research repository. Of course, this could have something to do with the fact that my memory doesn't seem to be what it used to be.

Should you discover that the family history Web site contradicts your research, don't be shy about contacting the compiler. In most cases, the person who has compiled the Web site has included an e-mail address. Use it. Ask what resources were used to come to the published conclusions.

ABSTRACTS OR TRANSCRIPTIONS

Many people are involved in volunteer projects to transcribe or abstract records and make them available on the Internet. There is a difference in these two methods.

A transcribed record is a verbatim copy of the record, including every word, misspelling, and punctuation mark. Such records are useful in that you do not have to wonder if the researcher left out a pertinent fact. Transcriptions take much longer to do than abstracts, so transcriptions are not as common.

When abstracting, the researcher records just the pertinent facts. These facts will vary depending on the type of record that is abstracted. For instance, in a land record, the pertinent facts include the names of the grantor(s) and grantee(s), the date of the instrument, the date of filing, the consideration, the land description, the names of the witnesses, and whether or not there was a release of dower.

To an experienced genealogist, the example of the land deed makes perfect sense. However, to a newcomer to genealogy, this information may not be common sense. Some of the people who created the Web pages you will discover online are newcomers to the field. They may not be aware of all the information to include in an abstract. Therefore, when you visit their Web sites, you may discover that they did not include the releases of dower, for example, in the abstracts.

This is an important lesson about researching on the Internet: **Never assume anything when working with compiled pages.** Always make note of questions. If you are new to genealogy and don't necessarily know the right questions to ask, assume that you will need to re-invent the wheel, so to speak, with information in each Web site that you find.

When you re-create the research, you not only verify what the compiler has shared, but you also begin to learn from others. Hands-on learning is often the best teacher, especially in genealogy.

SEARCHABLE DATABASES

Genealogists thrive on databases. They relied on them even before personal computing was so affordable and available. The *International Genealogical Index* or IGI has been available for many years. Its original format was microfiche. (See page 58.) This was one of the first databases that genealogists used.

Although the IGI was initially intended for members of The Church of Jesus Christ of Latter-day Saints to track Temple ordinance work, genealogists everywhere discovered that the IGI could serve in the capacity of an index to the world. The IGI is far from complete, but if you are fortunate enough to find your ancestor in this index, you will have an idea of where he was born or where he lived.

Over the years, the IGI has gone from microfiche to CD-ROM to the Internet, where you can now access it at any time. This is just one of the many databases that is available on the Internet.

When working with any online database, including commercial sites, there are a few questions to keep in mind: Where did the compiler of the database get the information? How was the information digitized? Are there source citations for the information included in the database?

Where?

Let's look at the first question—**Where did the compiler of the database get the information?** Is this information from original sources, or have individual genealogists been encouraged to share their own research? This will dramatically affect the validity of the data included.

The IGI is a perfect example of this. This database includes two different types of research: patron submissions and extraction entries. The patron submissions may cite sources such as "family knowledge," whereas the extraction entries have been carefully pulled from original records. The patron submissions come from information gathered by individual Latter-day Saints as they compiled their family tree as part of their beliefs. Individuals working with original records extracted the pertinent names, dates, and places to compile extraction entries.

A GLIMPSE INTO THE BELIEFS OF LATTER-DAY SAINTS

Members of The Church of Jesus Christ of Latter-day Saints believe that families can be together forever. They believe that when a couple is married in the Temple that they are not just married "until death do us part," but for "time and all eternity." A Church of Jesus Christ marriage is actually known as a sealing. When a couple who has been sealed in the Temple has children, those children are bound to them for eternity as well.

This begs the question: What about their ancestors who did not know about this religion? Latter-day Saints believe they can perform needed physical ordinances, including those of sealing husband to wife and children to parents, by standing in proxy for their ancestors.

After completing the necessary family history research, Latter-day Saints submit the names to their local Temple so that the work can be done on their behalf. Those Latter-day Saints who have proven worthy to go to the Temple can stand in proxy for their ancestors going through the special ordinances. These ordinances are considered necessary for the eternal progression and exaltation of all individuals. They are considered highly sacred. In fact, the Temple is not the normal house of worship for Latter-day Saints. It is considered to be a holy house to be entered only by the worthy.

The ordinances that are completed on behalf of ancestors include baptism for the dead, endowment, and sealing (spouse to spouse, child to parents). As these ordinances need to be completed only once for each person, they are recorded in the *International Genealogical Index*. Latter-day Saints then check this to avoid duplication when preparing the names for submission to the Temple.

In addition, when working in the IGI, regardless of what version, you need to pay close attention to the batch number. This number is the clue to the type of entry with which you are working. The batch number for an extraction entry often begins with a letter, such as *C* for birth or christening records and *M* for marriage records. (For help on decoding batch numbers, see page 56.) The computerized versions of the IGI (see page 59) will supply you with additional information, stating outright whether the entry is a patron submission or extracted from a given resource, such as birth records for a given town or county.

How?

The second question deals with how the information was digitized. Was it entered by hand? Did the group use scanners and optical character recognition (OCR) software? Are you looking at a scanned image of the original page of the book or census?

Each of these methods will alter the validity of the information with the exception of one. If the database holds scanned images of the original book or

Notes

DECODING THE BATCH NUMBER

The best way to understand where an entry in the IGI is from is to learn what the various batch numbers stand for. Back in the old days, before computers in the Family History Centers, we relied on a microfiche version of the IGI. Once you had the entry you were interested in, you then had to convert the batch number to an input source number (which was usually the microfilm or microfiche number where the original source could be found). The *IGI Batch Number Index*, a microfiche listing batch numbers in numerical order is still available at your local Family History Center. It is a valuable tool when trying to understand the origins of entries in the IGI.

Below is a table that details the beginning character or characters of a batch number and an accompanying description for batch numbers beginning with those letters or numbers.

A	Church of Jesus Christ Temple sealing, only available in Special Collections. Original record open only to certain church members.
C	Births and christenings from Church of Jesus Christ extraction work. Records usually on microfilm.
D	Patron notification. Should have another batch number listed, which is the one you would actually concentrate on.
E	Marriages from Church of Jesus Christ extraction work. Records may be available on microfilm.
F	Family group records that are available on microfilm.
H	Church membership records of deceased individuals.
J, K	Births and christenings from church extraction work. Records may be on microfilm.
L	Church Temple—originated record.
M	Marriages from church extraction work. Records usually on microfilm (with the exception of M17 and M18).
M17, M18	Early church Temple sealing records.
P	Births and christenings from church extraction work. Records may be on microfilm.
T	Information comes from family group records, work done by the special groups, such as work on Royalty, and information from the Temple Records Index Bureau (TIB).
0000001 to 0000023	Patron submissions to Temples outside the United States.

500	Similar to F on page 56. Family group records.
60 to 6899999	Patron submissions that were automated through Personal Ancestral File.
694	Early church ward and branch records available on microfilm.
6940405 to 6949426	Card index to early church ward and branch records.
69407	Early church ward and branch records from Scandinavia.
69409	Family group records.
696	Records not open to the public.
725	Marriages from England indexed by J.S.W. Gibson.
744	Several extraction projects.
745, 754	Extraction from statewide vital records indexes.
766	Patron submissions on Marriage Entry form or entries from extraction (requires 766 Batch Cross Index to get the actual batch number).
8–4 to 8–9	Patron submissions.

Once you have the film number, you can then use the Family History Library catalog on CD-ROM to search for the actual record by using the film/fiche number search option. You cannot type in the batch number and get the film number.

—Rhonda R. McClure
"Overheard in GenForum: IGI Batch Numbers"
http://www.genealogy.com/heard070199.html
Posted 1 July 1999

census pages, then there was no room for errors to creep in during the digitization. While the original book may have had errors, at least neither human nor machine when digitizing the resource has compounded them.

Fortunately, this is becoming more the norm in the digitizing of records. However, this was not always the case; and for those volunteering to work on projects to compile databases, the cost of such equipment may not be feasible.

Until recently, while genealogy CD-ROM companies were releasing more CDs of digitized images as described above, the majority of the Web sites were using another method, generally that of hand typing.

I have already confessed my own typing limitations. I am also sure that others

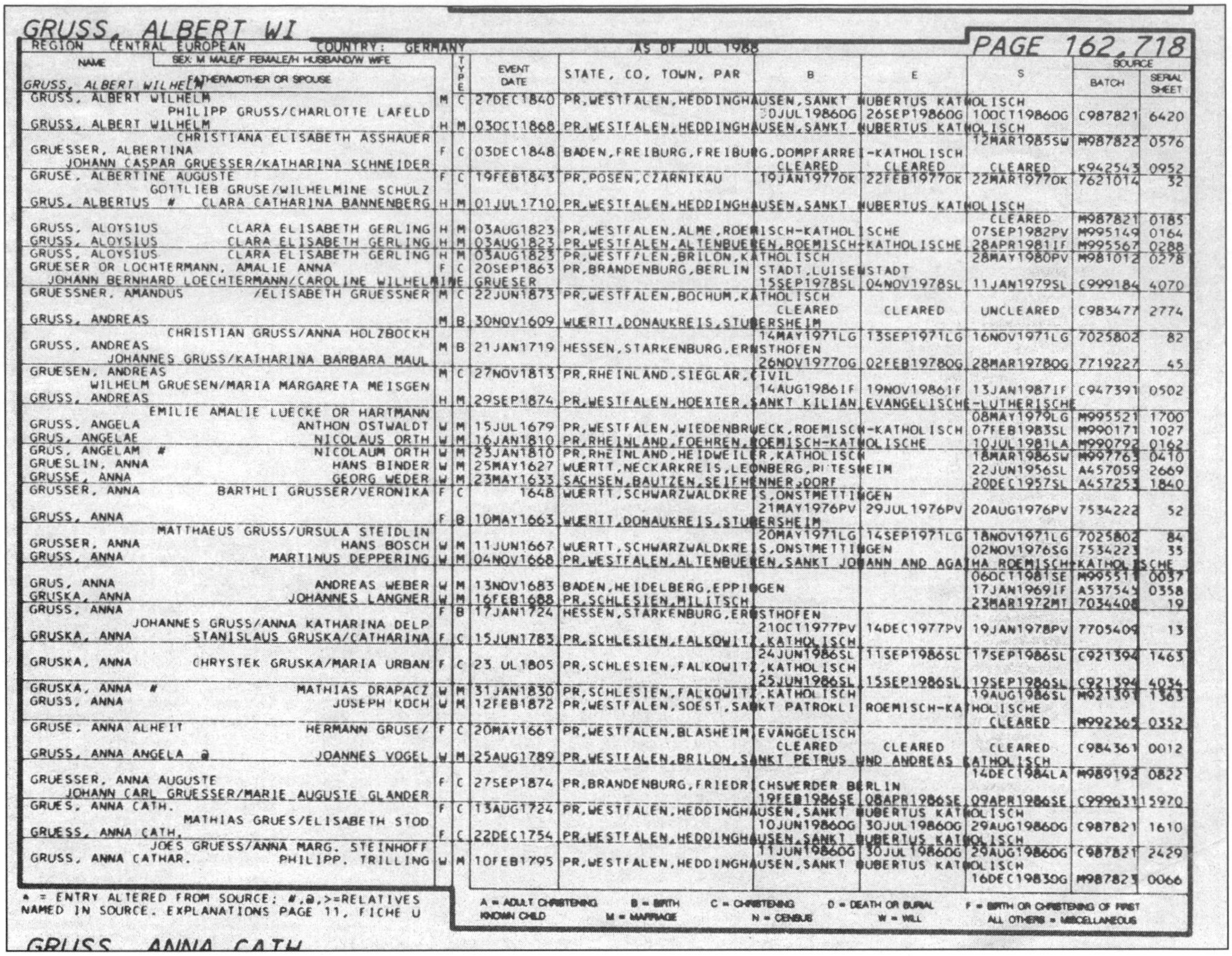
GRUSS, ALBERT WI
REGION CENTRAL EUROPEAN COUNTRY: GERMANY AS OF JUL 1988 PAGE 162,718
NAME / SEX: M MALE/F FEMALE/H HUSBAND/W WIFE / FATHER/MOTHER OR SPOUSE — TYPE — EVENT DATE — STATE, CO, TOWN, PAR — B — E — S — SOURCE: BATCH, SERIAL SHEET
GRUSS, ALBERT WILHELM
GRUSS, ALBERT WILHELM M C 27DEC1840 PR,WESTFALEN,HEDDINGHAUSEN,SANKT HUBERTUS KATHOLISCH
PHILIPP GRUSS/CHARLOTTE LAFELD 30JUL1986OG 26SEP1986OG 10OCT1986OG C987821 6420
GRUSS, ALBERT WILHELM H M 03OCT1868 PR,WESTFALEN,HEDDINGHAUSEN,SANKT HUBERTUS KATHOLISCH
CHRISTIANA ELISABETH ASSHAUER 12MAR1985SW M987822 0576
GRUESSER, ALBERTINA F C 03DEC1848 BADEN,FREIBURG,FREIBURG,DOMPFARREI-KATHOLISCH
JOHANN CASPAR GRUESSER/KATHARINA SCHNEIDER CLEARED CLEARED CLEARED K942543 0952
GRUSE, ALBERTINE AUGUSTE F C 19FEB1843 PR,POSEN,CZARNIKAU 19JAN1977OK 22FEB1977OK 22MAR1977OK 7621014 32
GOTTLIEB GRUSE/WILHELMINE SCHULZ
GRUS, ALBERTUS # CLARA CATHARINA BANNENBERG H M 01JUL1710 PR,WESTFALEN,HEDDINGHAUSEN,SANKT HUBERTUS KATHOLISCH
CLEARED M987821 0185
GRUSS, ALOYSIUS CLARA ELISABETH GERLING H M 03AUG1823 PR,WESTFALEN,ALME,ROEMISCH-KATHOLISCHE 07SEP1982PV M995149 0164
GRUSS, ALOYSIUS CLARA ELISABETH GERLING H M 03AUG1823 PR,WESTFALEN,ALTENBUEREN,ROEMISCH-KATHOLISCHE 28APR1981IF M995567 0288
GRUSS, ALOYSIUS CLARA ELISABETH GERLING H M 03AUG1823 PR,WESTFALEN,BRILON,KATHOLISCH 28MAY1980PV M981012 0278
GRUESER OR LOCHTERMANN, AMALIE ANNA F C 20SEP1863 PR,BRANDENBURG,BERLIN STADT,LUISENSTADT
JOHANN BERNHARD LOECHTERMANN/CAROLINE WILHELMINE GRUESER 15SEP1978SL 04NOV1978SL 11JAN1979SL C999184 4070
GRUESSNER, AMANDUS /ELISABETH GRUESSNER M C 22JUN1873 PR,WESTFALEN,BOCHUM,KATHOLISCH
CLEARED CLEARED UNCLEARED C983477 2774
GRUSS, ANDREAS M B 30NOV1609 WUERTT,DONAUKREIS,STUBERSHEIM
CHRISTIAN GRUSS/ANNA HOLZBOCKH 14MAY1971LG 13SEP1971LG 16NOV1971LG 7025802 82
GRUSS, ANDREAS M B 21JAN1719 HESSEN,STARKENBURG,ERNSTHOFEN
JOHANNES GRUSS/KATHARINA BARBARA MAUL 26NOV1977OG 02FEB1978OG 28MAR1978OG 7719227 45
GRUESEN, ANDREAS M C 27NOV1813 PR,RHEINLAND,SIEGLAR,CIVIL
WILHELM GRUESEN/MARIA MARGARETA MEISGEN 14AUG1986IF 19NOV1986IF 13JAN1987IF C947391 0502
GRUSS, ANDREAS H M 29SEP1874 PR,WESTFALEN,HOEXTER,SANKT KILIAN,EVANGELISCHE-LUTHERISCHE
EMILIE AMALIE LUECKE OR HARTMANN 08MAY1979LG M995521 1700
GRUSS, ANGELA ANTHON OSTWALDT W M 15JUL1679 PR,WESTFALEN,WIEDENBRUECK,ROEMISCH-KATHOLISCH 07FEB1983SL M990171 1027
GRUS, ANGELAE NICOLAUS ORTH W M 16JAN1810 PR,RHEINLAND,FOEHREN,ROEMISCH-KATHOLISCHE 10JUL1981LA M990792 0162
GRUS, ANGELAM # NICOLAUM ORTH W M 23JAN1810 PR,RHEINLAND,HEIDWEILER,KATHOLISCH 18MAR1986SW M997763 0410
GRUESLIN, ANNA HANS BINDER W M 25MAY1627 WUERTT,NECKARKREIS,LEONBERG,RITESHEIM 22JUN1956SL A457059 2669
GRUSSE, ANNA GEORG WEDER W M 23MAY1633 SACHSEN,BAUTZEN,SEIFHENNER,DORF 20DEC1957SL A457253 1840
GRUSSER, ANNA BARTHLI GRUSSER/VERONIKA F C 1648 WUERTT,SCHWARZWALDKREIS,ONSTMETTINGEN
21MAY1976PV 29JUL1976PV 20AUG1976PV 7534222 52
GRUSS, ANNA F B 10MAY1663 WUERTT,DONAUKREIS,STUBERSHEIM
MATTHAEUS GRUSS/URSULA STEIDLIN 20MAY1971LG 14SEP1971LG 18NOV1971LG 7025802 84
GRUSSER, ANNA HANS BOSCH W M 11JUN1667 WUERTT,SCHWARZWALDKREIS,ONSTMETTINGEN 02NOV1976SG 7534223 35
GRUSS, ANNA MARTINUS DEPPERING W M 04NOV1668 PR,WESTFALEN,ALTENBUEREN,SANKT JOHANN AND AGATHA ROEMISCH-KATHOLISCHE
06OCT1981SE M995511 0037
GRUS, ANNA ANDREAS WEBER W M 13NOV1683 BADEN,HEIDELBERG,EPPINGEN 17JAN1969IF A537545 0358
GRUSKA, ANNA JOHANNES LANGNER W M 16FEB1688 PR,SCHLESIEN,MILITSCH 23MAR1972MT 7034408 19
GRUSS, ANNA F B 17JAN1724 HESSEN,STARKENBURG,ERNSTHOFEN
JOHANNES GRUSS/ANNA KATHARINA DELP 21OCT1977PV 14DEC1977PV 19JAN1978PV 7705409 13
GRUSKA, ANNA STANISLAUS GRUSKA/CATHARINA F C 15JUN1783 PR,SCHLESIEN,FALKOWITZ,KATHOLISCH
24JUN1986SL 11SEP1986SL 17SEP1986SL C921394 1463
GRUSKA, ANNA CHRYSTEK GRUSKA/MARIA URBAN F C 23 UL1805 PR,SCHLESIEN,FALKOWITZ,KATHOLISCH
25JUN1986SL 15SEP1986SL 19SEP1986SL C921394 4034
GRUSKA, ANNA # MATHIAS DRAPACZ W M 31JAN1830 PR,SCHLESIEN,FALKOWITZ,KATHOLISCH 19AUG1986SL M921391 1363
GRUSS, ANNA JOSEPH KOCH W M 12FEB1872 PR,WESTFALEN,SOEST,SANKT PATROKLI ROEMISCH-KATHOLISCHE
CLEARED M992365 0352
GRUSE, ANNA ALHEIT HERMANN GRUSE/ F C 20MAY1661 PR,WESTFALEN,BLASHEIM,EVANGELISCH
CLEARED CLEARED CLEARED C984361 0012
GRUSS, ANNA ANGELA @ JOANNES VOGEL W M 25AUG1789 PR,WESTFALEN,BRILON,SANKT PETRUS UND ANDREAS KATHOLISCH
14DEC1984LA M989192 0822
GRUESSER, ANNA AUGUSTE F C 27SEP1874 PR,BRANDENBURG,FRIEDRICHSWERDER BERLIN
JOHANN CARL GRUESSER/MARIE AUGUSTE GLANDER 19FEB1986SE 08APR1986SE 09APR1986SE C999631 15970
GRUES, ANNA CATH. F C 13AUG1724 PR,WESTFALEN,HEDDINGHAUSEN,SANKT HUBERTUS KATHOLISCH
MATHIAS GRUES/ELISABETH STOD 10JUN1986OG 30JUL1986OG 29AUG1986OG C987821 1610
GRUESS, ANNA CATH. F C 22DEC1754 PR,WESTFALEN,HEDDINGHAUSEN,SANKT HUBERTUS KATHOLISCH
JOES GRUESS/ANNA MARG. STEINHOFF 11JUN1986OG 30JUL1986OG 29AUG1986OG C987821 2429
GRUSS, ANNA CATHAR. PHILIPP. TRILLING W M 10FEB1795 PR,WESTFALEN,HEDDINGHAUSEN,SANKT HUBERTUS KATHOLISCH
16DEC1983OG M987823 0066
* = ENTRY ALTERED FROM SOURCE; #,@,>=RELATIVES NAMED IN SOURCE. EXPLANATIONS PAGE 11, FICHE U
A = ADULT CHRISTENING B = BIRTH C = CHRISTENING D = DEATH OR BURIAL F = BIRTH OR CHRISTENING OF FIRST KNOWN CHILD M = MARRIAGE N = CENSUS W = WILL ALL OTHERS = MISCELLANEOUS
GRUSS ANNA CATH

Figure 5.2
The *International Genealogical Index* was originally released on microfiche. Reprinted by permission. © 2001 by Intellectual Reserve, Inc.

out there have been known to hit a wrong key from time to time. Usually such mistakes take place when my ancestors are indexed. This must be why my ancestors never show up in the databases.

Even with the most stringent of verification practices, mistakes will sneak in when records are being digitized by hand. Just as we have noticed mistakes in typed indexes of the land records or vital records that we view in the county courthouse, the same thing is happening today with computers.

Therefore, you need to keep two things in mind when working with such databases. First, remember to verify the information against original sources if at all possible. Second, do not give up on a source just because you cannot find your ancestor in an online index. Perhaps the name was not abstracted correctly, so your search will not reveal the entry under the spelling or spellings you know. For example, the surname Herendeen was included in a census index as Hundun. Until I found that, I had not thought of Hundun as an alternative spelling for Herendeen. I have since added it to my list of variant spellings, even though I have not seen it again.

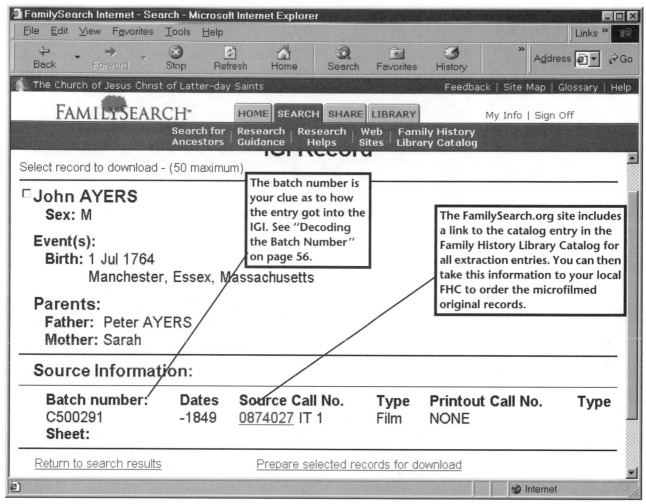

Figure 5.3
Many researchers stop after finding information at the FamilySearch Web site. Reprinted by permission. © 2001 by Intellectual Reserve, Inc.

The other method I mentioned was the use of OCR software. Optical character recognition software takes an image from your scanner and looks at the text on the page. It uses an internal alphabet to convert the graphic image to actual text, which can then be used in a word processing program.

While the OCR program has been trained, it will at times produce errors. The type on the scanned page may not come through clearly. The ink on the page may be splotchy, making the original hard to read. Such features of the scanned text affect how the OCR program reads it. In addition, because a computer is doing the majority of the work in this instance, there is not usually enough comparison from the original to the newly digitized version to notice the errors that do appear.

To you, the person working with the results, some words may look like nonsense. Either the words will be horribly misspelled or they will include extraneous characters such as those that appear above the number keys on the keyboard.

Warning

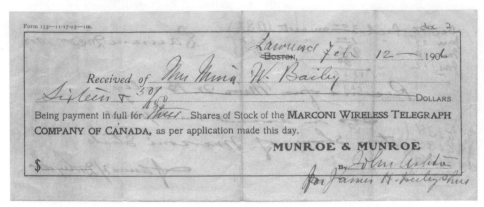

Figure 5.4
Digitization of original records is becoming more prevalent. Graphical digitization is the only option for handwritten records.

Sources?

In some instances, when working with commercial databases, it will be easy to tell where information was acquired. Much of the data added to the commercial sites comes from books or other such records. As you conduct your search, you will know from the title of the database listed where the information came from. However, this is not true of all databases.

One of the most commonly used databases is Ancestral File from the Family-Search CD-ROMs or the FamilySearch Web site, <http://www.familysearch.or g>. This database consists completely of patron-submitted GEDCOM files. Unfortunately, even if the individual making the submission included source citations, these were stripped out when the data was added to Ancestral File.

Individuals may submit the research to databases such as Family Tree Maker's World Family Tree or RootsWeb's WorldConnect. They may elect not to include their source citations, assuming they entered source citations in their computer in the first place. If you plan to use this information, **you must verify what has been shared.**

If this sounds like I am repeating myself, I am. This is something that cannot be stressed enough. I have seen too many people swallow information they found in one of these databases only to regenerate it on their Web site or in a GEDCOM they share with another researcher. Eventually the information is taken as fact, even if it isn't. In the end, this will only hurt the field of genealogy and family history.

Important

DISCUSSION AREAS

Many people overlook the value of the online discussion area. They feel that real information can only be found in some of the sites we have already mentioned. They concentrate completely on compiled family history pages or searchable databases.

My introduction to discussion areas and their wealth of information took place about thirteen years ago. It was my first night as an online genealogist. In fact, we had subscribed to the commercial online service that evening.

UNDERSTANDING GEDCOM

GEDCOM stands for GEnealogical Data COMmunication, and it is this standard that allows you to share your data with others; or send it to Salt Lake City, to the Family History Library for sharing in the Ancestral File and Pedigree Resource File.

GEDCOM files are very specific. Each line contains a detail about a person, family, source, or repository as found in your database. The Family History Library Department developed the GEDCOM standard in 1984. Its purpose was to make it easier for Church members to be able to share their data for inclusion in the *International Genealogical Index* through their own Personal Ancestral File program. As we have seen with many of the tools that have come out of the Family History Library, however, this one quickly took on a life of its own. Over the next thirteen years this standard has grown with the current version (5.5) now being used by most genealogy program developers.

COMMSOFT introduced Event GEDCOM that supported data that was event linked, as opposed to the lineage-linked support of standard GEDCOM. Event-linked databases link the individuals together through the various events in their lives. Lineage-linked databases link individuals through familial connections. While approved by The Church of Jesus Christ of Latter-day Saints, Event GEDCOM has never become a part of the GEDCOM standard.

OK, now we know what GEDCOM means. But how does it help you? I'll point out right away that it does not mean you can change back and forth from software to software without having a little cleanup, but it sure does save hours on the more basic entries for each person.

The basic structure is to take all the data in your database and break it down into single pieces of information. These are identified with tags so that the program reading the file knows where to put each of the lines of information, thus keeping all the family units together and all the events for each individual attached to the right individual. If you are truly interested in how the GEDCOM file compiles all your data, create a GEDCOM file and then open it in your word processor. It is a simple text file that can be read by any word processing program. Here is a short example to give you an idea of what it looks like.

```
0   HEAD
1   SOUR      UFTREE
1   CHAR      ANSEL
1   DATE      28 APR 1998
0   @TI2@     INDI
1   NAME      Charles Phillip / Ingalls/
1   NUMB      2
1   CHAN
2   DATE      28 APR 1998
```

continued

```
1   SEX        M
1   BIRT
2   DATE       10 JAN 1836
2   PLAC       Cuba, Allegheny, NY
1   DEAT
2   DATE       08 JUN 1902
2   PLAC       De Smet, Kingsbury, Dakota Territory
1   FAMC       @F2@
1   FAMS       @F3@
0   @I3@       INDI
1   NAME       Caroline Lake / Quiner/
1   NUMB       3
1   CHAN
2   DATE       27 APR 1998
1   SEX        F
1   BIRT
2   DATE       12 DEC 1839
2   PLAC       Milwaukee Co., WI
1   DEAT
2   DATE       20 APR 1923
```

Each person, event, source, repository, and family has a GEDCOM tag. As a genealogy program reads the GEDCOM file (always given a .GED extension), it knows what to do with the names, dates, places, repositories, and sources and how to keep them linked as you go from one software program to another.

I would like to be able to say that importing information from a GEDCOM file magically puts all the information into the proper place. Unfortunately GED-COM is more like a baseline standard which the developers have built upon. What this means to you is that not all the information may be recognized by your genealogy program. Items that your genealogy program cannot recognize are called exceptions, and information about them is put into a text file that you can read later to see what your program did with the unrecognized data.

When working with GEDCOM files from cousins, it is a good idea to open them as separate projects or family files. This allows you to look at the information for accuracy, possible duplications, and applicability to your own line. Then once you are sure you want to import the information into your database, you can either import the entire GEDCOM file or separate out those specific individuals you want to import.

The commercial services that existed then were a far cry from what we have now. There were no pictures; everything was done in text. The commercial services were also isolated communities. You had to join in order to use their resources. That meant that the genealogists who subscribed developed a community on their service.

Genealogists shared current research and asked questions. Others came along, read the questions, and offered their advice. This give-and-take was educational and useful.

Those who are new to the hobby of genealogy may know only the Internet as the online source. The Internet is quite different with the graphics, photographs, and sound that Web designers often include. It is also less personal than the communities of before.

We are all guilty of hit-and-run research. We do a search on a search engine, click a link in the search results, read through the site, then move on. We forget that there is a person behind that Web site. A genealogist, willing to share, is behind that Web site.

Discussion areas fall into one of four types. Each is a little different as to the manner in which you receive information and the type of information you are likely to receive. We will look at all four of them:

- bulletin boards
- mailing lists
- newsgroups
- chat rooms

Bulletin Boards

The easiest way to comprehend a bulletin board is to think of a physical bulletin board, such as one you might see in a college dorm or in the local library. Genealogists who have attended conferences could equate electronic bulletin boards to the physical ones that often contain messages from individuals looking for fellow conference attendees or a ticket to one of the luncheons or the banquet.

Just as you must walk to these types of bulletin boards, you must go find the electronic bulletin boards that exist on the Internet. You must visit them to read the messages. You must stay there to send a message. In the past, you even had to revisit them to see if there were any responses to your posts. However, now some of them offer e-mail notification when someone has responded to a bulletin board message.

Bulletin boards exist for many subjects, so you cannot type "bulletin board" into a search engine and magically get a list of all the genealogy bulletin boards that exist online. While the genealogy bulletin boards would probably appear, you would find them intermixed with many bulletin boards that do not interest you.

Page 64 has a list of bulletin boards to get you started.

Notes

Mailing Lists

Mailing lists are much as they sound. You receive e-mail messages when you pick up your regular e-mail. The difference from your regular e-mail is that the message has gone to many individuals instead of just one or a few. The tip-off for you is what appears after *To:* in the message address. Messages sent directly to you show your e-mail address or name after *To:*. Messages sent to people on a mailing list will show the mailing list's address after *To:* (see example letter on page 66).

This has confused many people. I remember one particular incident a couple

\di'fin\ *vb*

Definitions

BULLETIN BOARD SITES	
GenConnect	http://cgi.rootsweb.com~genbbs
Genealogy Exchange & Surname Registry	http://www.genexchange.com/index.cfm
GenealogyOutfitters	http://www.genealogyoutfitters.com/messages/index.cgi
Heritage Quest Query Center	http://www.heritagequest.com/genealogy/queriescenter
Yahoo! Genealogy Clubs	http://dir.clubs.yahoo.com/Family_Home/Genealogy/
About.com Genealogy site	http://genealogy.about.com/hobbies/genealogy/mbody.htm
GenForum	http://genforum.genealogy.com/
Genealogy Queries	http://ourworld.compuserve.com/homepages/Strawn/allqueri.htm

of years back, when I was the moderator of a mailing list for a genealogy program. This person had joined the list either late the night before or early that morning. I watched as the messages went back and forth.

First, I would read the message from someone with a question about the program or how to do something within the program. Next, I would see a message from this new person. The tone of the messages changed as the day continued. His first messages were helpful and friendly. About halfway into the day, the messages grew shorter, stating something like, "I'm afraid I don't know the answer to that question."

By the end of the day, the new person's messages sounded frantic and contained pleas for people to stop sending all of those questions. At this point I sent the individual a private e-mail and explained what was going on. Unfortunately, the new subscriber was under the misconception that the people were all writing to him personally. I explained that he was not expected to respond to each message and that the messages were going to many different people simultaneously.

Like the bulletin boards, there are mailing lists for all kinds of subjects. Included on page 67 are the names and URLs for servers that offer mailing list capabilities. No doubt, you will recognize some of them, as we have looked at them for other genealogical items.

One suggestion I offered the panicked individual was to change the format in which he received the mailing list messages. This would make it look different from regular e-mail and help remind that person of the mailing list subscription. While some mailing lists offer an ability to prepend the subject line with a bracketed abbreviation for the mailing list, not all mailing list administrators have turned on this option. Newcomers to mailing lists also do not realize that such a prepend—APG, for example—indicates that the message is coming from the mailing list.

Mailing lists come in two varieties. The first is the list mode, and each message that is sent to the mailing list will come to you as a single e-mail message. It may be difficult to differentiate it from your regular e-mail. The second format is digest mode. This method sends you perhaps one to three e-mail messages a day, depending on how busy the mailing list is. Each e-mail message consists of a table of contents of sorts at the front of the message. It may have ten

Notes

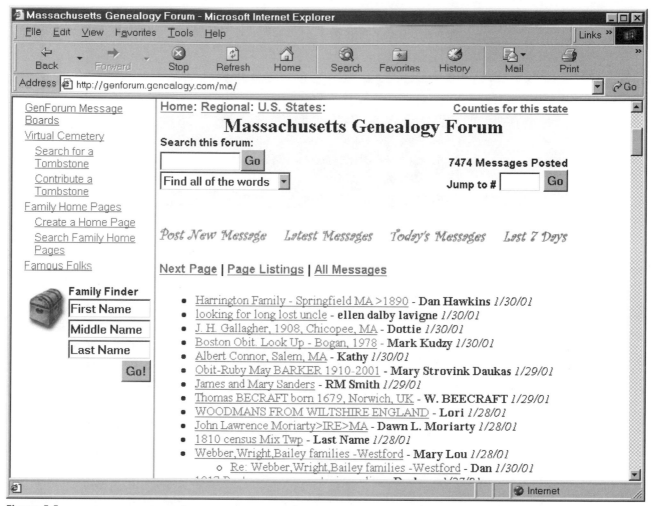

Figure 5.5
Bulletin boards offer genealogists a way to carry on a conversation with fellow researchers on a particular topic.

entries. These are the titles of the messages included in that digest. You can then read through the ten to twenty messages in a single e-mail.

Newsgroups

Newsgroups are probably more closely associated to bulletin boards than they are to mailing lists. You must seek them out as opposed to receiving e-mail from them. They also are threaded like bulletin boards.

Threaded messages show you the title of the first message, then below that and indented may be a response to that message. This indenting continues as individuals read and respond to the different posts. Threaded conversations allow you to get the complete research process. Mailing lists do not offer this as an option. You must either quote from the previous message or remember the ongoing discussion. My memory is often not up to the challenge.

I find that threaded conversations offer a valuable learning tool for new genealogists: They allow you to read a research problem and see how to resolve it. The suggestions shared by other researchers may clue you in to idiosyncrasies in the

X-From_: McClain-L-request@rootsweb.com Sun Jul 4 14:12:37 1999
Resent-Date: Sun, 4 Jul 1999 12:11:28 -0700 (PDT)
X-Sender: rhondam@thegenealogist.com
X-Mailer: QUALCOMM Windows Eudora Pro Version 4.1
Date: Sun, 04 Jul 1999 15:08:24 -0400
Old-To: McClain-L@rootsweb.com
From: "Rhonda R. McClure" <rhondam@thegenealogist.com>
Subject: Daniel MCCLAIN, PA 1749
To: McClain-L@rootsweb.com
Resent-From: McClain-L@rootsweb.com
X-Mailing-List: <McClain-L@rootsweb.com> archive/latest/426
X-Loop: McClain-L@rootsweb.com
Resent-Sender: McClain-L-request@rootsweb.com

Hello,

I am researching a Daniel McCLAIN. He was born in Pennsylvania, circa 1749. He married Aug 1770 in York Co., PA to Nancy (last name unknown). This information came from Annie W. Burns Bell, "Abstracts of Pension Papers of the Soldiers of the Revolutionary War, War of 1812, Indian Wars Residing in Scott County, KY."

He moved from PA to Scott County, Kentucky. Through surviving tax and land records and the pension abstract, I have been able to determine the names of four of his children:

1. Nancy McCLAIN, b. before 1780

2. Robert McCLAIN, b. 14 Dec 1780 in PA; m. abt. 1813 to Elizabeth VAN ZANT; d. 1864 Orange Co., IN

3. Ruth McCLAIN, b. 6 Sep 1782

4. John McCLAIN, b. 25 Apr 1786

I am descended from Robert, through his daughter Jane.

If anyone has any information on this line, I would appreciate hearing about it.

Thank you.

records for a given area or repository. It is always nicer to learn the easy way, from someone else, than the hard way, which is often more painful and expensive.

Unfortunately, there are not as many newsgroups as there are mailing lists. The subjects for newsgroups are generally broader than for mailing lists. You also must have the ability to read the newsgroups. Both Internet browsers support this under Mail.

Newsgroups and mailing lists have one thing in common: You may not want

MAILING LIST SERVERS	
Genealogy Resources on the Internet	http://www.rootsweb.com/~jfuller/gen_mail_info.html
FamilySearch—Collaboration E-Mail Lists	http://www.familysearch.org/Eng/Share/Collaborate/frameset_share.asp
Publicly Accessible Mailing Lists	http://paml.net/
List-Universe	http://www.listz.com/
Yahoo! Groups	http://groups.yahoo.com/
Mailing Lists (on Roots Web)	http://lists.rootsweb.com/
Cata List	http://www.lsoft.com/catalist.html

to read all of the messages. In chapter eight, we will look at some software utilities to aid you in finding just those messages in which you are interested.

Chat Rooms

My first experience online was in a chat room. They have developed a negative reputation over the years through the media, but for genealogists they can be a chance to get together with individuals who will share your excitement at the latest discovery.

Chat rooms are similar to bulletin boards in that you must go to them. That is the only similarity to the other discussion areas already mentioned. Everything about a chat room is different. You need different software. You need a different mindset. You may even need an alarm clock.

Reminder

Just as you have your e-mail software for reading your e-mail messages, you must also have software for accessing and joining chat rooms. Some of these are shareware programs, allowing you to try before you buy. The list shows just a few of the easy-to-find ones that you can download online.

Chat rooms, originally referred to as real-time conferences, allow you to visit with other genealogists live online. Unlike mailing lists, where a message is sent to everyone in the group and responses come back over a couple of days, the communication in a chat room is live and instantaneous. Of course, to get that instant response, people must attend the chat at the same time. Chats are run in real-time. Real-time is techno speak for "gotta watch the clock."

Chats are scheduled for specific times. The trick is to remember what time zone you are in and make any necessary adjustments to the time. If a chat is scheduled for 10 P.M. Eastern time and you live in California, you will miss it if you log on at 10 P.M. your time. No one will be there. In order to make that chat, you would need to log on at 7 P.M.

Also, daylight saving time can play into this. I have some friends who live in Phoenix. Since Arizona does not follow daylight saving time, my friends must further adjust their thinking in order to make it to the chats on time. At least one person I know sets his alarm clock so he doesn't miss a chat because of the time difference.

Chat rooms also vary in tone. Chats may range from a gabfest to a serious

---

MAILING LIST MESSAGE IN DIGEST MODE

Some mailing lists arrive in digest format. The top of the message is a table of contents of the messages included in that digest.

ROOTS-L Digest	Volume 00 : Issue 588
Today's Topics:	
#1 Re: 2nd Time Sending Message	[LaChance <lachance@ccis.com>]
#2 Ancestors in Scotland/How to search	["Kim A. Lance" <kalance@cc.owu.edu>]
#3 RE: Ingram	[CROBIN5008@aol.com]
#4 Ruelkes in Wisconsin	[NMClara@aol.com]
#5 Chronic Asotetis	[Orbie & Lorene <olhops@ipa.net>]
#6 Kelley	["Harlow" <harlow@hutchtel.net>]
#7 PHD's #584 message #6	[adrian s brisee <rottenralf@juno.com>]
#8 re, Chronic Asotetis	["S.T. Richbourg" <str@iag.net>]
#9 Harriet Morton Holmes	[MonaNAriz@aol.com]
#10 Re: Dunn	[LatWC@aol.com]
#11 Brenda Joyce Jerome	[Mary P Hammersmith <mphammersmith@earthlink.net>]
#12 SHIRLEY SCHMEHL	[GGulland@aol.com]
#13 PERKINS FAMILY OF VA., KY, MO.	[GGulland@aol.com]
#14 Re: [ROOTS-L] re, Chronic Asotetis	["MScheffler" <figaro@dreamscape.com>]
#15 LAKE FAMILY	["L J TONG" <p_earl@prodigy.net>]
#16 LDS help needed:	[kujawski@marywood1.marywood.edu]
#17 Thomas Harris of Colorado:	[kujawski@marywood1.marywood.edu]
#18 Grovenor WILLIAMS	[MaeMay510@aol.com]
#19 FINGER-BATHRICK	[MaeMay510@aol.com]
#20 John SETTLE/Mary (STRUDER) STROTHE	[Sharon Clark <clarksha@swbell.net>]

GENEALOGY NEWSGROUPS	
Scottish Clans	news:alt.scottish.clans
Denmark	news:dk.historie.genealogi
English Genealogy Newsgroup	news:news//england.genealogy.general/
Europe	news:fido.eur.genealogy
Germany	news:fido.ger.genealogy
Genealogy of French-Speaking People	news:fr.rec.genealogie
Norwegian Genealogy	news:no.fritid.slektsforsking.diverse
Norwegian Genealogy—searching for relatives and ancestors	news:no.fritid.slektsforsking.etterlysing
Norwegian Genealogy—computer software discussions	news:no.fritid.slektsforsking.it
Basque Culture	news:soc.culture.basque
African Genealogy	news:soc.genealogy.african
Australia & New Zealand	news:soc.genealogy.australia+nz
Benelux Region (Belgium, the Netherlands, and Luxembourg)	news:soc.genealogy.benelux
Great Britain	news:soc.genealogy.britain
Genealogy of French-Speaking People	news:soc.genealogy.french
German Genealogy	news:soc.genealogy.german
Hispanic Genealogy	news:soc.genealogy.Hispanic
Irish Genealogy	news:soc.genealogy.Ireland
Jewish Genealogy	news:soc.genealogy.jewish
Scandinavian Genealogy	news:soc.genealogy.Nordic
Slavic Genealogy	news:soc.genealogy.Slavic
Genealogy Research in the West Indies	news:soc.genealogy.west-indies
Swedish Genealogy	news:swnet.sci.genealogi
Welsh Genealogy	news:wales.genealogy.general

INTERNET RELAY CHAT (IRC) PROGRAMS	
mIRC	http://www.geocities.com/SiliconValley/Park/6000/index.html
OrbitIRC	http://www.orbitirc.com/
PIRCH	http://www.pirchat.com/
XiRCON	http://www.xircon.com/

discussion complete with a guest speaker. They may range from a party atmosphere where everyone chats at once to a controlled environment where you

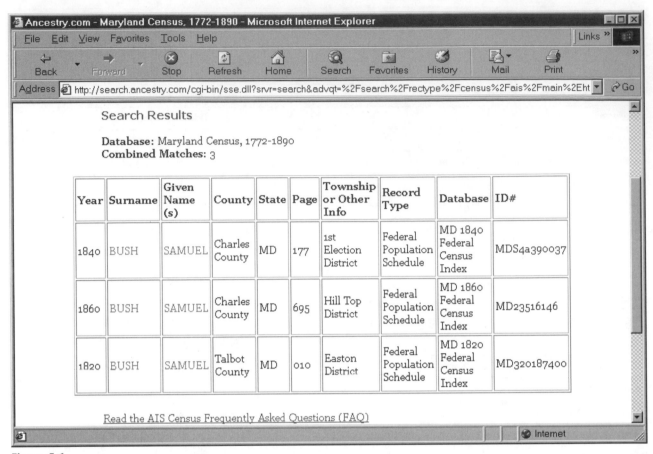

Figure 5.6
Census indexes offer us a way to search the available census indexes at a time that is convenient for us. © 2000–2001 MyFamily .com, Inc. Screen shot from Ancestry.com. Used by permission.

must use a command that equates to raising your hand before you speak. You must then wait for the moderator to set it up so you can speak. It is a good idea to visit the Web site for the chat in question and see what is scheduled before you jump in.

I want to share one warning about chatting, especially if you find yourself enjoying it and returning often: It will affect your manners in the real world. Chatting software allows you to type in your message while other messages are being displayed and then press Enter. Your message is inserted in turn in the conversation. The concept of interrupting is foreign to chatting software and most chatting environments. Of course, that is not true in the real world. Be cognizant of the fact that you may be interrupting people when talking with them face to face. This can happen with such stealth that you may not realize that you are being rude. Even after a few years of conscious thought about this, I still slip up from time to time.

\di'fin\ *vb*

Definitions

COMMERCIAL SITES

Commercial sites differ from other sites in that you must subscribe—that is, pay money—to access the wonderful information they have squirreled away. They may

allow you to run a complimentary search to see if your ancestor's name appears, but to see the actual information requires that you put your money where your mouse is.

Many people have asked me if these sites are worth the money. That is truly difficult to answer. Is the site worth it if I find a clue that allows me to break through a brick wall? Definitely. Is the site worth it if the bulk of its current resources excludes the localities where my ancestors live? Probably not.

As genealogists, we can justify any expense if it supplies us with one more ancestor to add to the family tree. Look at how much we spend on computer equipment, software, books, and trips to the library. How many of you have flown to Salt Lake City to experience the Family History Library? How many of you have rented microfilm or paid to borrow the film from Salt Lake City via your local Family History Center? Subscribing to an online commercial site is no different. You are paying for a service.

I have done the math—I even had my son check it with the new math he learned in school—and come to the conclusion that a year's subscription to these online commercial sites is still cheaper than going to the library on a regular basis.

Now, before genealogists jump on me for discouraging you from visiting your library, let me dig my way out of this. Some resources that we use frequently may be available in book or microfilm format at our local public or genealogy library. These may include census indexes, the censuses themselves, and compiled indexes such as *Periodical Source Index* or *The American Genealogical-Biographical Index*.

If that was all I needed to work with, then it would make more sense for me to work from home on the computer than it would to get in the car, drive thirty miles, pay the toll, pay to park the car, and use the library. I can't do all that, and feed myself, for less than the monthly cost of one of these online subscriptions.

Another factor to consider is the active addition of resources to these commercial sites. Each of the sites adds new databases each business day. These may include books, indexes, and digitized images of census or other popular records. What this means to you and me is that what is not available today may be available next month.

The sites may also offer resources that you do not have easy access to, such as AGBI, or resources in a format that is easier to use, such as PERSI. For years I have had access to both of these resources in their book format. For years I have suggested to people that they use AGBI in their research only to have them tell me they couldn't find it. I just discovered about three years ago that AGBI in book form was available in only two hundred libraries across the country. I was one of the lucky ones: The public library near me was one of those libraries.

What about those who live in another country or in a small town with a small library or no library at all? Perhaps business duties require it. Whatever the reason, we still hope to work on our genealogy. Unfortunately, the resources we need are all back on American soil or require a lengthy trip to a larger city.

AGBI AND PERSI: ALPHABET SOUP?

AGBI and PERSI are two useful indexes that genealogists have been relying on for years. Each offers its own unique contribution to the world of genealogy, offering insight into books and periodicals that may prove useful in your research.

The American Genealogical-Biographical Index is commonly referred to as the AGBI. In book format, this set has more than two hundred volumes and has been an ongoing publication for more than forty years. When AGBI was available in only book form, few libraries in the United States had this set. Those libraries that became interested in this set in the 1970s as interest in family history grew discovered that the earlier volumes were no longer in print. As a result only about two hundred libraries have the complete set.

AGBI was the brainchild of Fremont Rider of the Godfrey Memorial Library in Middletown, Connecticut. The earliest volumes were known to many as *Rider's Index* after their creator. The project began in 1952 and was not completed until 1999. Entries in the index were taken from a variety of published resources, totaling 850, including

- the "Boston Transcript" (a genealogy column from the early 1900s)

- 1790 U.S. Federal Census

- published Revolutionary War records

- published family histories

Each entry in AGBI may include the following information about a given individual:

- surname

- given name

- maiden name

- birth date (usually just the year)

- birthplace (usually the state or country)

- biographical information

- citations to references

The focus of AGBI includes New England, the mid-Atlantic states, and the Midwest. Many researchers have dismissed this as a New England–only resource, which is a mistake.

Ancestry.com has acquired the electronic rights to this massive database and made it available on both CD-ROM and its subscription services.

PERSI is the *Periodical Source Index*. This is an ongoing indexing project of the Genealogy and History Department of the Allen County Public Library in Fort Wayne, Indiana. Under the direction of Curt B. Witcher, this project adds at least 100,000 new entries each year.

First released in 1985, this project sought to index all periodicals with genealogical information. When first published, PERSI organized entries by surname, record type, and locality. It is not limited to genealogical publications. Periodicals included in PERSI are

- genealogical publications

- historical publications

- ethnic publications

- family and surname publications

If you locate your family or an individual in this index, you should first check to see if your local library has subscribed to the periodical in question. If not, and you cannot get it on microfilm via your local Family History Center, the Allen County Public Library does offer a copy service for a fee. (See Appendix C for the Web site.)

Like AGBI, PERSI is now available on CD-ROM and through Ancestry.com's subscription services. (See more on PERSI's CD-ROM below.)

The Internet offers a way for those genealogists to continue their research, and commercial sites play a big part in that.

Many researchers who have spent time using the PERSI volumes may wonder what the CD-ROM version offers as a benefit. The printed volumes are organized alphabetically by surname, record type, or locality. When researching, this limits what entries are seen as you look under these alphabetical headings.

The CD-ROM and online versions allow you to search every word of the entry for a surname. You will pick up additional entries this way that may not have been obvious when working with the books. The CD-ROM version also offers a variety of other ways to search this powerful index, including keywords.

By using keywords, you can narrow the focus of your search, eliminating those entries that do not pertain to the research at hand. The keyword search also allows you to more clearly define a search when working with a common surname, such as Smith, resulting in a more manageable list of possible entries.

Finally, commercial sites give you the opportunity to work on your own time. Recently, while giving a talk at a genealogy conference, I had a shot of an outgoing e-mail message up on the screen. Some women in the front could make out the time stamp on the e-mail. As I was talking, I noticed that one woman leaned over to the other, pointed, and said, "Look at the time when that e-mail was sent!" At that point, I confessed to the group that I was indeed up at 2 A.M. sending that e-mail.

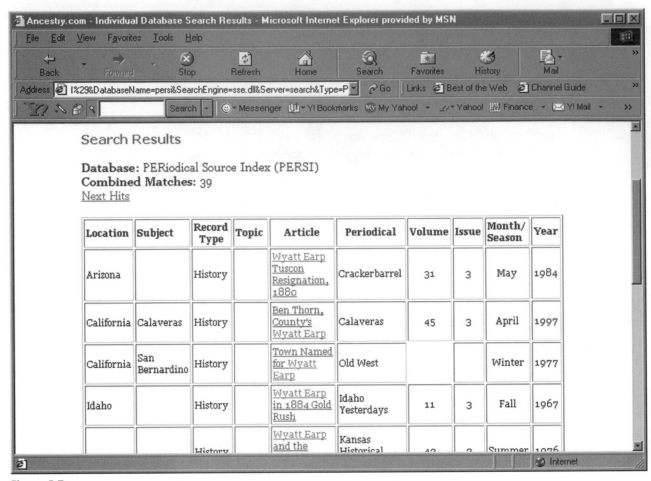

Figure 5.7
PERSI, compiled by the Allen County Public Library and available through Ancestry.com's subscription service, offers researchers the chance to locate articles on their ancestors in a variety of periodicals. © 2000–2001 MyFamily.com, Inc. Screen shot from Ancestry.com. Used by permission.

Timesaver

While I am just naturally a night person, some genealogists work that late because it is the only time they can work on their genealogy. This work must be squeezed in along with making a living (yes, our families insist that they have food, clothes, and a place to live), helping with homework, and generally participating in the land of the living. As such, it may be 8 P.M. or 9 P.M. before you get the chance to jump back into your research. Unfortunately, most libraries are closed or getting ready to close at these hours.

Data online is available anytime. There are no set hours of operation (although some sites have set downtimes for maintenance). I also find that the late-night hours (after 11 P.M.) and early-morning hours (before 9 A.M.), are some of the fastest processing times on the Internet because there's less traffic.

These are just a few of the reasons commercial sites are worth your money. I will not say that one commercial site is better than another. In fact, I have subscriptions to many of them. I suggest that you give each one a year's try. If you do not find that it offers you the records and resources that you need, you do not have to renew your membership. While they all offer monthly or quarterly

---

E-MAIL TIME STAMPS, OR YOU SENT THAT *WHEN?*

When you view incoming e-mail messages, you can determine how the date and time are displayed for each e-mail. You need to decide whether you wish to view them based on the sender's time zone or your time zone. There are pros and cons to both.

When you choose to view items based on the sender's time zone, you may discover that incoming messages don't appear to be chronological. They are organized chronologically by when they arrive according to your time zone; however, the time stamp that appears will be according to the time zone where the sender lives. Some find this disconcerting. I prefer this setting and seeing the difference in time zones. It also helps to remind me of my colleagues' time zones and keeps me from calling them on the phone too early if they have asked me to give them a call.

The flip side of this is displaying time stamps based on your local time zone. This will still result in some disorder to the chronology you see, but they will all represent your local time. Don't forget to convert the time difference if you grab the phone to respond to someone.

When it comes to e-mail that you send, unless you monkey with the clock and date setup on your system, there is no way to fool the world into thinking you were sleeping at 2 A.M. instead of typing at the keyboard. The time stamp that gets assigned to e-mail that you send is the time your computer shows when you click Send.

---

subscriptions, for those not sure they want to commit, these often end up being more expensive than the yearly subscription rates.

PICK A PLACE AND START CHATTING

You have been introduced to a number of different methods to communicate with other genealogists. Each method has both pros and cons. You won't know which method works best for you until you jump in with both feet.

To help you get started, I have created a comparison chart of the different types of sites and resources available for contacting other genealogists. (See page 77.) The chart includes some features and drawbacks and a couple of URLs to get you started.

USING WHAT YOU FIND

While we have looked at some of the more popular aspects of the Internet, this is not the be-all and end-all of genealogical research. This is but the tip of the iceberg. Through the Internet, we have many new resources at our fingertips, but it does not mean the end of legwork. What it does mean is that you can do much of your preparation at home, then take full advantage of a research trip to a library or courthouse. After all, it takes time and money to go to these places, and you want to make sure you get the most out of your trip.

COMMERCIAL DATABASE SITES	
American Civil War Research and Genealogy Database	http://www.civilwardata.com
Ancestry.com	http://www.ancestry.com
Everton's Genealogical Helper	http://www.everton.com
Family Tree Maker's Genealogy Site	http://www.familytreemaker.com
English Origins	http://englishorigins.com
Genealogy Library Subscription	http://www.genealogylibrary.com
Next of Kin	http://www.lineages.com/NextOfKin/default.asp

ONLINE ELECTRONIC OPTIONS

Online Area	Pros	Cons	Starting Points
Bulletin Boards	• Messages are often threaded, making it possible for newcomers to read the entire discussion. • Life of original message may be longer. • May offer a search engine for the specific bulletin boards of that site.	• The fill-in-the-form method sometimes causes researchers to be less than clear. • You need to go to the bulletin board; the messages don't come to you.	• GenConnect Boards http://genconnect.rootsweb.com • GenForum boards http://genforum.genealogy.com/
Mailing lists	• Messages come via e-mail with your regular e-mail. • You can elect to receive the messages one at a time or in groups. • Some people feel more comfortable conversing in this manner because it is e-mail. • May offer a searchable archive.	• Newcomers sometimes do not understand how the messages are sent and feel compelled to respond to each one. • People often either quote too much of the previous message or not enough.	• RootsWeb Mailing Lists http://lists.rootsweb.com/ • Yahoo! Groups http://groups.yahoo.com
Newsgroups	• Bring you in contact with others interested in the same subject. • Are archived and searchable. • Rely on the threaded system, so you can follow from the first message to the last.	• Even though they look a lot like e-mail messages, you must use a newsreader and seek out the messages. • There are not as many newsgroups as other online communication options.	• Google Groups http://groups.google.com/ • The Genealogy Infocenter: Newsgroups Finder Page http://members.tripod.com/~Genealogy_Infocenter/genealogy-discussions.html

SIX

Library Research From Home

Y ou have been introduced to the Internet's basics as they relate to genealogy. You should be familiar with some online terminology. You now know of some good sites to begin your research. You have also been introduced to some of the online databases. Many online genealogists stop there; however, if you do, you will miss out on the best part of the search.

In chapter seven, we will examine the reasons for going further. So much material has not been digitized. In order for something to be available on the Internet, it must first be converted to a digital format. In the last chapter, you read about some of the ways this is done and some of their inherent problems.

HEAD FOR THE CATALOGS

Some of the biggest and best genealogical libraries have recently put their catalogs online. For many genealogists who began their research before genealogy moved onto the Internet, these libraries were the mainstay of their preparatory research. Few of us live near enough to these libraries to visit them often. When we do go, we want to make every moment count.

The biggest and perhaps best-known is the Family History Library in Salt Lake City. I admit to having referred to it as Mecca from time to time. While I have been able to visit it often, each visit leaves me in awe. The amount of records at my fingertips is truly amazing. Visiting requires some planning, though, if I am to make each moment count. In the past my prep work involved spending days at the local Family History Center. That was the only place I could go to get information about the holdings of the main library so I could plan my research. (Go to <http://www.familysearch.org> to find a Family History Center near you.)

Volunteers staff the Family History Centers, so operating hours vary depending on how many volunteers the director can get. I have read many comments

Library/Archive Source

For More Info

See *Your Guide to the Family History Library* by Paula Stuart Warren and James W. Warren (Cincinnati: Betterway Books, 2001).

online from people who were frustrated by the limited number of hours their local Family History Center was open.

At the 1999 GENTECH conference (a conference devoted to technology in genealogy) held in Salt Lake City, the Family History Library held a meeting. It announced that within the next few months it would be unveiling a Web site that would make some of its digitized databases available on the Internet. As the conference continued, there was much speculation as to what would be released.

After much anticipation, the day for the unveiling of the Web site finally came, and so many people visited the site that it crashed. For weeks afterward, it was not uncommon to visit the site and see an error message that the server was too busy and visitors should try back later. At that time the FHL had made available only small portions of two of its databases, yet genealogists still flocked to the new site. They were eager to work with a database that until then could be accessed only through the Family History Library or one of its Family History Centers.

Now the FamilySearch Web site offers researchers the chance to search many, though not all, of the databases that are on CD-ROM as part of the Family-Search CDs available at all Family History Centers and at the Family History Library. As noted in the previous chapter, most people stop investigating the Web site after they have searched for their families in *Ancestral File*, *International Genealogical Index*, and *Pedigree Resource File*. This is a shame.

The Family History Library Catalog (FHLC) is the meat of this site for me. **Using the FHLC, I can prepare for my Salt Lake City trip at any hour of the day or night.** In the past I was limited by the hours of operation of my local Family History Center. I also either had to make sure to bring either my checkbook to pay for the copious printouts I made from the catalog or aspirin to relieve the writer's cramp that was sure to set in from hours of extracting the various catalog entries I planned to pursue.

Timesaver

Now much of your legwork, even for your next visit to a Family History Center, can be accomplished through the FamilySearch Web site at any hour. In fact, the information on the Web site may be more-up-to date than the CD-ROMs at your local Family History Center.

In addition to the database, the research aids available on the Web site offer a wonderful education, especially for those new to the hobby. You may not know that you can access census records for England. Perhaps you were unaware of the index to pensions for those Americans who served in the Civil War.

By searching the databases and the catalog at the FamilySearch Web site, you can make a quick trip to a Family History Center to order films. Then you will not need to schedule another visit to the Family History Center until you are notified that the microfilms have arrived. During that visit, you can spend your time working with the microfilm or microfiche.

The Family History Library Catalog can be accessed through the Family-Search Web site <http://www.familysearch.org> by selecting the Library tab and then the "Family History Library Catalog" link just below the tabs. Once at the catalog page, you will find you have a variety of search choices.

- place search

- surname search
- author search
- call number search
- film/fiche search

Through these searches, you can see all the resources cataloged and housed at the Family History Library in Salt Lake City as of the posted catalog entry date. These resources are in a number of different formats including books, CD-ROMs, microfilm, microfiche, and maps. Often you will find that a particular book is also available on either film or fiche. You want to look for such entries, as only the microfilm and microfiche can be ordered and sent to your local Family History Center.

One final note about ordering: Not all of the films and fiche are available for use at the local Family History Centers. When entering agreements with certain repositories, it was necessary to agree to restrict some film for use only in the Family History Library in Salt Lake City. If such a restriction on the film exists, it will be noted in the FHLC.

A New Library

While the Family History Library is perhaps at the top of each genealogist's wish list of places to visit, many other libraries have valuable genealogical collections. I would like to say that I plan every trip I make to any library far in advance, but there are times when I just can't look a gift horse in the mouth. That happened to me a few years ago. My husband had to go to Chicago on business. Since he had family nearby, we thought it would be an excellent opportunity to take the kids on a vacation. I was in vacation mode, even though I did have to bring my notebook computer along and keep up with my online job. Three days into this trip, my husband suggested that his mother and I take a day to go "do genealogy."

Chicago is home to the Newberry Library. I certainly wasn't going to say no, but I was kicking myself for not having planned ahead. Fortunately I had my database on my computer, and even better, I had a portable printer, and the Newberry Library's catalog was online.

The night before we were to go to the library, I spent a few hours running search after search to see what records were available. I also used up a bit of paper printing out those that looked the most promising for my research.

When we got to the library, the staff gave us an overview of how the library works. I was pleased to have my printouts when the librarian explained that the library is a closed-stack library. While closed-stack libraries may have some books and resources available for browsing, the majority of the collection must be requested.

To request a book, periodical, or other source, you must fill out a call slip. There is usually a drop box where you place the call slips. Pages, those working at the library who go into the closed stacks to pull requested materials, then get the materials from the closed stacks and bring them to your table. As you may have guessed, this takes time.

THE NEWBERRY LIBRARY

The Newberry Library was named after Walter Loomis Newberry, a pioneer real estate speculator and humanitarian of Chicago. The library itself is located on Walton Street. It sits opposite a lovely park, where hardworking researchers can take a break at lunchtime and enjoy the scenery.

Long considered one of the top ten libraries for genealogists, it holds a variety of treasures including two thousand books dating back to before 1500. Among the five million to six million manuscripts are works by Brahms, Wagner, and Mendelssohn.

While many researchers assume that the collection hinges on Chicago or the state of Illinois, the true scope of the genealogical collection covers the United States and Canada. The library also has a strong British Isles collection, especially local histories and published county records. The Newberry Library is one of the libraries with a complete set of *The American Genealogical-Biographical Index*, which was discussed in chapter five.

Due to the library's extensive family history collection, an index to those volumes published between 1896 and 1918 can be found in the *Genealogical Index of the Newberry Library*. This set of books is not a catalog to the holdings at Newberry, but it is a useful tool in looking for family histories. Many public libraries with genealogy collections have this index.

Like other libraries with valuable collections, the Newberry Library is a closed-stack library, meaning someone retrieves the books for you. The library is open to the public and charges no fees. Upon your first visit you will need to fill out a registration form and show a picture ID. The materials in this library do not circulate, so you can access them only by visiting the library in person.

The resources mentioned here merely touch the surface of a staggering and impressive collection. You can find out more by visiting the Newberry Library's Web site at <http://www.newberry.org/nl/newberryhome.html>.

By printing some of the resources the night before, I was able to fill out my first set of call slips within minutes of arriving at the library. Most libraries with this type of system limit the number of call slips you can submit at once. While the page went off to retrieve my first batch of requests, I spent time working with the reference and high-use resources that were out in the open. Thus, I made every minute of my unplanned visit to a new library count.

Even if you do not have a portable printer, if you have your notebook computer and an Internet connection you can still prepare. Simply write down the pertinent information about the sources of interest. Write down six to eight sources to get you started. Be sure to include as much information as possible about each source so that when you get to the library you can remember why

Timesaver

the source was of interest to you. Then, while you wait for these sources to be retrieved, you can either work in open stacks or peruse the catalog more fully to see what else may be available. If you are new to the library, it doesn't hurt to use this time to read any brochures or other publications that introduce you to the library, its holdings, and its rules.

Finding the Catalogs

Finding library catalogs online is a big Catch-22. In order to find the catalogs, you must use the biggest catalog of them all—the Internet. However, you already have some tricks up your sleeve to help you. You know about directories and search engines. You can use these tools to find the available catalogs.

When working with a search engine, take advantage of the Boolean operator *AND* to string together some words that pertain to the library you want to locate. For instance, you could use the following search string:

"Allen County" AND library AND genealogy

You might also take advantage of one of the free-form question search engines, such as Ask Jeeves <http://www.askjeeves.com>, and pose a question such as

Where is the Allen County Public Library?

When working in a directory such as Cyndi's List, you can do this in two different ways. First, you can look under the Library category. Cyndi's List shows in alphabetical order those libraries that are online. Mind you, not all of these will have an online searchable catalog. Some may only have information

Figure 6.1
Many libraries, such as the Allen County Public Library, are bringing the online library catalogs in-house. You search the same catalog at the library that you would from home via the Internet.

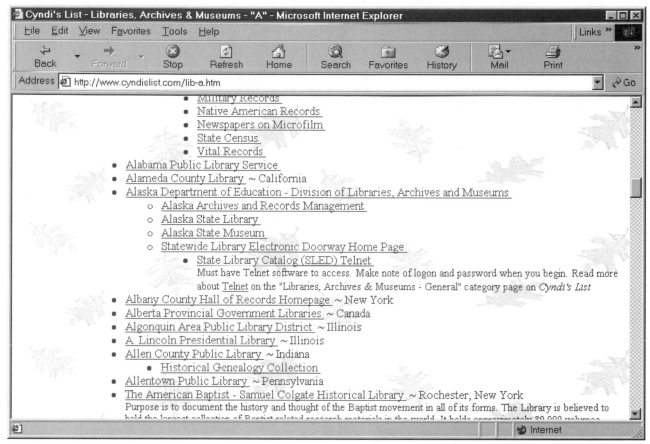

Figure 6.2
Using a directory such as Cyndi's List is an easy way to access online library catalogs.

about their location and hours of operation and tidbits about their holdings. Even if they do not offer a searchable online catalog, at least you will have a link to check.

The other method, which I find easier and more likely to generate positive results, is to use the appropriate locality category for the library in question. For instance, to find out if the Allen County Public Library has a Web site, I would begin in Cyndi's List by scrolling through the headings until I got to the United States category. While I could click on this, links to each of the states are in a chart on this front page.

The Allen County Public Library is in Indiana. Clicking on the Indiana link displays a list of links pertinent to Indiana. On this page the sites are further divided by standard headings such as Societies, Archives and Libraries, and so forth. You can either scroll down this page using your scroll bar, or you can click these heading links to go directly to the set of links you want—in this case click Archives and Libraries.

Clicking on the link for the Allen County Public Library will take you to its home page. The Allen County Public Library is not just a genealogy library; it is a fully staffed county public library. They do put a certain importance on genealogy on the site though. Having spoken with Curt Witcher, the manager of the Genealogy and History Department, a few times, I know that he cares that genealogists and family historians be able to find useful information on the Web site. Not all pubic libraries will include Web pages devoted to genealogy.

One other method for locating libraries is to take advantage of a Web site that does nothing but compile a list of libraries with online catalogs. Such lists omit those libraries that may have a Web presence but have not put their catalogs online. Keep in mind that sometimes being listed on these sites is voluntary.

FINDING ONLINE LIBRARY CATALOGS	
Libweb Library WWW Servers	http://sunsite.berkeley.edu/Libweb/
WebCATS—Library Catalogues on the World Wide Web	http://www.lights.com/webcats/
Webbed Catalogs	http://www.lib.ncsu.edu/staff/morgan/alcuin/wwwed-catalogs-Traditional.html
Gateway to Library Catalogs	http://lcweb.loc.gov/z3950/
Library of Congress: State Libraries	http://lcweb.loc.gov/global/library/statelib.html
Directory of Genealogy Libraries in the U.S.	http://www.gwest.org/gen_libs.htm

Get the Lay of the Library

Once at the library's Web site, what do you do? The first thing you need to do is determine whether its catalog is available online. Look for a search link on the home page. Fortunately some libraries have begun to include a catalog link or button, so there is no question.

Just as you learned in chapter four that different Internet search engines have different interfaces, so too you will find that each online library catalog is different as well. Of course, you are no longer intimidated by your computer or the Web; you are in control. You tell the computer what to do and where to go as you type a URL or click a link.

What Can You Find?

I love to watch some of the technology commercials on television. They point out how within a given company their various systems can't seem to talk to each other. I have come to view the Internet like that. Every place you visit is different. Each online catalog you discover will have a slightly different interface. Don't get discouraged. It will take some time and a little experimenting, but the more you work with the catalogs, the more success you will have.

As the interfaces are different, so too is the content of the online catalogs. Remember that computerized catalogs are relatively new. Many libraries, maybe even your local public library, have been around for many years. If you

Notes

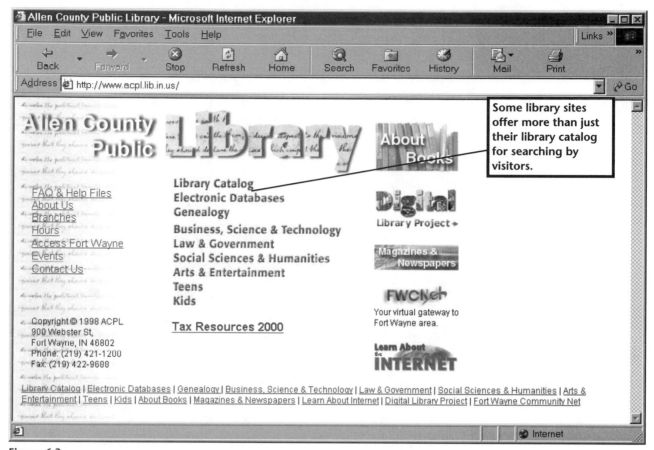

Figure 6.3
The Allen County Public Library has put the Library Catalog link at the top of its list of links, making it easy to get to the online catalog.

live in an older community, it is possible that your library has been around for a hundred years or more.

While it is a safe bet that any books that old are held in a special collections department, the incomprehensible number of titles housed in the library may not yet have made it to the computer catalog. This may not be mentioned in the details of an online library catalog, so I mention it here to make you aware that the catalog may not be complete. More information on this can be found in the sidebar "What's in That Catalog?"

Even libraries, such as the Family History Library, that have been cataloging their holdings on computer for years do not release their entire catalogs online at once. The Family History Library brought its catalog and most of the databases it has available online out in stages. Unlike other sites though, it made a point of mentioning what sections were available with each release.

If the library in question has a genealogy department, and its online catalog appears to be complete, then you should be able to search for books and other resources found in their holdings. Keep in mind that in order to control the strain on the computers that perform these searches, the library may have separated their catalogs. Some libraries separate out their periodicals. Others may separate out their microfilm holdings.

WHAT'S IN THAT CATALOG?

Here are a few tricks to help you determine how complete an online library catalog is.

1. Do a search on the word *genealogy*. Do this only to see what comes up in a general, not specific, search. Look to see if the results include only books or if the entries also include microfilm and periodicals.

2. Investigate the library catalog site. Does it have separate buttons or options for periodicals, media, and books?

3. When doing any search, look to see how old the copyright dates are for the volumes that appear in the list of results.

4 Look for an online help file. If there are limitations to the Web-based catalog, these should be mentioned in the help or frequently asked questions (FAQ) files.

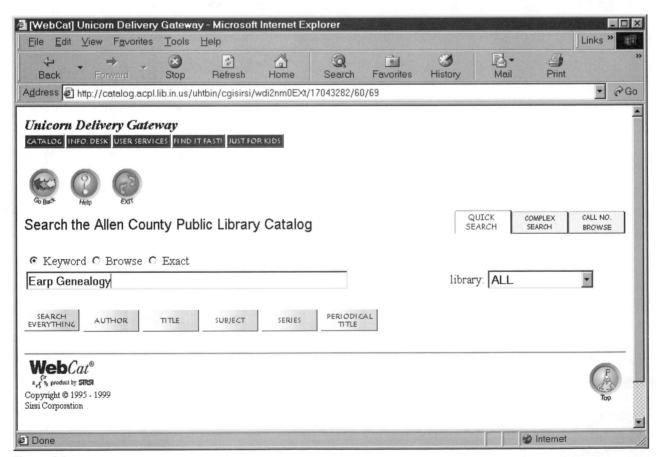

Figure 6.4
Each library's online catalog will feel different; however, you should be able to search on author, title, subject, and keyword at most of them.

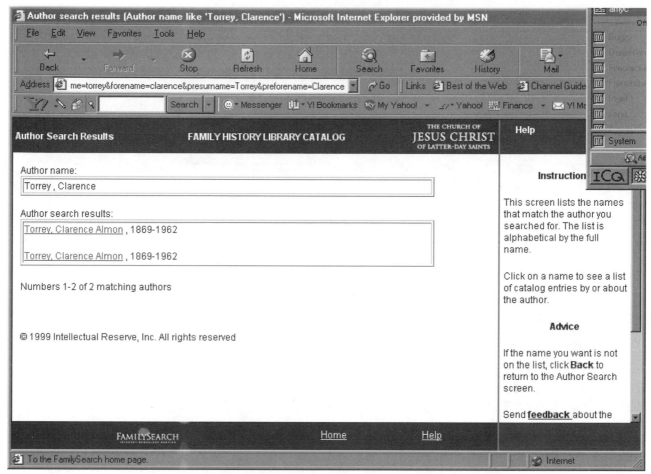

Figure 6.5
The Family History Library Catalog offers a search on authors. Reprinted by permission. © 2001 by Intellectual Reserve, Inc.

Avoid searching on the term *genealogy.* As we saw in chapter four, this is not an effective method of searching; it results in too many entries. The same will happen with the online catalog for any library that has a genealogy department. The sheer number of the entries tends to overwhelm, and you will have defeated your own endeavor with such a search. No one wants to spend hours looking at each entry. Get above about fifty hits, and you will find that your enthusiasm begins to wane.

Instead, approach your search of the library catalog just as you would your search on the Internet. Think about what you want to find. What is the locality or the surname in question? You can always combine the term *genealogy* with these other terms to eliminate nongenealogical entries, but it shouldn't be your only search term.

Warning

Authors and Titles and Keywords, Oh My!

One benefit of the online library catalogs is that they often have built-in filters that you do not see in the general search engines of the Internet. A library is made up of published works. Authors wrote the books. Editors compiled the periodicals. Singers sang the songs on the albums and CDs.

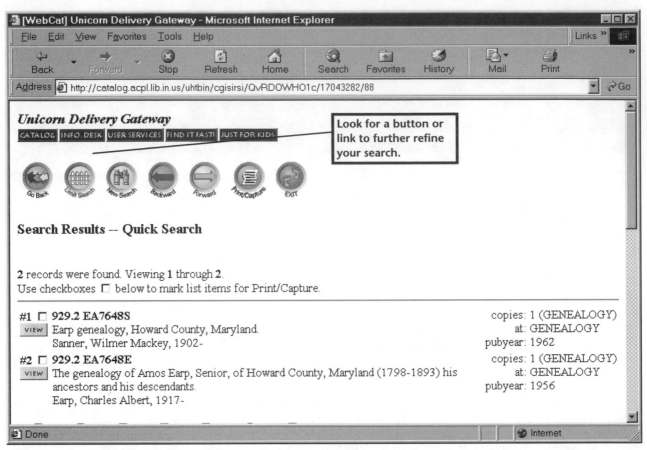

Figure 6.6
Sometimes a search result includes too many possibilities. Most catalogs have options for further limiting your search.

If you know the name of the author of a book you are trying to find, use that name in your search. Use a search for the author instead of a blanket search of all possibilities. Be warned: Spelling counts in these searches. Library catalogs do not list their authors by variant spellings of the surname.

Some online library catalogs will let you refine a search after the initial search has been completed. Take advantage of this if the search results in a number of entries so high that it knocked you off your seat.

Refining a search tells the library catalog to take the list of results and search through it for an additional requirement. For instance, despite my advice you did a search on *genealogy*. The number of results was staggering. You can use the refine option to specify an additional term, perhaps a surname or a county.

THERE'S NO STOPPING YOU NOW

Now that you know how to find the online library catalogs and search them, you are invincible. I have shown you how to make any trip a genealogy trip. Your job now is to convince the rest of your family that all flights go through Salt Lake City, and, yes, it is quite normal to have a three-day layover. I suggest that you vary the libraries when doing this. For instance, take one trip through

GET BOOKS FROM ANOTHER LIBRARY

One method for getting access to books not available at your library is through interlibrary loan. For an interlibrary loan your library requests a book, newspaper or other resource from another library, often out of state. That library then sends the requested item to your library, and you are allowed to view the item there.

Libraries around the country participate in this program, including the Library of Congress, which Librarian of Congress Herbert Putnam referred to as the "nation's library of last resort" when he began lending books from the library's collection in 1902.

Interlibrary loan must be done through your local library. Do not mistake your Family History Center for a library. Family History Centers are branches of the Family History Library, but they cannot do interlibrary loan with other libraries. In a few instances you will find that the local public library is a Family History Center, but this is uncommon.

Find information for the item in question, complete with ISBN and Library of Congress number, to facilitate the search and request of the book. In some instances the library you are aware of won't be able to lend the volume, so your librarian needs this information to find it through another repository.

Interlibrary loan is one more way to help you accomplish your research from home, or at least from your hometown. Searching for the desired resources can be done through online library catalogs at any time of the day or night. Armed with printouts from the catalogs, you should find that you can get many of these resources via interlibrary loan.

Salt Lake City. Make the next one go through Washington, DC, and the next time go through Fort Wayne, Indiana.

If your family absolutely refuses to take such outlandish side trips, check to see what libraries and archives are in the neck of the woods they have insisted on. You could be pleasantly surprised, especially if the trip is to visit family. Sometimes families stayed put for a long time. You may get a genealogy trip out of that vacation yet.

Convincing them to let you take a day to visit the library may take some effort. "Because" is not an effective argument. Believe it or not, there really are gems and treasure in them thar libraries.

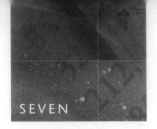

SEVEN

The Search Is On

Important

T here is a new breed of family historian—the online researcher. You may find yourself in that category. The good news is that because of the advances in technology, more people have been introduced to the hobby of researching their family trees. The bad news is that you may feel that the Internet is your only resource. **If you can't find your ancestor on the Internet, all is not lost.**

I'VE GONE AS FAR AS I CAN GO

Brick walls are not a new problem, and they cannot be blamed on the Internet, at least not completely. When I was the Sysop of the GEnie Genealogy Round-Table, I was monitoring a chat room when a frustrated individual entered.

We'd been talking for a little while when he mentioned that he had gone as far as he could go with his genealogy. He was relatively new to the hobby, so I asked him why he felt that way. His response was that there was nothing else he could find.

Having spent more time on this hobby over the last seventeen years than I am willing to admit to in writing, I was flabbergasted by his comment. He'd only been researching for a year, and he thought he had exhausted all the records already. I couldn't help wondering where I had gone wrong taking so long with mine.

As we continued to chat, I tried to get some information about where he was with his end-of-line ancestors. He described his English ancestry and mentioned that he had the line back to the early 1700s. I asked if he had checked into bishop's transcripts for the town where the family lived at that time. He said he didn't know what the bishop's transcripts were.

At this point I thought I had better get an idea of what he had been doing for the last year. He had searched for family in the Ancestral File database at his local

BISHOP'S TRANSCRIPTS

The Act of 1598 also specified that once a year a copy of all entries for that year should be sent to the diocesan registry at the bishop's office, and these are now known as the *bishop's transcripts.* In many cases, where parish registers have been destroyed or lost, the bishop's transcripts have been preserved. I am always a little amazed when I meet fairly experienced amateur genealogists who have only a vague knowledge of the transcripts and have never made use of them. . . .

Most of the bishop's transcripts are deposited in the county record offices most closely concerned with the areas of jurisdiction of the bishops. A notable exception is Kent, where those of the Diocese of Canterbury remain at Canterbury Cathedral. Those for the Diocese of Lichfield, which covered several counties, are all in the Lincoln County Record Office. In the diocese of London, no transcripts were kept before 1800, and in that of Winchester there are none before 1770. (This diocese also included the Channel Islands, so searchers in that area should remember this.)

From 1660 the parish registers are, generally speaking, complete. The only exceptions are those lost through natural disasters. Here again, bishop's transcripts are very useful—depending on the date of the disaster, and the date on which the transcripts were sent to the bishop (they were supposed to be sent after Easter in each year).

—Angus Baxter

Baxter, Angus. *In Search of Your British & Irish Roots: A Complete Guide to Tracing Your English, Welsh, Scottish & Irish Ancestors.* 4th edition. Baltimore, Md.: Genealogical Publishing Company, 1999.

Additional Research Help—English Ancestry

Many additional records and resources are available to you if you are searching for English ancestors. Many of the records will depend largely on the time period in which your ancestor lived. In addition to the book by Angus Baxter, you should read *A Genealogist's Guide to Discovering Your English Ancestors* by Paul Milner and Linda Jonas and published in 2000 by Betterway Books. This volume explores a variety of records unique to English research. It also devotes a chapter to accessing records of libraries and Family History Centers. You will soon discover that what you find in computerized databases and on the Internet is just the beginning.

Family History Center. He was completely unaware of the treasure trove of records on microfilm that he could access through the Family History Center.

NOT THE END OF THE ROAD

This story is indicative of online or computer researchers. They are generally new to the hobby and may know only what they have picked up in online

---

EVIDENCE! THAT SAYS IT ALL

As researchers of family history, we must always record reference information about where we found each date, place, name, and relationship. Without recording this vitally important information, we create two problems. First, when we share our data with someone, that person cannot tell how accurate our research is or see where we found what we claim to be true. Second, we may not remember everything we have already done and may end up repeating research in resources that we have already searched.

I suspect that most of us had to do at least one research paper when we were students. But how much of what we were taught did we retain? And how much of what we retained can we apply to citing sources in our research? After all, we tend to use some very unique resources in tracking down our ancestry.

Many genealogists have picked up Richard S. Lackey's *Cite Your Sources*, an answer to a prayer for guidelines on citing books, periodicals, pamphlets, and much more. However, technology has come so far that many resources we now use weren't around when Mr. Lackey's book was published. So, it was with excitement that I consulted Elizabeth Shown Mills's *Evidence! Citation & Analysis for the Family Historian* (Genealogical Publishing Company, 1997).

In her introduction, Mills states, "Successful research—research that yields correct information with a minimum of wasted time and funds—depends on *a sound analysis of evidence.* Source citation is fundamental, but it is not enough. The validity of any piece of evidence cannot be analyzed if its source is unknown. Citing a worthless source is an effort that produces worthless results."

In addition to the detailed examples of every conceivable source you might encounter, this volume also looks at the fundamentals of both citation and analysis. Even experienced genealogists would be wise to have this volume.

conversations. Since many people they converse with are also new to the hobby, it is almost like the blind leading the blind.

Important

The Internet and the computerized databases such as Ancestral File or WorldConnect, RootsWeb's equivalent to Ancestral File, are not the end of the research road. In fact, they are just the beginning. They are marvelous tools to garner clues for your research. I equate them to the published family histories because they include names, dates, and places.

When I began researching my family tree, all I cared about was adding more names, dates, and places to my pedigree chart. When I first started, I wrote it all by hand. I would pore over those pedigree charts, taking pride in the six or seven generations I had for my mother's side. I would swell with excitement to see the branches spread out further and further. I would jump from one published family history to another trying to add more names.

This is a natural reaction. In the beginning, the names often come more easily

FROM IGI TO ORIGINAL RECORDS

In chapter five you were introduced to the *International Genealogical Index*. This tool is as close to a worldwide index as we are likely to get. Many people stop once they find an ancestor listed in the index, but this is a mistake. Like all indexes, it is merely the first step in the research process. Following these steps is good practice in research methodology.

1. Locate your ancestor in the IGI, either on CD-ROM at a Family History Center or online at the FamilySearch Web site <http://www.familysearch .org>.

2. Print out the pertinent entry, paying close attention to the film number.

3. Turn your attention to the Family History Library Catalog. Use the Film/ Fiche Search option, and type in the film number. If you use the online IGI, you can simply click on the film number on the entry.

4. Read the catalog entry. Understand that not all entries in the IGI have been extracted from original records. Most entries are from patron submissions.

5. If the film is an original record, such as a church record or marriage record, print out this entry and order the film through a Family History Center.

6. If the film mentions patron submissions, you may want to order the film to view the patron submission form. Submitters are supposed to include sources for the information they submit. Sometimes these patron submission forms list probate records or other resources you may be able to view on microfilm.

7. After reading the patron submission from microfilm, you may need to return to the Family History Library Catalog to search for probate records or vital records for a given locality.

than other facts. We are swayed by the ease and lulled into a false sense of security. As I continued my research, I began to question some of what I had. Dates didn't seem to jibe. I had discrepancies I couldn't solve. That was when I began to learn the art of research.

The Internet is very similar to those early stages of research. It's so easy to type in a name and find all sorts of entries in a database. In fact, you begin to get so much information that you don't stop to see what it is. Online research is addicting. It is also misleading. While some of the information is probably correct, sometimes misinformation is rampant. While you feel that you recognize the names or the lineage appears to make sense, until you begin digging in the original records you won't begin to get a feel for the family as a unit and as real individuals. They lived, they may have fought, they worked hard, and then they died. Their legacy is you.

VENTURING BEYOND THE INTERNET

I think the Internet is a marvelous tool for genealogical research—notice that I used the word *tool*. Every Web page you find your ancestry on, every database that has your lineage in it, and every query that gets answered is a piece in the ultimate puzzle: your family history puzzle.

Warning

As you search for family lines on the Internet, you get clues to your research. The next step is to verify the information you find. **Few Web sites and even fewer databases that are available online offer any form of source citation.**

Without a source citation, you don't know where the information came from. You don't know how accurate the conclusions are. As a result, you need to verify the "facts" found. This means you must go beyond the Internet: You must turn to the original record.

In chapter six you learned about library catalogs that are available online. This was not just to give you practice using a different kind of search engine; it was to prepare you for the next step. The Internet can still help you with the preparation, but eventually you will need to venture forth a library or other respository.

WHY ISN'T IT ALL ONLINE?

This past year I wrote an article about ways to locate people in the 1910 census in those states that were not included in the Soundex. If all of your research so

CAN YOU SEARCH THE SOUNDEX?	
Census Year(s)	**Available Soundex**
1790–1870	No Soundex projects were complete for these years. Published head of household indexes may exist; they may be available online through commercial services.
1880	Soundex project was completed for all households with a child age ten or younger.
1890	Majority of the census schedules were destroyed by fire in 1921, prior to the Soundexing projects of the 1930s. There is an alphabetical index to the few surviving schedules. This index is available on microfilm.
1900	Soundex completed for each household in each state and territory that existed in the United States at that time.
1910	The following states were Soundexed: Alabama, Georgia, Louisiana (except Shreveport and New Orleans), Mississippi, South Carolina, Tennessee, and Texas. The following states were Miracoded (computerized Soundex system): Arkansas, California, Florida, Kansas, Kentucky, Louisiana (Shreveport and New Orleans only), Michigan, Missouri, North Carolina, Ohio, Oklahoma, Pennsylvania, Virginia, and West Virginia.
1920	Soundex complete for each household in each state and territory that existed in the United States at that time.
1930	The following states were Soundexed: Alabama, Arkansas, Florida, Georgia, Kentucky (Bell, Floyd, Harlan, Kenton, Muhlenberg, Perry, and Pike counties), Louisiana, Mississippi, North Carolina, South Carolina, Tennessee, Virginia, and West Virginia (Fayette, Harrison, Kanawha, Logan, McDowell, Mercer, and Raleigh counties).

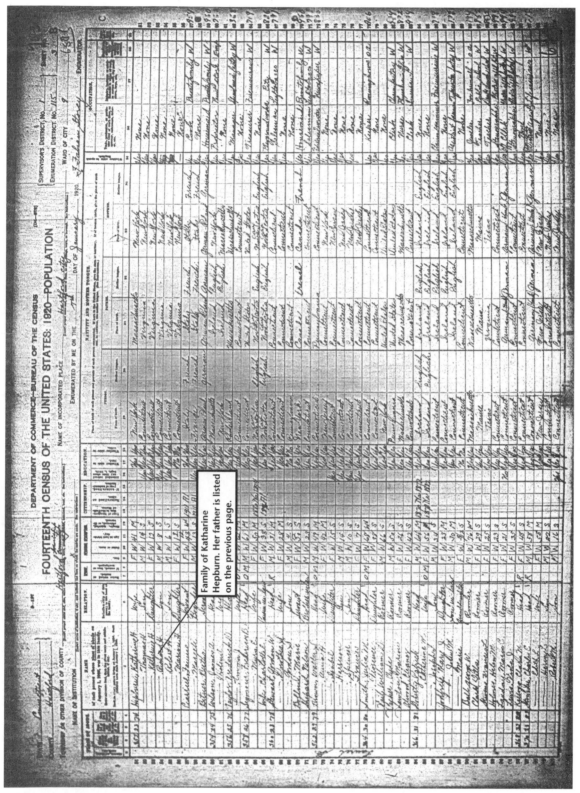

Figure 7.1
Every ten years since 1790 census enumerators have recorded information about people living in the United States. Even those destined for stardom, like Katharine Hepburn, were enumerated.

CENSUS—AROUND THE WORLD

While those researching their ancestry in the United States know that there are census records to aid them in their research, these same researchers when faced with research in other countries tend to forget about this basic resource, and many other countries have census records.

Canada

While some of the provinces have taken censuses over the years, the first official Canadian census was that taken in 1871. They were taken every ten years until 1971, and they have been taken every five years since then. The Canadian government, like the U.S. government, protects its census records for a given number of years. At present, you can access the 1871, 1881, 1891, and 1901 Canadian census records. These census records are available on microfilm. If you have easy access to a Family History Center, visit it and search the catalog. Remember to search on the province level as the individual provinces tended to take censuses prior to 1871.

England

While England has had censuses every ten years since 1801, the first census of genealogical value is the 1841 census. One of the peculiarities of the 1841 census was the rounding down of the ages. The enumerators rounded down ages over fifteen to a multiple of five. So a person who was actually forty-three years old would have been listed in the census as forty. The censuses of 1851 and later did not do this. If you are interested in the pre-1841 census records, read Colin R. Chapman's *Pre-1841 Censuses & Population Listings in the British Isles* (4th ed. Dursley, England: Lochin Publishing, 1994).

France

The earliest census taken in France was in 1772. Those taken from 1795 to 1836 are statistical censuses and do not include names of individuals. From 1836 to 1936, France had a national census every five years, except in 1871 (it was taken in 1872) and 1916 (which was skipped entirely). Unfortunately, these census records have not been microfilmed and indexed.

Germany

Germany has not taken national census enumerations. However, some enumerations exist for specific places and time periods. The 1819 census of Mecklenburg-Schwerin can be found on sixty rolls of microfilm at the Family History Library. Because Schleswig-Holstein was under the government of Denmark until 1864, it has a large number of census records taken by the Danish, also available on microfilm through a Family History Center.

Spain

For the colonies of Spain, at least one major census was taken during the colonial period, which covers the years 1492–1825. Some of these censuses are extant and may be available on microfilm. To find out what is available in Latin America and the Hispanic United States, consult Lyman D. Platt's *Census Records for Latin America and the Hispanic United States* (Baltimore, Md.: Genealogical Publishing Company, 1998).

—Rhonda R. McClure
Family Tree Finders
Posted 14 September 1999

far has been on the Internet, you may not even be aware of census records and the Soundex.

In a nutshell, the United States has been taking enumerations of the population of the country since 1790. Every ten years—we just filled out the form in 2000—census takers have canvassed the country gathering information on the citizens. In the beginning it was all just numbers, but as the census progressed it began to include the names of everyone in the household and other information as well.

The census is one type of record that every genealogist should be familiar with as it is one of the core records relied on by researchers. Taken every ten years, it sometimes offers a constant record. Experienced researchers know that it has its problems, and sometimes there are tricks to working with the census. You may want to read "Research in Census Records" in *The Source*, edited by Loretto Dennis Szucs and Sandra Hargreaves Luebking (Ancestry, 1997). A more recent publication that deals only with census records is William Dollarhide's *The Census Book: A Genealogist's Guide to Federal Census Facts, Schedules, and Indexes* (Heritage Quest, 1999).

Not surprisingly, as the population grew, so did the census schedule. During the Depression, individuals, as part of the Works Projects Administration (later named the Works Progress Administration), were directed to index the census beginning with 1880. This was not so that genealogists fifty years later would be happy. It was done to see who would be eligible for the soon-to-be instituted Social Security program. Each successive census through 1930, which will be released to the public in 2002, has an index, though these indexes may not be complete.

The 1910 census was not completely indexed. Many states were not included in the indexing program. As a result, if you wish to find someone in that census, you need to narrow the search, especially if they lived in a big city such as Philadelphia or New York.

The article "Help With Unindexed Census Records" describes how to pinpoint your ancestors using city directories and other resources as alternatives when Soundex is not available. The point of the article is that you can locate

SOUNDEX—JUST WHAT IS IT?

Ask a question about census records and pretty soon you will see a response that probably has to do with the term *Soundex*, especially if your question had to do with the 1880, 1900, 1910, or 1920 census. Unfortunately these very helpful people never seem to explain just what the Soundex is or how to use it.

Soundex is an index. It is based on phonics rather than spelling. In other words, like-sounding surnames will be grouped together. This was done to keep those like-sounding names together regardless of spelling variations, which cropped up during the census recording phase.

The Soundex is one of those projects that came out of the WPA groups during the 1930s, during the Depression. Those hired to work in this group would look through the pages of the census and record certain information on preformatted cards. These cards were then grouped together based on the surnames, which were each given a code based on the letters found in the surname. The code is broken down as follows:

1 b, p, f, v

2 c, s, k, g, j, q, x, z

3 d, t

4 l

5 m, n

6 r

You will notice that not all of the letters in the alphabet are included in the list above. Certain letters, primarily vowels, are ignored in Soundexing a surname. These letters are a, e, i, o, u, w, y, h. If the same letter appears consecutively, ignore the second occurrence.

The Soundex code consists of a letter and a three-digit code. The letter is the first letter of the surname. The three digits follow the list above, substituting a number for the letter it represents.

To Soundex a surname, start with the first letter and work to the right. So to Soundex the surname Standerfer, I begin by using the *S*. That is the first digit. Then I look at the table and see that the letter *t* is represented by the number 3. So my code now looks like S3??. I next skip the letter, *a* (vowels are always excluded). The next letter is *n*, which is represented by the number 5. So, now my code looks like S35?. The next letter is the *d*. This is represented by the number 3. So the Soundex code for Standerfer is S353.

It doesn't matter how many letters are left over, once you have filled all four of the digits, you have the Soundex code. The same is true if you run out of letters. You must always have four digits.

So let's code the surname Pifer. The first digit is *P*. The next letter is *i*, which we ignore. The next letter is *f*, represented by the number 1. Ignore *e*, the fourth letter. The next letter is *r*, which is represented by the number 6. Right now we have a code of P16?. This is not a complete Soundex code. When you run out of letters, then you add one or more zeroes. That means that the Soundex code for Pifer is P160.

You will find the Soundex indexing system used on many different indexes in the government. In addition to census records, you will find Soundex used in passenger list indexes and other records. In fact, your driver's license may even have the Soundex code at the beginning; many states use this system for assigning driver's license numbers.

an individual even if you don't have an index. One reader of the article missed that message. His e-mail message to me pointed out that "in this day and age, there is no excuse for the 1910 census not being indexed."

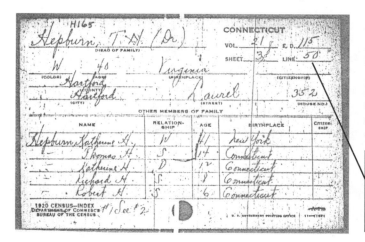

Figure 7.2
The Soundex card offers an overview of the household. Use the E.D., Sheet, and Line numbers to finish the research by going to the original page in the census.

Soundex cards include everything necessary for locating a family in the census.

He was caught up in that whole idea that the computer could do everything. Computers can't do everything. If they could, we would all be out of jobs and they might govern us. In most cases a computer can only do what a human has told it to do.

In chapter five we discussed the new programs used to digitize census records and make them available online. These projects are massive undertakings and have cost more money than most people will make in their lifetimes. In addition to the computers and the scanners, there are humans eyeballing the scanned images to make sure they are as clear as possible.

That is the problem—computers can't digitize the information without help from humans. Few people grasp the concept of how much has been made available on microfilm and published on paper over the centuries. While the United

Figure 7.3
The mechanical shelves located in the subbasement of the Allen County Public Library are filled with books, directories, maps, and more that genealogists use all the time.

Reminder

States is relatively young, the first Europeans to step on its shore and survive that first year arrived in the early 1600s; other countries have existed for thousands of years. A lot of records have been generated in that time period.

Even if you have visited a library and seen the holdings on its shelves, **it is sometimes hard to grasp the true concept of the millennium that would be necessary to digitize all of those books, microfilms, old ledgers, and boxes of unbound manuscripts that exist.**

There is so much paper that many repositories are now feeling the crunch. They are running out of room. They have used every shelf and are now putting things in boxes that they label and stack.

Even the Family History Library has moved all of its published family histories to another building. The microfilm on the second floor, where they have the U.S. and Canadian films, has run out of room and spilled over onto another floor. These are just microfilm reels. My hands twitch as I mention this. I love to go to the Family History Library for this very reason; there are so many

HELP WITH UNINDEXED CENSUS RECORDS

We have relied on indexes to the federal census records for so long that we sometimes panic when we discover that the census we need is not indexed. I am referring directly to the 1880 census (which indexed only those houses that had children age ten or under) and the 1910 census (which was indexed for only twenty-one states). However, even the 1900 and 1920 census indexes are not 100 percent accurate. As such, even with these indexes, you may find yourself needing to go to the actual census pages without having an exact page to turn to. What to do?

There are some often overlooked aids that can be of use to you in this situation. For the 1880, 1900, 1910, and 1920 censuses, there are descriptions of the enumeration districts on microfilm. They are also sometimes referred to as enumeration district maps, though they do not actually have graphic maps as you might expect.

Instead each state is broken down by supervisor's district and thereunder by enumeration district (ED). For each enumeration district is some sort of description, followed by the county and possibly any special instructions. In some cases the population for the particular ED is also included.

To be able to effectively use this aid, you need to know the street address for your ancestor. Impossible you say? Not necessarily. Addresses can be found in many ways. They are sometimes found on vital records. One researcher I know was researching an immigrant ancestor. That ancestor listed his brother as his sponsor and included his street address. Another resource for finding street addresses is city directories, which often have the added benefit of being able to tell you what ward or other geopolitical division the city may have been divided into.

Once you have the street address, you can turn your attention to the enumeration district descriptions. When using these, you may not find the name of the street. That is why finding the ward in the city directory can be so helpful. Generally the description of the enumeration district includes the outer boundaries for that ED or the city ward. This is why it is possible for the street to be included but not listed.

Here is an entry found in the 1910 enumeration district descriptions. This particular one is for Pennsylvania.

ED 9
East Providence township (part of)—All north of the center of the Chambersburg and Bedford turnpike.
Population 766
County Bedford

continued

> So how do you find your person without going line by line? The street names are included in the census. This means you can scan the census pages looking for the street name rather than having to search names of all the people on the page. This can greatly reduce the time it takes to search a census for your ancestors.
>
> These microfilms can be ordered through Family History Centers and may be found at public libraries with good genealogy collections.
>
> —Rhonda R. McClure
> Family Tree Finders
> Posted 1 April 1999

records available. But even with more than two million rolls of microfilm, it still doesn't have every record.

NOW I SEE

Perhaps you are beginning to understand the sheer magnitude of the project of digitizing the world. As such, it will not happen any time soon. And I confess that there is something special about cranking the microfilm. If you are fortunate enough to work with the original record, you will find that even more magical.

The chase after the records is what makes genealogy fun. Sure there are frustrating moments when you are certain your great-great-great grandfather was dropped off by aliens, but imagine the thrill and sense of accomplishment you will get when you do prove that he had human parents after all.

VERIFY, VERIFY, VERIFY

The digitized census records are a major breakthrough. Unlike transcribed records that include a potential for error during transcription, the digitization of the census makes the original record available in a different medium. Nothing

Figure 7.4
This is just one of the many rows of microfilm filing cabinets located on three floors of the Family History Library. Reprinted by permission. © 2001 by Intellectual Reserve, Inc.

has been changed on the census page. You still view it as though you had it in front of you on paper or microfilm. Generally though, the information on the Internet is not in this format. This is the biggest reason for turning to the libraries, archives, and county courthouses to verify the names, dates, and places as they have been shared.

Genealogy and family history is largely a study in deductive reasoning. Many of us are also hooked on mystery novels. We thrive on the entire thought process. If you are not taking your research that extra step, you may not have yet discovered the real fascination of family history.

Each name, date, and place you discover on the Internet should be verified, especially when the compiler of that family history Web site has not included a list of the sources used to construct the family history. This is one of those lessons in the hobby that you often don't learn in time. You may have already amassed a healthy number of individuals in your genealogy database but not yet verified the conclusions of others.

Important

Genealogy software, as shown in chapter three, is designed to make compiling and publishing family histories easy. In some instances, the companies that own these software programs encourage you to dump the data from their CD-

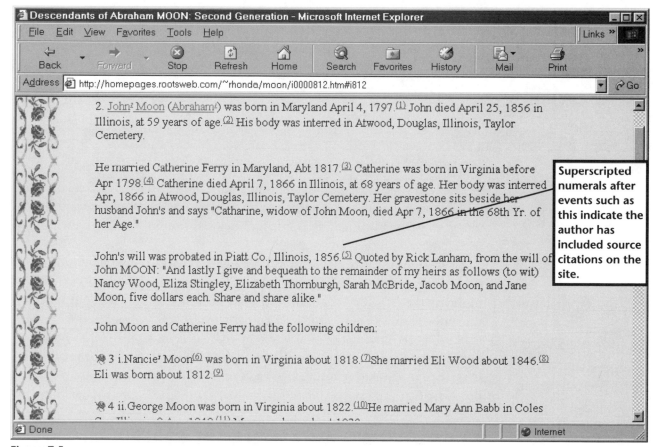

Figure 7.5
When searching compiled family history pages on the Internet, be mindful of any available source citations. Be sure to click on these links to see the sources used.

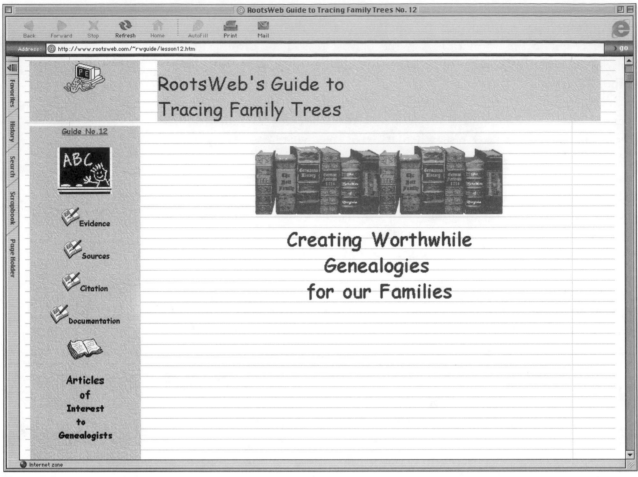

Figure 7.6
Online guides and lessons, such as RootsWeb's Guide to Tracing Family Trees allow you to augment your genealogical education at your convenience. © 2000–2001 MyFamily.com, Inc. Screen shot from Ancestry.com. Used by permission.

ROMs into your database and then spit it back out in a database that you share with them, to be put in a database or on a CD-ROM in the near future. While this is all well and good, it is a little like a closed circuit. Nothing new is going to be added with such an approach.

Because these software programs make this so easy, many family historians do not yet understand the importance of verifying the information that was found on the CD-ROMs or in the other electronic databases. Without verifying this information as you get it, you perpetuate a myth. Erroneous information is like a myth. Information you have entered based on family stories may turn out to be mythical. All of this information needs to be verified. That verification usually comes from visiting libraries, archives, courthouses, and other repositories.

GET OUT THERE AND SMELL THE PAPER

Once you have begun to locate family members in these online and CD-ROM databases, create a file of them on your computer. I advise against immediately

In my work as chair of a lineage society, I have seen the research of a lot of different people. Some of them submit applications that are approved right away; others need several letters sent to them explaining why they haven't been accepted and what they still need to do. The major difference between the two is the ability to analyze sources.

There are times in our research that we need to have a hypothesis, a working theory, of how the family relationships were aligned. When you have a framework to base your research—is John the father of Samuel?—your research can be more efficient.

The problem comes in when you forget which is the hypothesis and which is the research. The most common problem that I see applicants have is reading too much into a source. Instead of analyzing what the source actually says, they make it fit their hypothesis: "John has to be the father because Samuel is living in his house in 1850."

Successful applicants—and successful researchers overall—are the ones who realize that the 1850 census doesn't state relationships and that young Samuel could be a son, grandson, nephew, cousin, etc. They use their theories as guides, not as molds for the sources they uncover.

—Amy Johnson Crow, CG
Chair, First Families of Ohio

dumping all of these individuals into your family file. In fact, I downright discourage it. It is a lot easier to put in at a later date the ten or twenty people that do turn out to be related to you than it is to try to delete three hundred people that you discover aren't in your family tree.

The only way that you will determine the relationship of these individuals is to do research of your own. **Begin the true adventure by learning about the various record types and what they offer you.** You can even learn this online, at your own pace, and at a time that works best for you.

Idea Generator

Understanding what records exist and how they aid in moving back a generation or two on a family tree is the first step to understanding how conclusions are drawn from these records. If you have not worked with any of these records, you will have trouble evaluating another researcher's Web site even if they did cite sources, because you are unfamiliar with the resources.

The numerous of books available to introduce you to genealogical records include

Crandall, Ralph. *Shaking Your Family Tree.* Dublin, N.H.: Yankee Publishing Company, 1987.

Croom, Emily Anne. *Unpuzzling Your Past: The Best-Selling Basic Guide to Genealogy.* 4th ed. Cincinnati: Betterway Books, 2001.

LONG-DISTANCE RESEARCH NEED NOT BE OVERWHELMING

There is something intimidating about discovering that our ancestors lived in a state far from where we currently reside. We believe that we will be unable to gather records on this line. This couldn't be further from the truth.

If you have access to a Family History Center, you have access to records of the world. To locate a Family History Center, check the phone book. Look in the yellow pages under *Churches*, then look for *Church of Jesus Christ of Latter-day Saints*. Within the listings of facilities in your area, you may find a listing for a Family History Center.

Another way to find your local Family History Center is to visit the FamilySearch Web site at <http://www.familysearch.org> and select the "Find a Family History Center near you" link in the middle of the right-hand column. Fill in the fields for the country, state, county, and city where you live. Click Search, and a list will display. This list may include Family History Centers that are not nearby, so pay attention to the addresses.

The address supplied for each center is not a mailing address, but the physical address where the Family History Center can be found. I encourage you to call before you go. While the hours are posted on the Web site, hours can change as volunteer staff members find they can no longer participate. Other times there may be an emergency preventing the volunteers from being there on their normal day and time. You do not want to spend time traveling to a Family History Center only to discover it is not open.

While the Family History Library does not have all the records of the world, its collection is most impressive. You will find records from the United States and most foreign countries. How many records and what they cover varies from county to county, state to state, and country to country.

For more on getting the most from working on long-distance genealogy from home, read Christine Crawford-Oppenheimer's *Long-Distance Genealogy* (Betterway Books, 2000).

Greenwood, Val D. *The Researcher's Guide to American Genealogy*. 3d ed. Baltimore, Md.: Genealogical Publishing Company, Inc., 2000.

McClure, Rhonda. *The Complete Idiot's Guide to Online Genealogy*. Indianapolis: Alpha Books, 2000.

Rose, Christine and Kay Germain Ingalls. *The Complete Idiot's Guide to Genealogy*. New York: Alpha Books, 1997.

Rubincam, Milton. *Pitfalls in Genealogical Research*. Salt Lake City: Ancestry, Inc., 1987.

Stevenson, Noel C. *Genealogical Evidence*. 2d ed. Laguna Hills, Calif.: Aegean Park Press, 1989.

A LOOK AT THE SOCIAL SECURITY DEATH INDEX (SSDI)

The Social Security Death Index is often misunderstood both in its scope and the information you should expect to find in it. This index is available online through Web sites like Ancestry.com at <http://www.ancestry.com>, Roots-Web.com at <http://www.rootsweb.com>, and Genealogy.com at <http://www.genealogy.com>. It is available on CD-ROM through Family History Centers as part of the FamilySearch system and as part of many genealogy software packages.

The first misconception surrounding the SSDI is whom you should expect to find in the database. Many people think that it is an index to all individuals who have died in the United States dating back to the 1600s. Those people are often disappointed.

Social Security was signed into law in 1935 by President Franklin D. Roosevelt. Since that time, over 370 million Social Security cards have been issued.

In an effort to track all of these individuals, the Social Security Administration (SSA) also began to track individuals who were reported to the SSA as deceased. This list of deceased individuals is known in the SSA as the Social Security Death Master File, what we refer to as the SSDI.

Your ancestor may not appear in the SSDI for a number of reasons. The SSA may not have been notified of the death, the death may have occurred too early, or the deceased individual may not have ever had a Social Security number. The Social Security Death Master File was not computerized until 1962. This was not a retroactive index; computerization began in 1962, and very few pre-1962 entries have been included.

Some occupations did not require registering for a Social Security number, and for some occupations a number was assigned in a special category. For instance, long-term railroad employees received a pension through the railroad. They were given Social Security numbers that begin with 700. Medical doctors were not eligible for Social Security benefits until 1965.

When searching the SSDI, keep a few things in mind. First, the Issuing State is the state in which the person applied for a Social Security number. The Place of Last Residence is not necessarily the place of death. My grandfather Thoulough Ayer is a perfect example of this. He is listed in the SSDI with the Place of Last Residence as Manchester, New Hampshire. At the time of his death, he was on vacation. He died in Florida, more than twelve hundred miles away from Manchester.

continued

The true gift of the SSDI is the ability to locate an ancestor and get the birth and death dates and the Social Security number. Armed with this information, you can request a copy of your ancestor's Form SS-5, the application for a Social Security card. This small form gives you your ancestor's birth information, signature, and parents' names. Ordering the Form SS-5 online is easy. Each of the sites mentioned on page 107 offers an option that creates a letter you can print out with the necessary information for requesting the form, including the address where you need to mail it. Be patient. Some requests take up to six months to be fulfilled.

ORDER ONLINE

While going to a repository in person is exciting, some records will require just a little of your online time and your credit card. You can now request certain necessary forms via e-mail. More and more is coming to the Internet—if not the actual records, the methods for getting those records.

Vital records have long been a staple to genealogical research. While they do not go back to the 1500s, for the years that they do exist for a given county, state, or country, they are a marvelous resource. Many researchers have visited courthouses or written letters. Now some of those county courthouses, state vital record offices, and other repositories accept online orders.

Understand that you may pay a little extra for the convenience. Also know that not all counties or repositories with vital records take online requests. **One place for ordering records in the United States is through VitalChek.com at <http://www.vitalchek.com>**. It has a list of the states and counties from which you can select. You then fill out a form with information on yourself and the individual whose vital record you want. The cost is charged to your credit card.

Internet Source

I did this recently for a death certificate I needed. I had discovered an ancestor in the Social Security Death Index. Her last place of residence was listed as Macon County, Illinois. While the place of last residence is not always the place of death, this family had been in the county for well over a hundred years, so I decided to take a chance. On a Tuesday night (I would say "evening," but it was almost midnight) I went to VitalChek.com and saw that Macon County was one of the Illinois counties that would accept an online order. I filled out the form, gave my credit card number, and anticipated delivery of the certificate.

I expected to wait three or four weeks for this record. That was not the case. I was pleasantly surprised to receive the death certificate that Saturday in the mail. Now, not all orders will move that quickly, but it certainly was easier than writing the letter, writing a check, and mailing them—knowing I would have to wait a good three weeks or more for the certificate.

The National Archives, while not yet making its pension records and other resources available through an online ordering system, has made it possible to request the necessary forms via e-mail. Now when I run low on the military

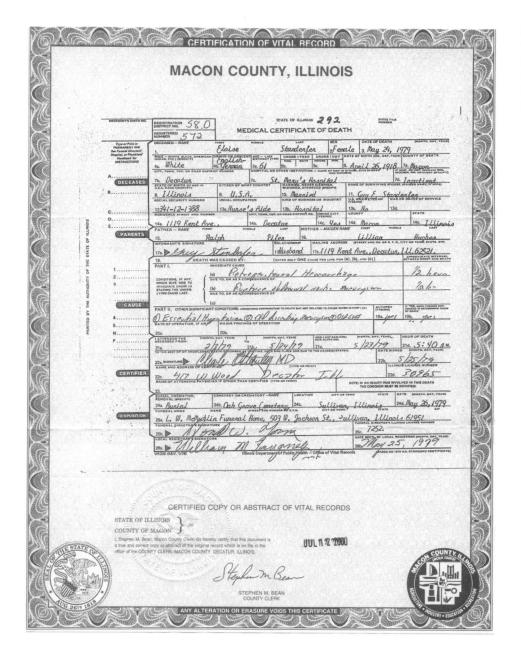

Figure 7.7
Vital records are one of the main record types that genealogists use. Now it is possible to order some of them online.

records forms or the passenger list forms or the land entry forms, I can e-mail a request for more forms. (Because these are multi-part forms, you must use the original forms as sent by the National Archives.) I can request up to six copies of a form at a time.

It is a good idea to limit your e-mail to the request for the specific form. I also request only one type of form in each request; I try to make it as straightforward as possible. Usually I have the forms within a couple of weeks.

KEEP TRACK OF YOUR RESEARCH

Before you can accomplish much at a given repository, you must have a plan. You need to know what information you have to verify. You need to have an

Supplies

REQUESTING RECORDS

A short request to the National Archives is the best way to assure receipt of the wanted forms.

To: inquire@nara.gov
From: "Rhonda R. McClure"
rhondam@thegenealogist.com
Subject: Form Request

I am writing to request the following form:

NATF Form 85—5 copies

Please mail this to:

Rhonda R. McClure
P.O. Box 700295
St. Cloud, FL 34770-0295

Thank you,

Rhonda R. McClure
http://www.thegenealogist.com

---

idea of what records exist at the repository you are visiting. You also need to keep track of your research as you do it.

We already looked at researching library catalogs, so that takes care of knowing what records exist at the repository you will visit. Now it is time to learn about the different programs that can assist you in planning and tracking your research.

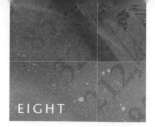

EIGHT

Genealogical Aids

U p to this point, when discussing software, we have looked at programs that deal specifically with either tracking your ancestors or getting you onto the Internet. When you walk into a software store, it is easy to understand how small a percentage of the total software on the market this really is. There are so many other types of software, and you can use some of them to help you with your research. In addition, some software utilities are devoted to aspects of genealogical research, offering you the chance to computerize some things that in the past had to be done by hand.

Once you begin to incorporate these programs into your research regimen, I suspect you will become more organized, accomplish more with your research time, and have a better overall grasp of your family history. While these utility programs are not miracle workers, what you will learn about them in this chapter will help you understand different aspects of your research. The different utilities will force you to concentrate on the given task, thus helping you to better understand it. As you begin to understand land records or evaluation of a source, you will grow as a researcher.

As you learn how to plat a land description, you will begin to understand that land records hold more for us than just proof that an ancestor owned land or was living in a given community. You will see how the land changed hands. You may see how the father divided up his property amongst his children. Perhaps when combined with the will, the land records will prove that he had more children than those mentioned in the will. You will begin to understand that the price of the land is often a clue as to any relationship between the grantor and the grantee.

WHAT'S AVAILABLE

Earlier chapters concentrated on genealogy software and what it can do for you. You rely on the genealogy software to create and track the familial relationships you uncover as you research. When you work in your genealogy software, your focus is on trying to connect the individuals in some form of a family unit. There are times when your focus needs to be less on family and more on the individual. That is sometimes a hard concept for those new to family history research to grasp. Some of the software utilities described in this chapter take just a single facet of the research process, thus allowing you a vacation from the constant search for that family connection, that ever-present need to force an individual into a family unit.

Notes

The different software programs and genealogy utilities discussed in this chapter are categorized to help you differentiate the focus of each program type. For each software type, you will be introduced to how this program may expand your genealogical endeavor. Sometimes even a single additional clue is all it takes to push the brick wall back one more generation. The four types of utilities to be examined are

- mapping utilities
- abstracting utilities
- image software
- organizational utilities

You can create some of the forms and unique features found in these software utilities by using the word processing, spreadsheet, and database software packages you may already own. As each focus is explored, look for comments on how to use your software to do something similar. The goal here isn't to force you to buy more software; it is to get you to think about what your computer should be doing to aid you with your research. Your computer should be more than an expensive paperweight or a glorified notebook full of family group sheets. Yet, this is the most that many genealogists do with their computers. Oh sure, they may go online, but they have not truly tapped into the power of the machine.

NO NEED, I'VE ALWAYS DONE IT THIS WAY

While genealogists have clamored to the Internet, many still refuse to change how they go about researching. Genealogists definitely don't like change. We don't like anything that requires us to stop researching while we learn a new software program or research method. Never mind that this new knowledge may in the end save us time. It might even offer us a faster way to call up some forgotten piece of information. We simply don't want to change.

I was like that for a long time. There are still some things that I don't want to see change. I have already confessed to the length of time it took me to move from my first genealogy software program to a much better one. I am going through a similar decision again, as the program I have used for some time has been discontinued. It's never easy, but this time I am more open to the prospect of finding something that works better.

A few years ago, as I was getting more involved in lecturing to genealogical societies and at genealogical conferences, I created all of my transparencies using my word processing program or my publishing program. I was using Microsoft Word and Microsoft Publisher. They offered me many nice features, and best of all, I was familiar with them. There were few things I couldn't do in these two programs.

My husband, always looking for ways to make things easier for me—no doubt so I will return to the life of domestic servant in our home—encouraged me to try Microsoft PowerPoint. It came with my Microsoft Office suite of programs, but it didn't seem all that great as far as I was concerned. I believe my retort was, "It just does a bunch of bullet charts. *My* lectures are much more than bullet charts."

What I was really saying was, "No thanks. This is the way I have always done it." I didn't want to do anything that might deviate from what I knew. I didn't stop long enough to think about the possibilities that such a program might offer me.

He was persistent, and eventually I gave in and began to play with the program. I took one of the lectures I needed to update and began to copy things out of Microsoft Word and paste them into PowerPoint. I even got a book on the program—not the manual, but a book written by "a real person." Little by little, I began to see potential in this bullet chart software.

Today I not only create all of my lectures in PowerPoint, but I also purchased my own projector so that I would never be without a way to run PowerPoint presentations. I just can't live without the animated circles, arrows, and other features that I can turn on when running the presentation. I could never go back to just printing out transparencies.

In case you were wondering, yes, my husband loves to remind me of how I summarily dismissed the program as useless in the beginning. And yes, we still eat as much takeout as we did before I discovered the wonders of PowerPoint, so, no, he still hasn't found a way to lure me back into the kitchen.

In addition to the fact that confession is supposed to be good for the soul, this little story exemplifies how my narrow focus precluded me from seeing the true potential of a program that was already on my computer. While working in the other programs often required some creative twists on my part, I wasn't willing to change. I knew how to get those other two programs to do what I wanted. I didn't want to waste time learning a new program. Also, since everything was printed to transparencies at the time, I hadn't yet thought to the future and the features I would find I couldn't live without.

Since this episode I am a little more open to suggestions by others, even my husband, about a possible alternative software program or method of accomplishing a given task. At times, though—usually when I notice that the clock has somehow jumped ahead four hours (four hours that I didn't really have to spare)—I must remind myself that the time I ate learning how to work the new software will be made up ten times over once I have mastered the program. It will make me a better genealogist or a better lecturer whether I better understand a land record or learn how to make a lecture more interesting. I will acquire knowledge and experience that I will continue to build on.

UNDERSTANDING THROUGH MAPS

When you work with your family history, do you find yourself sometimes doodling on a pad to understand what you are reading? Often those lengthy and almost foreign land descriptions found in the deeds for your ancestors are what you would like to envision. Sometimes you are simply trying to determine what county your ancestor was actually in when he was born or married. Remember that when it comes time to get the birth record or the marriage record, you need to check the county that existed at the time the event took place. Your ancestor's family could have lived on the same farm for two hundred years and possibly recorded births, marriages, the buying and selling of land, and wills in more than one county.

While there are ways to manually plat land, you must have all the necessary measuring devices. Sometimes this is easy—simply drawing a square and then dividing it. Other times the land description almost defies understanding. Why not have the computer do the work for you?

THE LAND RECORD SAID WHAT?

Notes

There are two different methods of surveying land. One method is found in most of the public land states, where the federal government owned the land first and the first individual to receive a parcel of land bought it from the federal government or received it as a bounty of some kind. This method is known as a rectangular survey. Another method of measuring the land is found primarily in the original thirteen colonies. Known as metes and bounds, this system describes the land through measurements and markers. Of the two systems, the metes and bounds method is much more difficult to use to create a graphical representation.

Working with land records, however, may be the one tangible connection you find among certain individuals. Land records have been used to prove relationships of children to fathers time and time again. At times it is necessary to research the land records for years after the individual who owned the land died. This may be because the children of the deceased, who received portions of the land through the probating of the estate, did not sell the land for some time. Thus they do not show up in the land records until they sell the land.

The recording of land deeds is not as we know it today. Sometimes a deed was not recorded until the time came to sell the land. Or the deed simply stated that the grantor had the right to sell the land from inheritance and then mentioned the deceased.

Case Study

Land records solved a riddle in my own research that had plagued me for a number of years. Early on in my research I was able to trace my direct paternal lineage back to my great-great-great-grandfather Benjamin Standerfer. From here the trail grew exceptionally cold, and for years I was not able to make any headway. Despite having found a land record early in my research, I did not stop to see what it said. In my zeal I had, of course, copied any deeds I could find with his name on it as grantor or grantee, but I never stopped to read any of it. I never

BUT HE DIDN'T MOVE

When working back in time, one pitfall you need to avoid is thinking that the county in which a town is now located is the same county in which the town was created. Those new to researching often fall into this trap, but it also happens to others who should know better. I have received correspondence that includes a county name as it is today. In many cases, since the research dates back to the early 1800s or late 1700s, I discover that the county name in question is incorrect.

This problem relates to the changing boundaries of the counties. As more people moved into a given area, the population grew. When the population got to a certain size, a new county or counties would be created from those counties currently existing. While your ancestor may not have moved, he may have found himself living in a new county.

The problem lies in where the records will be found. In most instances, records are housed in the courthouse of the county that existed at the time of the event. This is why it is so important to determine what county existed at the time.

AniMap (see <http://goldbug.com/store/page1.html>) offers you a way to watch the counties change. Through the maps included in this program, you can see how a given state or county looked from one year to the next. You can also use the Site Finder list of more than 200,000 place names in the United States to pinpoint a given town. You can then place a marker on your map where that place is now. Since the towns didn't move, when you change the date of the state's map, you will see what county your town was in at that time.

Many researchers relied on *Map Guide to the U.S. Federal Censuses, 1790–1920* by William Thorndale and William Dollarhide to do just what has been described. While this volume is a great asset to researchers, many changes took place in some of the states before 1790. Also, because you must estimate the locality of the city or town in question, it is possible that when working with the book's maps you may not estimate properly. You could end up chasing a line in a county where the families never were.

stopped to ask if I had I accounted for the same number of acres purchased as those sold.

Notice that the land description in the land record on page 117 mentions "the undivided sixth part" in a parcel of land. At the time I found this land record, I did not yet know enough about land records and the transfer of land to understand that this land record was as close to a smoking gun as I was likely to find. When I did stop to think about that, I realized that I should have been asking myself some questions. I should have been asking how he got this land in the first place. I should have been asking how he could own only a sixth of the undivided property.

SURVEYING SYSTEMS

Metes and Bounds Surveys

"Metes" refers to the measurement of boundaries of a tract of land by direction (given in degrees, minutes, and seconds) and distance. "Bounds" refers to physical objects such as trees, creeks, and adjacent tracts of land. Here is an example of a metes and bounds description:

> Beginning at a white oak head of branch that falls into Difficult. North 85 degrees West 54 poles to white oak side of branch. South 19 degrees West 220 poles to white oak in poison field. South 64 degrees East 110 poles to red oak on a levell [*sic*]. North 6 degrees East 254 poles to the beginning. [Mitchell, *Beginning at a White Oak . . . Patents and Northern Neck Grants of Fairfax County, Virginia*. (Fairfax, Va.: McGregor and Werner, 1977), p. 6.]

Rectangular Survey System

The thirty public land states are divided into thirty-six separate survey systems, each beginning with an initial point from which a baseline runs east-west and a principal meridian (P.M.) runs north-south. Secondary east-west lines six miles apart lie east and west of the P.M. and are called range lines.

These intersect to form townships thirty-six miles square. Townships are described by the number of the tier north or south of the baseline and by the number of the range east or west of the P.M., such as Township 3 South, Range 1 East, or T3S, R1E.

6	5	4	3	2	1
7	8	9	10	11	12
18	17	16	15	14	13
19	20	21	22	23	24
30	29	28	27	26	25
31	32	33	34	35	36

Each township is divided into one-square-mile sections numbered one through thirty-six, starting in the upper-right corner. Each section contains 640 acres and may be further subdivided into half-section (320 acres), quarter section (160 acres), half-quarter section (80 acres), or quarter-quarter section (40 acres). A complete legal land description should refer to the subdivision of the section, township, range, and the name or number of the Principal Meridian (P.M.); for example, Southwest quarter of Section 36, Township 3 South, Range 1 East of the Sixth Principal Meridian; or, SW1/4 S36, T3S, R1E, 6th P.M.

—Julia M. Case, Myra Vanderpool Gormley, and Rhonda R. McClure. "RootsWeb's Guide to Tracing Family Trees, No. 29: American Land Records," http://www.rootsweb.com/~rwguide/lesson29.htm

---

DEED ABSTRACT

Courthouse: Moultrie County Courthouse

Locality: Sullivan, Moultrie, Illinois

Volume: Book I   **Page:** 73   **Instrument:** Warranty Deed

Acres: 120

Grantor: Benjamin Standerfer   **Residence:** no residence listed

Grantee: Jacob Seass   **Residence:** no residence listed

Consideration: $300.00

Description: The following described lot, place or parcel of land situated in the County of Moultrie, and State of Illinois and known and described as follows, to wit: The undivided sixth part of the west half of the North West quarter and the South East quarter of the North West quarter all of section twenty two Township Fourteen North Range six East the two tracts containing one hundred and twenty acres.

Dated: 18 Sep 1856   **Signed:** Benjamin (his X mark) Standerfer

Witnesses: John A. Freeland

Recorded: 19 Sep 1856   **By:** John A. Freeland, Co. Clerk

Release of Dower? No

Record viewed on microfilm #1313221 at the Family History Library.

Finally the lightbulb came on, and I realized I should be searching through the land records until I could account for the entire parcel of land.

The other five pieces of the property led me on a merry chase in many volumes of the deeds for Moultrie County. I also returned repeatedly to the index to attempt to find those parcels as my reading of the land records themselves revealed that I still didn't have all six pieces. After finding all six pieces based on the information in the deeds, I was able to make a case for Benjamin's percentage.

Of course, this was a relatively easy puzzle to put together, at least as far as the land description was concerned. This land had been measured by the rectangular survey method. This system takes a big square and divides it. When it comes to the metes and bounds method, this description is not always as clear, especially if the land was divided and sold off in smaller pieces. Enter a program like Deed Mapper.

PUT THE DEED INTO THE COMPUTER

While we are far from the ability to scan that age-old writing of the seventeenth and eighteenth centuries and have the computer convert it to modern text, we

---

DEED ABSTRACT

Courthouse: Madison County Courthouse

Locality: Wampsville, Madison, New York

Volume: Book BY   **Page:** 147   **Instrument:** Quit Claim Deed

Acres: 40 and 20/100

Grantor: Clark Whitney, Mary (his wife)   **Residence:** no residence listed

Grantee: Frazier Cutler   **Residence:** no residence listed

Consideration: $1.00

Description: All that part of Lots no. 45 & 38 in the second allotment of the New Petersburgh Tract & bounded as follows. Beginning exactly one chain and thirty-two links south four degrees & fifteen minutes west, from the northeast corner of Lot No. 45 aforesaid and in the highway: Thence south fifty one degrees & forty five minutes west six chains & fifty two links: Thence north two degrees and fifteen minutes east one chain and eighty four links: Thence south eighty two degrees fifteen minutes west one chain & eighty two links: Thence south sixty two degrees forty five minutes west five chains thirty six links to a stake: Thence north four degrees fifteen minutes east thirty three chains sixty seven links to a stake: Thence south eighty six degrees twenty five minutes east fourteen chains & seventy five links: Thence south four degrees and fifteen minutes west twenty eight chains fifty eight links to the place of beginning.

Dated: 16 Aug 1854   **Signed:** Clark Whitney
                                             Mary Whitney

Witnesses:

Recorded: 16 Aug 1854   **By:** Lucius P. Clark, Clerk

Release of Dower? Yes

Record viewed on microfilm #0404328 at the Family History Library.

---

can at least use the computer to translate the gibberish in a land deed into a map showing the general shape of the land. Land measured using metes and bounds is seldom in the shape of a square.

As you can see by the land abstract, by the time you get to the end of the detailed land description, you've forgotten where the beginning was. You have made so many turns that you aren't even sure the description will create an enclosed geometric figure of any kind.

There are some excellent reference works that can be of help with this endeavor. Even with the available software programs, I encourage you to go the extra mile and read some of these so you'll understand what the computer does for you when you type in the pertinent details from the land record. **Find one or more of the following:**

Elliott, Wendy L. *Using Land Records to Solve Research Problems*. Bountiful, Utah: American Genealogical Lending Library, 1987.

Hone, E. Wade. *Land & Property Research in the United States*. Salt Lake City: Ancestry, 1997.

Lawson, Charles E. *Surveying Your Land: A Common-Sense Guide to Surveys, Deeds, and Title Searches*. Woodstock, Vt.: Countryman Press, 1990.

Miller, James W. Jr. "Platting Land Grants and Deeds." *The North Carolina Genealogical Society Journal* 16 (2) (May 1990).

Read, Helen Hunt. *Property Deeds for Genealogy*. Toledo, Ohio: the author, 1985.

Szucs, Loretto Dennis and Sandra Hargreaves Luebking, eds. *The Source: A Guidebook of American Genealogy*. Rev. ed. Salt Lake City: Ancestry, 1997.

Land platting is one of the best ways to understand your ancestor's land and that of his surrounding neighbors. These neighbors are the individuals with whom he most likely interacted the most. His daughters may have married their sons. His sons may have married their daughters. They may have moved together from one community to another.

DeedMapper (see <http://www.ultranet.com/~deeds/>) uses the gibberish of the land description and plats it for you. If you do go that extra step and gather information on other people in the community, you can use the features in the program to discover neighbors and see how close their land was. The properties may actually border one another.

Deed-mapping software should handle the different methods of measuring the land. After all, you didn't think that land measurement was done using just a single system, did you? In addition to metes and bounds, you may find that

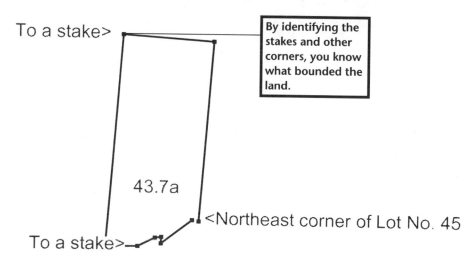

Figure 8.1

Platting land is made easier with programs such as Deed Mapper. Viewing a graphical representation of the land sometimes makes it easier to understand the acreage of the property.

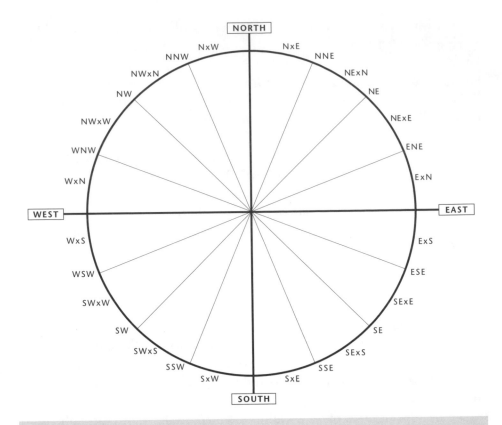

THE COMPASS POINT SURVEYING SYSTEM

Unlike other metes and bounds measurements, the compass point surveying system relies on compass points as opposed to those listed in degrees and minutes. This does not mean that there are not degrees in these descriptions. The above compass wheel is divided into thirty-two equal parts; each point on the wheel is 11.25 degrees from the next one. Once in a while, you will see a further breakdown by surveyor's into ¼ points. Each ¼ point is about 2.8 degrees from the next one.

land has been described using the compass point system. In other cases, you may find the land described using degrees/minutes/seconds in conjunction with the compass points. The land record abstract earlier in the chapter is based on this system.

While the deed-mapping software works the miracle of platting the land, it is up to you to input the correct description. Pay close attention to the numbers and letters you type into the deed-mapping software.

Of course, when you display the plot it is sometimes difficult to understand just how much land this may have included. Sure the program usually tells you how many acres in total there were, but it begs to be said, just what is a perch? When most of us purchase property we buy lots within city limits. When our ancestors purchased land, they were lucky if they had a neighbor only five miles away. You

Reminder

LAND MEASUREMENTS		
1 square foot	=	144 square inches
1 square yard	=	9 square feet
1 square rod, pole, or perch	=	30¼ square yards
1 rood	=	40 square rods, poles, or perches
1 acre	=	4 roods (4,840 square yards)
1 square mile	=	640 acres
1 square link	=	62.726 square inches
1 square pole	=	625 square links
1 square chain	=	16 square poles (10,000 square links)
1 acre	=	10 square chains
1 square mile	=	6,400 square chains

will find yourself reading about chains, links, rods, poles, and perches. If the degrees, minutes, and seconds didn't throw you, these terms might.

That little geometric shape on your computer screen begins to take on a new meaning when you know how big a chain is.

This is one of few genealogy software utilities that does not easily lend itself to an alternative in more mainstream programs. The closest I could come would be to use something like AutoCAD, a design program. If you are an architect or other designer, then you may be familiar with this type of program, which is used in designing homes, cars, and virtually anything else that has to be designed. Such programs usually bring a hefty price tag to the checkout as well. In this case, it is usually easier and cheaper to go with the deed-mapping software.

GET THE IMPORTANT STUFF

In a perfect world photocopies would be free, airlines wouldn't enforce weight limits for luggage, and genealogists would have photocopies of everything they ever used in compiling their family tree. Oh yes, and as long as we are dreaming, this perfect world would supply genealogists with a nifty perk—the ever expanding office. As your files grew, so too would your office.

Of course we live in a much different world. Photocopies aren't free, and we can't always get copies of everything that we would like. While transcribing is the next best thing, it is often tedious and time consuming. Instead, genealogists rely heavily on abstracting, a method where only the pertinent details are taken from a given record. When the land record was discussed earlier in this chapter (on pages 117 and 118), you saw abstracts of the original records.

Abstracting is designed to give you all the pertinent information without any of

\di'fin\ *vb*

Definitions

the fluff. Usually you are interested in names, dates, places, dollar amounts, and descriptions (such as cause of death on a death record). Often the original records are fraught with legalese, which only serves to give you writer's cramp if you write it all. Abstracting, when done correctly, leaves the rhetoric behind without sacrificing the important information. If you need to look at the record again years down the road and you don't have all the pertinent facts, you will have to find the original record again, duplicating past research—something we want to avoid.

The benefits of using one of the programs designed for abstracting relate to these omissions. Someone new to genealogy may not know which facts to gather from the different record types. We learn as we go in this hobby. Many of us have had to redo our early research because we realized we did it wrong. There is no shame in that, but wouldn't it be great if you didn't have to worry about whether you had abstracted all the important details? Instead you could concentrate on abstracting the information accurately.

That is the purpose of the abstracting programs. You can, of course, abstract using your word processing program or forms you create in a spreadsheet or database program. If you decide to go this route, create your templates before you travel. Travel can cause confusion; no doubt this has to do with the change in routine. (There's that word again—*change*.) Create any files at home while you're in your normal routine, and you can seek help from others, via e-mail or mailing lists, and from your collection of genealogical books.

The research value of these abstracting programs increases when you have a notebook computer, because you can abstract the information directly into the program on-site. If you abstract by hand and then input the information into the program later, you will duplicate your efforts unnecessarily.

ABSTRACTING WHAT?

Some abstracting programs are devoted to a single record type or resource. For instance, it may handle only information taken from a census form. Another may have been developed to abstract tombstones in a cemetery.

Imagine how many cemeteries the Daughters of the American Revolution (DAR) could have abstracted if they had had small computers to take to the cemeteries with them. I don't know any genealogist who hasn't relied on the tombstone abstracts that the DAR has done over the years. Some of those done during the 1960s and microfilmed by the Family History Library are now difficult to read. The ink has bled some on the onionskin, making the entries hard to read. Many of the earlier endeavors were not indexed either. Indexing is such a major undertaking and was not feasible on top of the work they had already done. Computers make many of these chores, such as abstracting a cemetery, easier.

Internet Source

Design Software <http://www.designsw.com> is one developer of abstracting software. It offers a program for abstracting census records. Design Software Family Census Research 3.0, a DOS (Disk Operating System) program, is actually more than an abstracting program. The templates for the census include every column used in every U.S. federal census. You actually transcribe the census page when you fill in the blanks. When you refer to this information, you will find that having all of the columns gives you peace of mind.

Another program by Design Software is Aspen 2000. This is its cemetery program. You abstract the pertinent information from a given tombstone, and you can also include pertinent details about the cemetery itself, such as driving directions, which will make returning at a later date should you so desire easier. Because Design Software Aspen 2000 is a Windows program, you can call up previously entered information, such as the cemetery, while you are working in the program. This means less duplication, which is one reason for using your computer to help you.

FORMS, FORMS, AND MORE FORMS

Genealogists rely heavily on forms when abstracting. Some of the computer software we have looked at includes forms for specific records, thus offering a template for abstracting. A recent addition to the Design Software catalog is the Genealogy Charts & Forms program.

The program offers many different forms to use for abstracting. Each form can be printed out and filled in by hand, but the program's appeal is that information can be input directly to the forms on the computer. The form can then be printed or saved as a file. Imagine if you could take all your abstracts with you on a research trip. As your research progressed, you could select the appropriate form without wondering if you remembered to bring it. You wouldn't have to pack the various forms, so your luggage might be a little lighter—the skycaps will certainly appreciate that too.

Many of us can type faster than we can handwrite. You are less likely to get discouraged in a major abstracting project if you use your notebook computer and a software program such as this one.

MOLD THE DATA INTO A CONCLUSION

One benefit of working with most of these programs over abstracting with your word processing program deals with manipulating the data after it has been entered. Abstracting is more than just writing down details. You will use the data to help you draw a conclusion about an individual. Is a person related to your family? Sometimes the data as it appears in its original listing does not lend itself to seeing correlations. When you can tell the computer to show you all the individuals with a given name or buried in a given plot, you may see a link that was previously hidden in the arrangement of the information.

Tip

YOUR SCANNER AND YOU

Scanners have come a long way over the last few years. I think back to the first one I had; I was impressed with it. It was a flatbed scanner, but it was a low-resolution, black-and-white scanner. That was about ten years ago. Now scan-

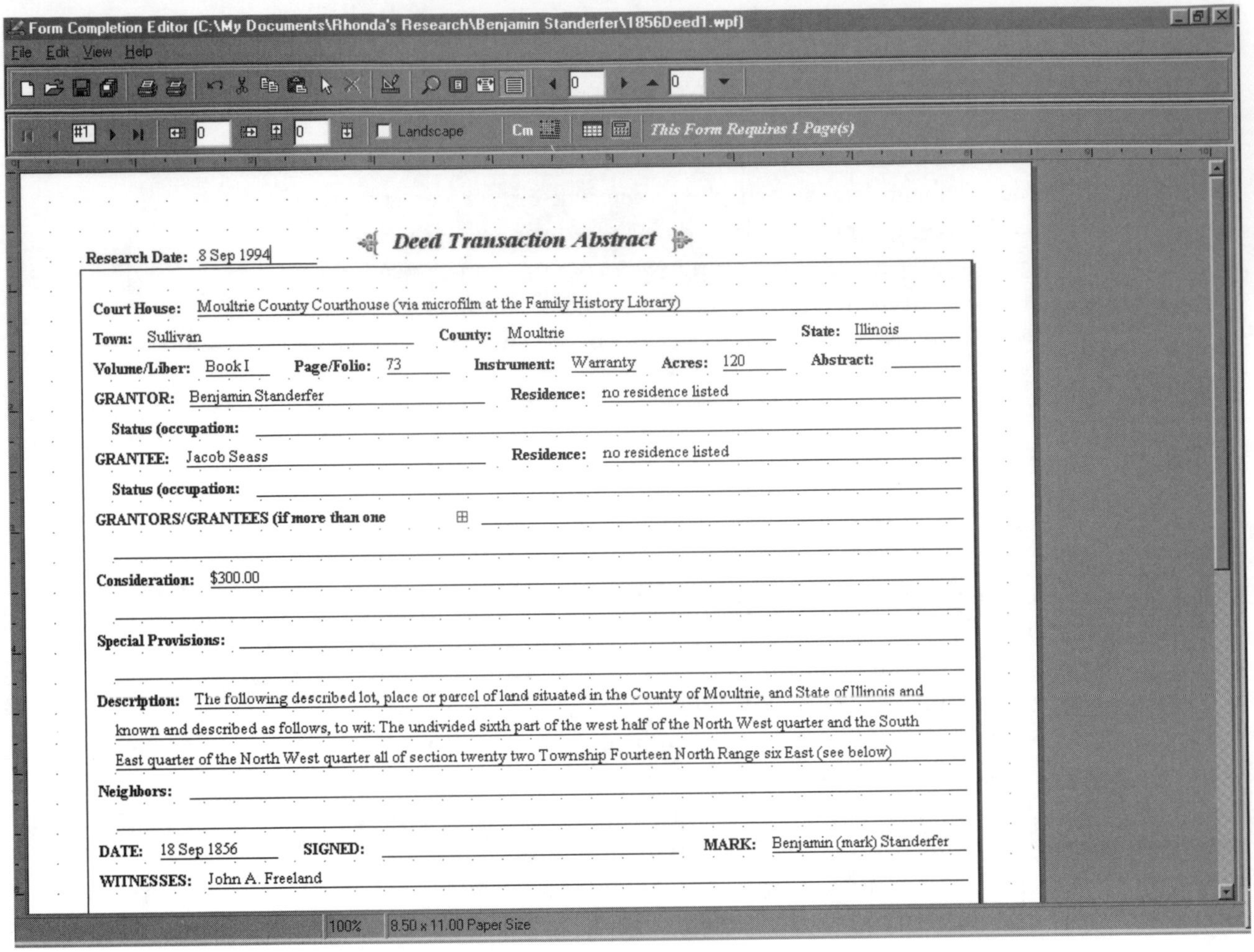
Form Completion Editor (C:\My Documents\Rhonda's Research\Benjamin Standerfer\1856Deed1.wpf)
File Edit View Help
Landscape Cm This Form Requires 1 Page(s)

Deed Transaction Abstract

Research Date: 8 Sep 1994

Court House: Moultrie County Courthouse (via microfilm at the Family History Library)

Town: Sullivan County: Moultrie State: Illinois

Volume/Liber: Book I Page/Folio: 73 Instrument: Warranty Acres: 120 Abstract:

GRANTOR: Benjamin Standerfer Residence: no residence listed

Status (occupation:

GRANTEE: Jacob Seass Residence: no residence listed

Status (occupation:

GRANTORS/GRANTEES (if more than one

Consideration: $300.00

Special Provisions:

Description: The following described lot, place or parcel of land situated in the County of Moultrie, and State of Illinois and known and described as follows, to wit: The undivided sixth part of the west half of the North West quarter and the South East quarter of the North West quarter all of section twenty two Township Fourteen North Range six East (see below)

Neighbors:

DATE: 18 Sep 1856 SIGNED: MARK: Benjamin (mark) Standerfer

WITNESSES: John A. Freeland

100% 8.50 x 11.00 Paper Size

Figure 8.2
With abstracting forms, you need never wonder if you have recorded all of the pertinent information.

ners scan in color, and the output can be of such high resolution that you can do justice to the family photos you scan.

If your family photo collection is like mine, some of the pictures are fading, especially the color photos. Others may have cracked or been damaged some other way. Wouldn't it be great if you could restore them?

There are companies that specialize in photo restoration. I encourage using them for photographs that are in serious disrepair. With a scanner, graphics package, and a steady hand, you may be able to handle photos with more minor problems. Just scan the photo, fix it on the screen, and print out a quality duplicate.

Image software packages vary in almost every way possible. Some are easy to use; others are more difficult. Some offer many more features than others do. Some have a much higher price tag than others do. The good news is that they are easy to find. Almost any store that sells software will carry at least a few different graphics packages.

Image software offers you options for cleaning up and restoring your photo

IMAGE-ENHANCING SOFTWARE	
Adobe Photoshop	http://www.adobe.com/products/photoshop/main.html
Kai's PhotoSoap	http://www.scansoft.com/products/soap/
Jasc Paint Shop Pro	http://www.jasc.com/products/psp/
ScanSoft PhotoFactory	http://www.scansoft.com/products/photofact/
Ulead PhotoImpact	http://www.ulead.com/pi/
MGI PhotoSuite	http://www.mgisoft.com/photosuite/index.asp

graphs, but using it requires a little bit of practice. Image software requires patience, a steady hand, oh, and did I mention patience?

The image software supplies you with the tools, but it is up to you to work the magic. You select the right tool for the job, perhaps a smudging tool, and then your movements with your mouse, trackball, or track pad make the changes. For some, myself included, this is the hardest part. My touch usually affects more than what I wanted to change. I am, and will forever be, graphically challenged. My daughter, on the other hand, who is not enamored with computers like her mother is, can sit down and do wonders with an image-enhancing program.

If you are easily frustrated, you may want to take a class on the software. Let an experienced teacher guide you through the best way to work with a program. You get to learn from their mistakes without having to make those mistakes yourself.

Usually your scanner will include more than just the software used for scanning the image. Scanners often come with an image-enhancing program. It may be a "light" version of one of the major commercial packages. These light versions are usually not as powerful as the total packages. This is a good way to try a program before you invest in the complete package.

The scanning software may offer some additional features. While these built-in utilities work well for much of your general scanning, they cannot alter an image to the extent that an image program can to produce photos that are fine and do not show any distortions.

The scanning software's focus is to scan the item into a digitized format. In many cases this will be graphical. Once the scan is on your computer, you can use image-enhancing software to alter the contrast, bring out or restore the colors, and hide any scratches.

Once you have finessed the scanned image, you can do many things with it. Most genealogists import the image into their genealogy program, then place it in a book or on a Web site.

WHY CAN'T I FIND IT?

I have long maintained that genealogy is the safe man's mystery. We get the thrill of the hunt and the deductive reasoning without risk of getting clobbered

THINKING OF GETTING A SCANNER?

Things to Keep in Mind

Talk to almost any genealogist today and you will learn that he or she has a scanner. In many cases the scanner was part of the package when they purchased their computer system.

Scanners offer many benefits to genealogists. Scanners allow us to digitize our photographs of our ancestors. In the past, the output of the scanned image was often disappointing. The printed images often appeared grainy, and the picture quality was degraded. The newest group of scanners scan at much higher resolutions, so it is easier to get a quality digitized image.

Some things to keep in mind if you are thinking about purchasing a new scanner:

- How often will you be scanning? If you plan to scan the eight hundred photographs you have stored in a box, a speedy scanner is a must. Keep an eye out for a computer magazine that publishes a comparison of scanners. Such articles often compare speeds for scanning and for working with computers. A major factor affecting speed with a scanner is the connection. There are three types: SCSI (pronounced "skuzzy"), parallel port, and USB.

- What do you plan to scan? If you have a lot of slides, you will need a scanner that offers a transparency reader. Transparency readers use a backlight to illuminate the slide so that as the scanner's ray swipes by it, the scanner's ray will pick up the image. For more on scanning images, specifically photographs, see chapter ten.

- Where will you put your scanner? If you already work in a tight space, you may not be able to clear enough room for a flatbed scanner. The flatbed scanner generally offers the best and most versatile options, allowing you to scan something in a book or other bound volume. The other option is a sheet feeder. These scanners take up much less space than flatbed scanners. In some instances you can purchase a sheet feeder attachment for your flatbed scanner, giving you the best of both worlds.

- What is your budget? The good news is that scanner prices have come down dramatically. You can often find a scanner that will give you acceptable results for under two hundred dollars. If you want top-quality photoduplication options, you are probably looking at a cost of more than five hundred dollars.

over the head by some big hulking bad guy. Admit it: You love the chase. You feel pride and a sense of accomplishment when you finally put your hands on the record that brings two generations together on a pedigree chart.

Unfortunately, as author and lecturer Sharon DeBartolo Carmack, CG, points

---

TYPES OF CONNECTIONS FOR PERIPHERALS

USB: Universal Serial Bus: This type of connection takes the place of serial and parallel port connections on your computer. The benefits are (1) you can plug something in without having to reboot your computer and (2) the throughput of data is faster than that through a parallel port or serial port.

SCSI (pronounced "skuzzy"): Small Computer System Interface: This is a standard interface between many computers and certain peripherals, including scanners and tape backup units. SCSI requires the installation of a computer board on the motherboard.

Parallel Port: A connection on the computer, usually in the back, where you can plug in a cable for something such as a printer or scanner.

---

out, seldom is the thrill as great the second time around. If you are disorganized, you will probably spend more time trying to put your hands on your copy of a census record or will than you spent finding the original record. Your frustration level will escalate, and by the time you do find it, all you will think about is the time you wasted searching for it.

We have all been there, I think. While the computer cannot keep your house clean or your papers filed, it can help you organize your research. Genealogy software incorporates some features to aid us in our research; a key feature is the source citation capabilities. If nothing else, a cited source will point you to the original record should you ever need to return it. Ideally the source will be in our own files, but that doesn't always happen.

There are many different approaches to organizing paper files. You will find articles and books on this subject; each offers a different approach. Lectures are given on this subject. Some lectures are devoted to a single method; others include information on many different methods so that each member of the audience may learn of one that best suits his needs. Perhaps none of the methods will suit your needs, so you will create your own from bits and pieces of the different systems. **For more on some of these systems, consult the following sources:**

For More Info

Carmack, Sharon DeBartolo. *Organizing Your Family History Search: Efficient & Effective Ways to Gather and Protect Your Genealogical Research.* Cincinnati: Betterway Books, 1999.

Dollarhide, William. *Managing a Genealogical Project.* Baltimore, Md.: Genealogical Publishing Company, Inc., 1999.

Kerstens, Elizabeth Kelley. Get It Together: "Naming and Numbering Your Documents," <http://www.ancestry.com/library/view/columns/together/95 5.asp>, posted 20 April 2000.

McClure, Rhonda R. "Avoiding the Paper Trap," *Heritage Quest Magazine* 28 (May/June 1990).

Each of these publications offers a different approach to organizing your family history files. Some genealogists elect to store information in ring binders organized by surname and locality. Others elect to store information in manila file folders. Of those researchers, some create folders for surnames, others create them for specific families, and still others create them for surname and record type. The various ways to organize your files are endless. The key is to do *something*.

COMPUTERIZING YOUR FILING SYSTEM

As genealogists rely more heavily on their computers, new methods are arising that put the computer to work in organizing the information traditionally stored in our paper files. A software program that does this is Clooz <http://www.clooz.com>. Clooz, developed by Elizabeth Kelley Kerstens of Ancestor Detective, is known as the electronic file cabinet for genealogical records.

Many confuse Clooz with the other genealogy database programs available. The genealogy database programs are designed to organize your families into a lineal descent or ascent. The individuals are linked through their family connections or the events in their lives. The focus is on the people. While individuals are entered into it, when it comes to Clooz, the focus is on the documents.

Clooz offers a number of templates. Using these templates, you can abstract information from record types including censuses, city directories, vital records, and more. When you use Clooz in conjunction with your genealogy database program, you will never again wonder what records you used in your research.

Ideally, you will use Clooz on a notebook computer while you are at a repository such as a library or courthouse. With your genealogy program and Clooz open, enter in your genealogy program the new individuals you discover. The supporting evidence you will then transcribe into Clooz. By working with both programs at the same time, you will keep both of them up-to-date.

Lest you think that Clooz is intended just for those researching American ancestry, you will find that the templates cover more than just records of the United States. Besides the U.S. census records, Clooz has templates for censuses in the United Kingdom (1841–1891), Canada (1852–1901), and Ireland (1901, 1911). The program includes two generic census templates as well.

Clooz, however, is not just for census work. If you take advantage of the template for photographs, you will end up with a catalog of all the photographs in your possession or that you have seen. The template has space for pertinent information about a photo. Do you have the negative? Is your photo an original or a copy someone has made for you? Did you digitize it? If so, where is that stored on your computer? After you fill out the pertinent information about the photo and link the appropriate people to it, you can generate a report to answer any question you may have about a photograph.

The photographs don't even have to be in your possession. Perhaps you found a photograph at a historical society or at one of the National Archives branches. You can record information on the repository where you found the

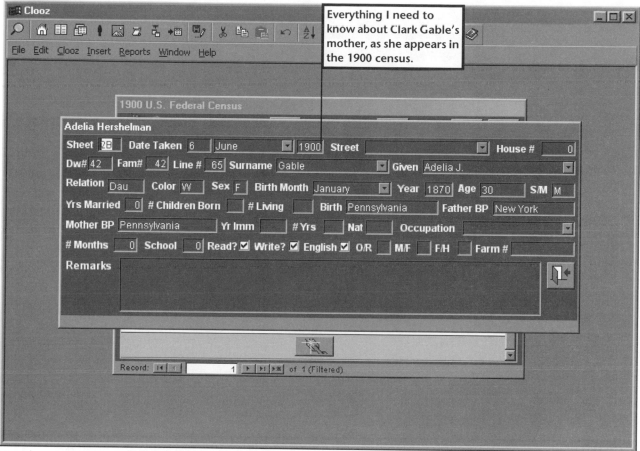

Figure 8.3
Clooz offers a fill-in-the-blank template for transcribing census records. Unlike with a form, you can manipulate the data once you have entered it into Clooz.

photograph. Even if you requested a copy of the photo, you should know where to return to replace the photo should something happen to it.

When you digitize photos, as we discussed earlier, keep Clooz open. As you work with each photograph, record where you are saving it in Clooz. In the end, you can generate a report to make it easy to pull up these digitized images later.

When it comes to organization, it is possible to create similar tools in a word processor, a mainstream database program, or perhaps even a spreadsheet program. To decide which of these to use, consider the strengths of each program.

Other records that you can transcribe in Clooz include city directories, vital records, land records, wills, correspondence, and Irish valuations (see page 130). As you work with these records, you may add new sources or people to your data. Include source citations for all of the many miscellaneous documents. Unlike the census templates that include the pertinent source documentation at the beginning of the census template, the other templates included have fields for source documentation built into the templates themselves. If you do not take advantage of these fields, you will do yourself a great disservice.

IMPORTING A GENEALOGICAL DATABASE TO CLOOZ

While Clooz is designed to help you track the documents of a person, you have to input the people in Clooz somehow. If you have a large genealogical database, you may feel that it is not worth your time and effort to type the people into Clooz. While you can enter the individuals manually, your genealogy software can be of help.

Most genealogy programs allow you to create lists. You tell the program what information on each person you wish to include in a list. You can send this list to a file, which you can open with a word processing program.

In the Clooz manual you will find step-by-step instructions for including information in the list and working with the file you create. The steps are clear, and you must follow them exactly.

While this may seem like an advanced project, if you follow the directions, you can successfully complete it. In the end, it is worth your time to import your genealogical database into your Clooz file. This will make it that much easier to stick with using Clooz in your efforts to get organized.

To be effective with a program such as Clooz, understand that it is designed to give you answers to questions you will have at a later date. Take a few extra moments to type in the full source citation so that when you have a question or need to do additional research in an area, the source may already be there. You may even solve a discrepancy when you look at the source of the information.

THE DO-IT-YOURSELF METHOD

You do not *need* a program such as Clooz. I am a big proponent of the use-the-right-tool-for-the-job theory; Clooz happens to save me time. I am not too proud to take advantage of the knowledge and creativity of another if he or she will help my genealogy efforts. I am a genealogist first, a writer second, and a computer person third. My expertise in computers does not lie in the land of

Notes

IRISH VALUATIONS

Irish valuations, also known as Griffith's Valuation, are surveys of land and property. Officially known as the Primary Valuation, these surveys took place between 1848 and 1865 to determine taxes. The assessments supported the Poor Law administration. The Poor Law Union books are available through the Family History Library.

programming; I would not spend time redesigning a wheel that has been crafted by experts. Some of you may prefer the comfy feeling of a form or database that you have created. **If you have some of the more powerful office suites or if you know that your database program or word processing program is up to the challenge, then go ahead and take advantage of the programs you already have.**

Database programs, such as Microsoft Access, are designed for tracking this type of data. They are hearty programs intended for rearranging information into different reports focusing on the different aspects of an entry. For instance, in your collection of photographs, you may wish to see which photos include a specific individual or family. This will probably be easier to handle in a database program.

A spreadsheet program may be easier to use to create a table, but it may not offer the important search and manipulation features you will need to evaluate the information. A spreadsheet program is also likely to be more limited as to the type of reports you can generate.

Finally, the word processing program may seem to be the best choice, but that is probably because you are quite familiar with it. While it can certainly generate a table, that table is not as robust when it comes to manipulating the data. Your word processing program will allow you to quickly search for a specific word or phrase. Is that all you want to be able to do, or do you want to be able to generate a report of just that information? If you answered yes to the latter, then you may be disappointed using a word processing program for your research.

BY LOOKING BACK, WE GO FORWARD

You have been introduced to many different software programs that will enhance your research experience. Many of them are designed to help you work more efficiently in the research phase. Through the different abstracting programs and forms programs, you will save time. Collecting the information with minimum effort on your part will help to keep you fresh during the research phase, and you will be able to abstract more information quicker. You can then spend more time on the evaluation of the research as you do it. The programs may help you get more research done when you visit a repository for the first—and perhaps the only—time.

As we review the research work we have already done, we must record our thoughts and concerns for future research. Don't let those questions get overlooked.

NINE

Look Toward the Future

F or each answer we find on our pedigree, we generally have at least two new questions. That's right, the farther back we go in the generations the more questions we have to research. As we look to the past, we must also look to the future. As we research we must consider the research we need to do in the coming days, months, and years. It may be easy to remember that day two at the library will include checking the census records for Great-Great-Grandfather Darst. Would you remember to check that census record if you plan to do it in two months?

QUESTIONS, ALWAYS QUESTIONS

Sometimes we don't come up with questions that our research didn't answer until we're back home reviewing research we just completed at a repository. As we input the names of the newly discovered children, we realize that the oldest child appears to have been born before the parents married. We must do further research to address this potential discrepancy.

When you receive a death certificate in the mail, you notice the date and cause of death for your Great-Great-Great-Grandfather Sickafus, and you see that he was buried in a cemetery you were not aware of. You learn the names and possible birthplaces of his parents. You now have more questions that must be answered. If you have used all of your vacation days for the year or have family commitments that will prevent you from pursuing the answers until six months from now, what do you do? **You need a method to track not only your past research, but also your future research.**

Research Tip

WHERE HAVE I BEEN? WHAT HAVE I DONE?

I was introduced to genealogy in the early 1980s. When I began my research, I had two advantages. First, I had a grandmother in the Daughters of the American Revolution. The DAR, one of many lineage societies, had required that she prove her descent from an ancestor involved in the American Revolution. Once she had completed the research, she filled out and submitted the DAR forms.

She did all of this work in the 1960s, when I was just a small child. I remember going with her to a couple of her meetings. Little did she know that I would become so infatuated with our family tree.

When I began working on genealogy, I naturally turned to her. She sent me a copy of her DAR application, and I set about re-creating her research. I was lucky to find some of the published volumes she used in my local public library.

My second advantage was the genealogical knowledge and experience of the two people who introduced me to this hobby. In addition to showing me how to fill out family group sheets and pedigree charts—at that time everything was done on paper—they both impressed upon me the importance of documenting all my sources. Over the years, my mentors and other professional genealogists have reinforced and expanded upon this message.

These people saved me from making a major mistake—not recording where I found information. While my early attempts at research logs may have been a bit lax, I did record enough information to allow me to recall where I found a given fact.

LEAVE A TRAIL OF BREAD CRUMBS

In chapter four you learned about saving Web sites in your browser. You learned that if you organize these favorites, you can easily return to a given site. The Internet is but one source, and it presents unique problems due to the ease of publishing and the constant evolution. Pages come, pages go. Print out any Web page that you rely on for information in your genealogy. The page may not exist at a later date, so you may not be able to consult it again online.

Keeping track of the Web sites you use is just one part of tracking your research. Whether you are working on the Internet or in a courthouse, you should keep a log of the Web sites, files, books, or other resources you have checked in your ongoing search for members of your family.

Citing Sources

In the story, Hansel and Gretel left a trail of bread crumbs so they could find their way home. Your bread crumbs aren't to lead you back home; your trail is for seeing how you arrived at your destination. You need a way to look back over the years of research that will allow you to see what have or have not accomplished.

IN THE BEGINNING

In the beginning, you may think that you will always remember everything there is to remember about your research. In the beginning you have perhaps thirty people in your database. It is likely that the information on them came from personal information; you probably know all of them personally. That is the beginning, when everything about genealogy is small: small database of names, small pile of file folders. Everything about genealogy is easily contained in the beginning.

FINDING THE RESEARCH LOG AT THE FAMILYSEARCH WEB SITE

Many valuable tools are buried in the layers of the FamilySearch Web site at <http://www.familysearch.org>. Many people use only the main search functions and never dig deeper. If you want to find the research log, you need to click on a few of the links at the site.

1. Access the FamilySearch Web site at <http://www.familysearch.org>.

2. Click on the Search tab.

3. Click on the Research Helps link.

4. Click on the Sorted by Document Type link.

5. Click on the Form link. The list of available documents will change.

6. Scroll through the alphabetical list until you find "Research Log." Notice that you can either view it in your Web browser, view a PDF file (requires Adobe Acrobat Reader), or order paper copies. You can order a package of one hundred paper copies for less than five dollars.

In the beginning you do not worry about filing systems, research logs, or organization. This is a shame because if you start out with such tools, you won't have to take time away from your research later to learn how to organize your information, keep track of your past research, and plan for upcoming research trips and projects. If you never develop these skills, difficulties you encounter in assembling your family tree will seem insurmountable.

Chapter eight addressed the theory of organization. I encourage you to read the various books and articles mentioned in that chapter. If you were not organized from the start, you will find that getting organized now is doable.

YOUR PAST RESEARCH

As I mentioned, the best genealogical advice I ever got was to record every source I ever used. It took me a few years to settle on a system that worked best for me, but during those years I at least made notes about resources I used. In the last ten years, I have relied on using a research log to organize my research.

Tip

A research log tracks your research. The best way to work with one is to maintain it as you work. A number of different research logs have been published. An easy one to locate is the one available through the Family History Library at its Web site, <http://www.familysearch.org>.

A good research log includes columns for certain information, such as when you completed the research, where you did the research, the source you used, and the results of that source. Beyond this, you may think of other useful information to document in your research log. When working with a preformatted research log, such as the one available from the Family History Library or one included in

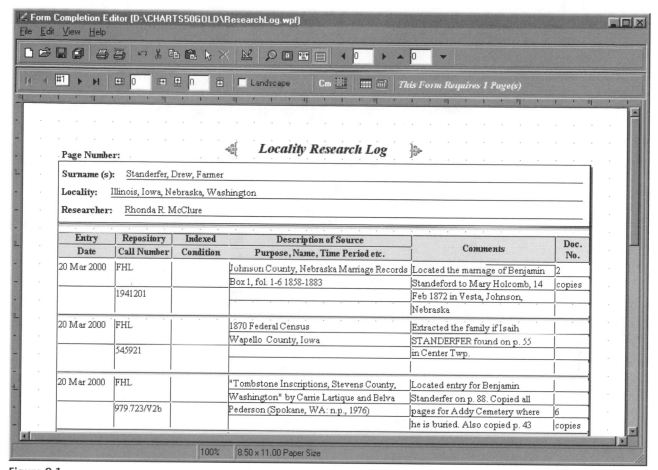

Figure 9.1
It is important to maintain some type of research log. This one, found in Design Software's Genealogy Charts & Forms, allows you to record the research as you work on it.

Genealogy Charts & Forms by Design Software <http://www.designsw.com>, you may not have control over what columns are included. You may want to try more than one before you decide which one to use.

A number of research logs or research calendars are available free of charge on the Internet (see page 136). Print out a few, experiment, and see which one works best for you.

Some of these forms have been developed for use in word processing programs. This makes them even more appealing, as you can use them with a notebook computer. I maintain my research log on my notebook computer now. I find that this way I am more apt to keep it current. I find it much easier to type into the computer all of the information found in a research log than to handwrite it. In the past, I sometimes took the easy way out by reverting to a form of shorthand to get the information into the research log with minimal time away from the research itself. Now that my research log is on my computer, I no longer resent the time I must take to work on it. I can quickly insert a full source citation in a column of my research log. I also make it a point to record names as I find them in the actual record in detailing the results of my search.

Figure 9.2
It is not unusual to find you have worked your way through a large number of books or microfilms during a research day. Research logs help you keep track of each resource searched.

Reminder

Another benefit to having your research log on the computer is that you can control the information entered. With preformatted forms, you are limited by the size of a given column, row, or box. When the log is on the computer, you can often change the sizes to suit your needs.

Of course, the "research log police" are not watching you use these logs. When working with a preformatted form, you can use two rows for the details of a source. We have been taught never to color outside the lines; however, it is better to go outside the box and be thorough than to skimp. If you read the log next year and cannot tell what you accomplished or why you looked at the resources you did, then the research log will not have served its purpose.

Perhaps the biggest benefit to working with a form you create yourself is that you choose the columns. If you wish to include a column about the condition of a record or the number of photocopies you made, then you have that freedom. Using your word processor's table function, you can create a research log that best suits you.

ONLINE CHARTS & FORMS (available free of charge)	
Ancestor Detective Freebies	http://www.ancestordetective.com/freebies.htm
Ancestry.com Charts & Forms	http://www.ancestry.com/save/charts/ancchart.htm
Family Tree Magazine	http://www.familytreemagazine.com/forms/download.html
Lineages First Steps	http://www.lineages.com/FirstSteps/Basic.asp
Family History Research Log	http://www.lds.org/images/howdoibeg/Research_Log.html

DON'T IGNORE YOUR INNER VOICE

As you work on a particular family, you tend to focus on that family. You constantly evaluate what you know about that family and consider what else might be out there. At this point your inner voice may begin to shout its thoughts on additional research you need to do on an individual or a family.

Unfortunately, we tend to push aside that inner voice. We think we will remember these questions the next time we visit a library or other repository.

SAMPLE RESEARCH LOG				
ANCESTOR'S NAME Standerfer, Drew, Farmer				
OBJECTIVES Locate records on these families			**LOCALITY** IL, IA, NE, WA	
Date of Search	**Location/Call Number**	**Description of Source (Author, title, year, pages)**	**Comments (Purpose of search, results, etc.)**	**Copies Made**
20 Mar 2000	FHL 1941201	Johnson County, Nebraska Marriage Records Box 1, fol. 1–6 1858–1883	Located the marriage of Benjamin Standeford to Mary Holcomb, 14 Feb 1872 in Vesta, Johnson, Nebraska.	2 copies
20 Mar 2000	FHL 545921	1870 Federal Census Wapello County, Iowa	Extracted the family of Isaih Standerfer found on p. 55 in Center Twp.	
20 Mar 2000	FHL 979.723 V2b	Births and Deaths of Stevens County, Washington 1890–1907	Searched for entry of Benjamin Standerfer who died in 1904 in Addy, Stevens Co., WA, but did not find an entry.	
20 Mar 2000	FHL 979.723 V2b	*Tombstone Inscriptions, Stevens County, Washington* by Carrie Lartique and Belva Pederson (Spokane, WA: n.p., 1976)	Located entry for Benjamin Standerfer on p. 88. Copied all pages for Addy Cemetery where he is buried. Also copied p. 43, listing of Highland & Calvary Cemetery with Standerfer entries.	6 copies
20 Mar 2000	FHL 0988360	Iowa County, Iowa Land Records Index to Deed Lots, 1855–1885	No entries for the Standerfer surname, though many of the entries were hard to read and some were completely faded.	
20 Mar 2000	FHL 0988362	Iowa County, Iowa Land Records Index to Deed Lands, 1871–1888	No Standerfer entries in this volume. There were many Sherlock entries (maiden name of Mary), but I did not extract any of them.	
20 Mar 2000	FHL 0988208	Iowa County, Iowa Birth Records Register of Births, 1880–1911	No Standerfer entries listed. Had expected to find the birth listing of the twins born 1881.	
20 Mar 2000	FHL 1769035	Iowa County, Iowa Birth Records Delayed Births, 1870–1937	No Standerfer entries listed in the index.	
20 Mar 2000	FHL 1674602	Des Moines County, Iowa Divorce Records 1835–1930	No Holcomb divorce file.	

Step By Step

CREATING A TABLE IN MICROSOFT WORD

Creating a table in Microsoft Word is fairly straightforward. Place your cursor where you would like the table to appear. There are two ways to insert a table. The simplest way is to click on the Insert Table icon on the toolbar. You can move your pointer to highlight how many columns and rows the table will have. The maximum table size with this method is five columns by four rows.

You can add rows and columns by using the Table menu. From this menu, you can insert rows above or below the cursor and columns to the left or the right. If you know that your table is going to be more than five columns wide or more than four rows long, it is easier to create the table from scratch using the next method instead.

The Table menu in Word 2000 includes many different options. In this menu, select Insert, then Table. You can then choose how many columns and rows your table will have and set the width of the columns. The Auto setting will create columns of equal width, and the columns will fill the page between the left and right margins. To override this setting, simply enter a width in that field. Later, if you need to add columns or rows, you still have that option using the steps outlined above.

In most tables, varied column width will be more effective; the column for the date doesn't need to be as wide as the column for the repository name. Once your table is created, you can set the size of each column. Position your cursor over a vertical line separating the columns. When your cursor changes into two vertical lines with left and right arrows, you can hold down your left mouse button and drag the column border to change the column width. You are limited by the widths of the other columns, so you may need to make some columns narrower before you make other columns wider.

Once you have created a table, you may want to take advantage of the AutoFormat option. Table AutoFormat is an option on the Table menu. This allows you to select from a number of preformatted tables that include font variations, column separation, colors, and more. You can easily design a clean, easy-to-use table with this feature.

However, most of our lives are too full and busy. (If we weren't, the companies that design and sell organizers—both electronic and paper—wouldn't be so successful.) We are busy with work, children, activities, and play; we are constantly on the go. As a result, it is a safe bet that on your next research trip you will *not* remember the questions your inner voice was shouting.

To save time, listen to that inner voice and write down what it says. There is no point in going to the library only to find that you must review the family group sheet and your past research before you can begin the research of the day. When you look over your notes as your research day progresses, it should

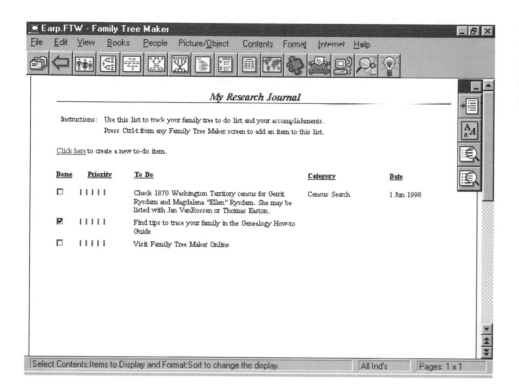

be only to assimilate any newly discovered information. Redoing at a research site the analysis you did at home is a waste of time. Keeping a log of research tasks you need to accomplish during your next research trip can save you from being doomed to repeat your efforts.

WORKING WITH TASK LISTS

A task list, or "to do" list, is an option in many genealogy software programs. It isn't there just because the developer of the program didn't have anything better to do. This list option is part of the program to make the program a better tool for your research. You do your research a disservice by ignoring this feature in your program.

You may be uncomfortable with this whole concept of multitasking. Maybe you like to use, or even have open, only one program at a time. You may prefer to use programs in full-screen mode. Perhaps your genealogy program does not include a task list. Are you at a disadvantage? Not at all.

First, double-check your software. The program may refer to this feature as a research log. While we think of the research log as a record of past research, some developers may have assumed that, since we cite our sources while we work in the program, we need a research log only to remind ourselves of impending research.

If your genealogy program does not offer any such feature, then you can make a to do list with your word processing software. Print a few copies of this form. Keep them beside you at the computer. As you work, write down anything that comes to mind for future research. I encourage you to keep your to do

Timesaver

Idea Generator

SOFTWARE WITH BUILT-IN RESEARCH LOGS (or To Do Lists)		
Name Family Origins	Contact Information Formal Soft, P.O. Box 495, Springville, UT 84663	Web Site Address http://www.familyorigins.com
Family Tree Maker	Genealogy.com, 39500 Stevenson Place, Suite 204, Fremont, CA 94539-3103	http://www.familytreemaker.com
Generations	SierraHome, 3060 139th Ave. SE, Suite 500, Bellevue, WA 98005, (425) 649-9800	http://www.sierra.com/sierrahome/familytree/
The Master Genealogist	Wholly Genes, Inc., 5144 Flowertuft Court, Columbia, MD 21044, (410) 715-2260	http://www.whollygenes.com

lists in some order, such as in the same order as you keep your files. If you have decided on an organizational system based on one highlighted in chapter eight, then you should coordinate your to do lists with that. This will save you time in the future. If all of your papers follow the same system, you won't need to stop and think about how to file your to do list or any of your other papers.

If you find a to do list that you like on one of the sites mentioned earlier, use it. You can always work with notebook paper; however, I advise against using a spiral-bound notebook as you can't reorganize the pages. Loose-leaf pages allow you to reorganize following whatever system you have set up.

USE YOUR COMPUTER'S POWER

Idea Generator

Even if your genealogy program does not offer you a to do list or a research log, you can create a computerized one. **You can use a word processing program, a spreadsheet program, or a database program.** Just remember to open the file whenever you work in your genealogy database program.

One of the easiest ways to create a to do list is to use a word processing program. This is one program you probably spend a lot of time with. Perhaps you write your letters in it or use the same program at work. Regardless of why, this may be the program you are the most comfortable using. It makes sense then to set up in that program a table or form you can use over and over again. When you open your master file, remember to immediately save it as a file with a new name, something that applies to the tasks you will include in it. This file may be determined by the organizational system you have selected.

Of course you will have more power to manipulate your data in a database program. Microsoft Access is one such program. If you have an office suite product that includes various programs, it is likely you have a database program. Some people shy away from database programs because these programs are too "computer-like." You must learn to think in terms of pieces of data rather than in entire records.

For instance, a to do item that you type into a word processing document or write on a form or other piece of paper is a complete thought to you. When

THE LAPTOP—AN EFFECTIVE TOOL

There was a time when, if you wanted to have all of your data with you at the library or courthouse, you had to carry several three-ring binders or boxes of file folders. Personally, I'm glad those days are past.

My laptop computer is one of my most effective tools. When I have it, I have access to all of my research notes, the data in my genealogy program, and e-mail from fellow researchers. With my modem, when I'm on a research trip I can log onto the Web from my hotel and peruse a library's online catalog late at night after digesting the day's discoveries.

In the days BL—before laptop—I wrote down all of my findings on research logs that I kept in three-ring binders. This wasn't very cumbersome until I added more families, which was approximately two weeks after I started to do research. Not only did this method take up a lot of space on my bookshelf, it also made it impractical to have all of my notes with me when I went to a library, especially one that limits how many items researchers can bring into the research area.

Analysis is much easier with a laptop. Land records are valuable in research, and with my laptop, I can easily abstract deeds and sort them by location to get a chain of ownership. I can also combine land records of different families. Sorting by location or date can show if they lived near each other or if they migrated at the same time. You can also see if they had associates in common.

Yes, this can be done by hand, but that has two drawbacks. First, this takes a lot longer, and time is something you never have enough of when you're researching. Second, doing this by hand requires writing. Every time you record something, you run the risk of having an error creep in. Did you write down "Range 17" when you really meant "Range 18"? Sorting the data directly—without having to reenter it—means less risk of transcription errors occurring.

My laptop has saved me countless hours. I don't duplicate previous research efforts because I brought the wrong notebook to the library. I can also do "analysis on the fly" by being able to tell exactly why I think Henry is Noah's father. The hardest thing to do is making sure that the battery is fully charged for those long days. A word of caution: Although many libraries have electrical outlets available for use, many courthouses do not. It is a good idea to call ahead to find out. To be on the safe side, bring a spare battery if you'll be there longer than your battery's life.

—Amy Johnson Crow, CG

you want to create a to do list in a database program, you must take apart that complete thought. Your to do list may have fields for surname, the given name, the event, your question, a deadline, the repository to search, and a completion date or some indication that the task has been completed.

Separating the tasks allows you to manipulate your to do list in a variety of ways. Imagine that you are planning a trip to the Family History Library. You could separate those tasks that need to be completed in the Family History Library (as noted in the "repository" field) and print a report of just those tasks. Those of you taking advantage of task list features in your genealogy programs may also have a similar capability.

CORRESPOND WITH OTHERS

Reminder

Another log that you need to keep is one that tracks your correspondence. Some people think you should have separate logs for online mail and regular mail. I think that correspondence is correspondence, and the two types should be kept together. The idea is to keep together everything that is similar, so you won't waste time searching in many different files to find an answer.

A good correspondence log should have space for you to include the

- date you wrote to the person
- address you used (either postal or e-mail)
- purpose for contacting them
- date you received a reply
- results of the reply

I suggest that you also include a column as to where you filed the letter and the reply. If the form you use does not offer such an option, put this information in the results section after your notes on the results.

If your ancestors emigrated from Europe, then at some point you will need to write a letter either to a repository or official in the country from which your ancestors came. This can seem daunting, especially when you are not fluent in the language of that country. The computer and the Internet offer a variety of methods to help with just such a problem.

CORRESPONDENCE LOGS	
Online Forms (available free of charge)	
Ancestry.com Correspondence Record	http://www.ancestry.com/save/charts/correcord.htm
Family Tree Magazine Forms	http://www.familytreemagazine.com/forms/download.html
Software Programs	
Genealogy Charts & Forms	http://www.designsw.com/charts50.htm
Clooz	http://www.clooz.com/

WRITING CONCISE LETTERS

When writing to anyone for the first time, it is generally a good idea to keep the letter short and to the point. This is true whether you are writing to a potential cousin or to a county clerk, though I maintain it is even more essential when contacting a clerk. After all, your potential cousin may be more interested in and more willing to read the family stories you include in the letter. The county clerk or librarian has many things to do, including reading requests from other genealogists, and therefore appreciates it when your letter is direct.

When contacting a county clerk or librarian, a good model is the one that is included below:

Dear Sir or Madam,

I am writing to request a copy of the death certificate for my great-grandfather. Below is the pertinent information for the requested record:

Name: Oliver Marion Standerfer
Death Date: 6 June 1931
Death Place: Sullivan, Moultrie, Illinois
Name of Spouse: Sarah Adaline Standerfer

I am including a check in the amount $8 to cover the cost. Please let me know if this is not enough. I am also including an SASE for your convenience.

Thank you for your time.

Such a letter generally gets a response. In fact, I have always received a response, though a couple of them were negative evidence. In one instance the check I enclosed was even returned because the information I was seeking was not found. Generally though, they will cash the check to cover the expense of the search.

—Rhonda R. McClure
"Ask Rhonda: Genealogy Questions Answered,"
http://www.genealogy.com/genealogy/askr011801.html
Posted 18 January 2001

BRING IT ALL TOGETHER

If you have a notebook computer, you can bring all of this together. If you are thinking about purchasing a new computer, **consider a notebook computer with a docking station** (see the sidebar "Docking Your Notebook"). The ability to work at your computer as much as possible while in a given repository is a time-saver, and I have found it helps me focus on what I am trying to do.

When I sit at a microfilm reader, I keep the following software open on my notebook computer:

Idea Generator

REQUESTING INFORMATION FROM OTHER COUNTRIES

One problem that many researchers encounter comes up when they begin to research immigrant ancestors. Unless the researcher grew up in a bilingual home, she may not possess the skills needed to converse with those in the home country. This makes writing to request records from the repositories in the home country a difficult task.

When working with microfilmed records from a foreign country, you may find that the FamilySearch Web site at <http://www.familysearch.org> has a word list for the language used in that country. These word lists, found in the Search section under the Research Helps option, offer a glimpse into the language. The word lists pertain specifically to words most commonly found in the various records genealogists use in their research. Even when using these word lists, from time to time I have had to refer to a more in-depth dictionary with English translations.

Of course, the word lists and an English-Italian Dictionary, for example, do not help you format a letter requesting documents from the civil authorities or some other repository in the home country. Constructing meaningful sentences when you do not really understand the language seems an insurmountable task. It is no wonder some genealogists do not pursue the parts of the family lines that crossed the ocean to come to the United States.

Fortunately, there are a couple of alternatives. The first is using online foreign-language converters (see the table on page 145). These convert simple sentences into another language. If you are going to rely on one of them, keep your sentences devoid of slang. Try to avoid contractions as well.

The second alternative is offered by the Family History Library. The FamilySearch Web site has many useful research tools to aid a researcher with all aspects of genealogy. The letter-writing guides are such a tool. These guides allow you to copy certain key phrases into a letter that you can mail to the appropriate agency. To find these guides

1. Visit the FamilySearch Web site at <http://www.familysearch.org>.

2. Click on the Search tab.

3. Click on the Research Helps link.

4. Click on the Sorted by Document Type link.

5. Click on the Letter-writing Guide link.

6. Select language from the list that appears.

Once you locate the language you need, you have three options for viewing the phrases: Web page, PDF format (requires Adobe Acrobat Reader [see <http://www.adobe.com/>]), and a published pamphlet that you can purchase.

If you write the letter as you look at the options, the Web page will be the easiest way to copy the appropriate phrases into your letter.

Some of the phrases you will find here include

1. My ancestor (*fill in ancestor's **name***) emigrated from your region in (*fill in year*).

2. I have not been able to identify this place, which appears to be in your area. Perhaps I do not have the correct spelling. Do you have any suggestions?

3. Can I write to you in English?

4. Please find enclosed a family group sheet with all the information I have.

Each language's guide has phrases devoted to different types of letters. For instance, you will find phrases for

- contacting a professional researcher

- writing to a genealogical society

- writing to a civil authority

Depending on the language you select, you may find additional letters, each with phrases unique to such types of letters.

FOREIGN LANGUAGE TRANSLATORS	
AltaVista World/Translate	http://www.altavista.com/r?F09
Dictionaries & etc.	http://www.cis.hut.fi/~peura/dictionaries.html
Free Translation.com	http://www.freetranslation.com
OnLine Translation	http://www.online-translation.dk
Translator Online	http://www.pinksoftware.com/trans
Web-a-Dex Universal Language Translator	http://www.web-a-dex.com/translate.htm

- Genealogy database program
- Clooz or Genealogy Charts & Forms (sometimes both)
- Research log (done in Microsoft Word)

I switch back and forth among these programs. As I abstract information, I use either Clooz or Genealogy Charts & Forms. I decide based on what I want to do with the final product. If the project will not require a lot of data manipulation, then I use Genealogy Charts & Forms. If I will need to manipulate the data, perhaps look at all the documents I have for a given individual, then I work in Clooz. When working on my own research, I duplicate some of this

DOCKING YOUR NOTEBOOK

When notebook computers, more often referred to as laptops or luggables, entered the computer scene, their limited capabilities required anyone purchasing one to also have a desktop computer. For genealogists, this was often the reason why laptop computers were not added to the tools used in researching the family tree. After all, the budget can stand only so many purchases to support the hobby. When it came down to a laptop vs. a desktop, the desktop computer, which was often cheaper, usually won.

Notebook computer prices began to come down, and the power and abilities began to go up. Smaller notebooks replaced the larger, older versions. Genealogists began to take a second look at this portable computer. Again some questioned whether they could justify spending so much on a second computer. They questioned purchasing a second, seemingly a duplicate tool when they weren't yet sure that the first one was going to be of much help.

Prices have continued to come down, and when you look at the power and features in today's notebook computers, you can see that they strongly resemble their desktop counterparts. As genealogists see more laptops invading their favorite repositories, they begin to hunger for their own.

One way to have the best of both worlds is the notebook computers that offer docking stations. A docking station enables a laptop computer to replace a desktop computer. Through the docking station, a genealogist can take advantage of a larger keyboard, a full-size monitor, and other peripherals such as printers and scanners.

The laptop connects to the docking station, which, when it has the peripherals connected, takes the place of the larger, stationary desktop model. Researchers who use a laptop and a docking station do not have to worry about synchronizing files between the laptop and the desktop.

Whether you use a laptop or a desktop, it is important to back up your data. You can use a Zip drive or Jaz drive to do this. If your system comes with a recordable or rewritable CD-ROM drive, you can back up your data to a CD-ROM.

When it's time to travel detach the notebook computer from the docking station and head out. While you won't have the larger keyboard and monitor on the road, you will have the freedom to take your computer from repository to repository.

When traveling, take advantage of one of the free storage sites. Online storage sites allow you to store files, free of charge, online. At such sites you can store important files, such as your family history database, and then download them should you have a problem. Two online storage sites are FreeDrive, <http://www.freedrive.com> and Xdrive, <http://www.xdrive.com>. You should also upload any changed files before heading home. You never know what might happen when you travel.

When researchers hankering for a notebook computer to make research trips easier are ready to purchase a new computer, a notebook computer and docking station may be a wiser investment than a new desktop.

work to be sure that I have all the data in Clooz. Finally, everything that I look at, work in, or investigate I record in the research log. I keep track of necessary future research in my genealogy program as I use a program that offers such a feature.

DON'T FORGET ABOUT TRAVEL PLANS

Up to this point, this chapter has addressed dealing with past research and planning for upcoming research. Your computer and the Internet can help you with the other aspects of future research. In chapter six you learned how to do some preparatory work at home or in your hotel room. You learned that online library catalogs offer you a chance to see in advance what a repository may have. **Your computer and the Internet can help you in other ways with your research trip including airline tickets, hotel accommodations, and car rentals.**

Tip

I haven't booked a flight by calling an airline or a travel agent in the past four years. I rely on the variety of online methods at my disposal. I can shop for the best fare from one airline or from many airlines at the same time. I can play with my dates and times of departure to see how they affect the overall cost of my flight.

Check the airline's Web site after you have narrowed down your flights before booking with one of the travel sites. Many of the airlines' sites offer incentives for booking through them. If you are a member of a frequent-flyer program, you may earn bonus miles by booking online at that airline's site.

Before you book your airline ticket, verify that you have a place to stay. Hotel reservations can usually be cancelled or altered without a penalty. Airline reservation changes, however, often mean paying an additional charge.

If you wish to stay in a specific hotel during your visit, start with that hotel's Web site. When I don't know the URL for a hotel chain, I simply experiment, using the name of the hotel and attaching .com to it. For instance, if you want to stay at the Best Western Plaza in Salt Lake City, Utah, you could try <http://www.bestwestern.com> and see what happens. Usually you will get what you expected on the first try. If not, you can use a search engine to find the URL.

If your hotel of choice does not appear to have vacancies or if you are unfamiliar with the area, use one of the travel sites. There you can select a city and the days you wish to be there. Take advantage of the maps included to determine if the recommended hotel is anywhere near the repository you plan to visit.

For a recent visit to the fair city of Fort Wayne, Indiana, I did have trouble

TRAVEL SITES	
Miscellaneous Travel Sites	
Expedia.com	http://www.expedia.com
Lycos Travel	http://travel.lycos.com
Priceline.com	http://www.priceline.com
TicketPlanet.com	http://www.ticketplanet.com
Travelocity.com	http://www.travelocity.com
Yahoo! Travel	http://travel.yahoo.com
Airlines	
Airwise Airline Web Sites	http://travel.airwise.com/info/airlines/index.html
American Airlines	http://www.aa.com
Delta Air Lines	http://www.delta.com
Frontier Airlines	http://www.flyfrontier.com
Southwest Airlines	http://www.southwest.com
TWA	http://www.twa.com
United Air Lines	http://www.ual.com

getting into my hotel of choice. In fact, since I had been assured that I would have no problem getting a room, I had ignored my own tenets and booked my flight before securing a hotel room. When searching the hotel's site, I learned that there were no rooms available for the days I was going to be there. Not one to panic, I called the hotel directly, and they confirmed this terrible fact. They offered to book me in a sister hotel, and I accepted. The problem? The hotel was thirty miles away. I took the reservation, though, as it was obvious that something big was happening in Fort Wayne that week.

Since I would be staying outside walking distance to the repository, I went to a travel site to rent a car. There I got the brilliant idea of looking for any hotels in the city of Fort Wayne that would take poor little me. While not within walking distance of my target, the hotel I got was about four miles away. Between the kindness of friends at the Allen County Public Library and the hotel's shuttle, I accomplished a great deal in my two days in Fort Wayne. I was able to cancel the other hotel reservation and the car rental reservation as well.

So you see, it pays to shop around. Don't accept the first hit you get from a travel site or a hotel site. If your plans are flexible, sometimes a change of a day or two can mean a major change in the cost of your flight or hotel room.

For lodging, look at all the room rates offered, especially when considering an individual hotel. Unlike the travel sites, which usually display the list of rates with the lowest rate at the top, the hotels often mix them up. Be sure to read all the fine print for each entry. Some rates require you to have a special membership, perhaps a AAA membership, or be a certain age. Other rates may require payment at the time of booking for one or all of the nights. Sometimes you can find some very low rates if you look hard enough at the search results. Some of these low rates may not appear on the travel sites' results lists.

When you need a car, again do some checking. Compare the rates between the travel sites and the individual company sites. Also, see what the rental prices are for offices that are not at the airport. Often additional fees or taxes are charged when the car rental place is on airport property. To see if there is a difference in rates, run a search for cars at the airport as well as for cars not picked up at the airport.

KEEP THAT COMPUTER WORKING

Hard to believe that all of this can be accomplished from your computer while you sit in your home, isn't it? You really can get a handle on your ancestry. You can keep track of everything that is important to your research, from Internet sites to books and other resources you use at the library. You can even plan a research trip using your computer.

While we have discussed a little about how you can use your computer to publish your family history, we haven't dealt with ways to perk up all those names, dates, and places. One of the best ways to make your genealogy come alive is through pictures. Let's look at how to use them, preserve them, and share them.

TEN

Put the Computer to Work for You, Part II

For More Info

See *Preserving Your Family Photographs: How to Organize, Present, and Restore Your Precious Family Images* by Maureen A. Taylor (Cincinnati: Betterway Books, 2001).

O ne of the benefits of computers is their ability to digitize images. We can share those precious photographs without letting them out of our hands. Digitized images can be printed out, e-mailed, or incorporated into a Web page. If you join an online community such as MyFamily.com <http://www.myfamily.com>, you will have a place to share photos of your children and grandchildren with family members living far away.

Scanners and the software that works with digitized images have improved dramatically over the years. Like everything else related to computers, the technology has been screaming along. Genealogists tend to be some of the last

MYFAMILY.COM

There is much concern today about personal privacy. As more people get involved in family history, more personal information about living individuals gets posted on Web sites. If the purpose of your Web site is to share the photo of Johnny's goal at the last soccer game, then you may want to check out MyFamily.com at <http://www.myfamily.com>.

The appeal of this site is that it is designed for that kind of sharing. You control, through a password system, who can log into your Web site. If you tell Johnny's grandparents the password, then they can log in and see his winning goal. The good news is that unwelcome, less scrupulous individuals cannot log in and learn all about Johnny.

The MyFamily.com Web sites offer more than just a place to share your family photos. Membership, which is free by the way, offers you message boards and other ways to communicate with your family members regardless of how far away they live.

people to learn of the most recent advances. This is primarily because our focus is on something else. We are more concerned with adding names to the family tree than upgrading our gadgets. There is a new breed of family historian, though, that looks to enhance those names with photographs and other multimedia features. There are so many ways to enhance a family history, both in printed form and on the Internet.

A TRIP DOWN MEMORY LANE

Like computers, scanners have gone through extreme changes. Many of those changes have taken place in the last ten years. In the last five years we have seen pushes toward top quality when it comes to a scan of a photograph. That level of quality is still a little pricey, but you can find many scanners at a reasonable price.

About five years ago, a software development company sent me on a trip to demonstrate a genealogy program. The software was to be featured in a magazine article. The article told about the experiences of a regular family (not a family of computer geeks) with the software package. The magazine was striving to bring a family together with a goal, in this case a wish to computerize their genealogy, with software and some hardware. The family had the computer already, but the magazine provided a computer program, someone to show them how to run it, and some additional hardware. For this article the hardware was a scanner. The scanner was a Hewlett-Packard 4P flatbed color scanner.

Since my husband has long worked with Hewlett-Packard (HP) in his real job (which is *not* tech support for his wife's computer), we have long had Hewlett-Packard products—both printers and scanners. My first flatbed black-and-white scanner was a Hewlett-Packard. In fact, I had a nice discussion about my HP scanner—a diehard at the time—with the HP representative on this magazine assignment.

As he began to show the family this new scanner, I confess that I fell in love with it. It was a flatbed color scanner. I hesitantly asked him the price—prepared to grab a seat when I heard the retail cost and went into cardiac arrest—and I was pleasantly surprised. The scanner was $450. You may think that was a lot for a computer part, but compared to other scanners of its day and considering the power and the color options it offered, it was a major breakthrough. Many similar color scanners were running $800 and up.

I returned home from that trip convinced that I would have the HP 4P scanner before the month was out. I needed a new scanner, we had discussed getting one, and now I had my heart set on a specific one. That scanner worked beside me for the next five years. I just recently purchased a new one.

ALLOW ME TO PRESENT YOUR SCANNER

When it comes to digitizing photographs and documents, your scanner is one of the most important pieces of the equation. **If you are considering a new scanner,**

Notes

you need to keep some things in mind. Unfortunately, some of what you need to remember is the technical aspects of scanners. You were shown in chapter two how to determine if your computer could run a certain software package. Now you need to consider your scanning objectives so that you get the one that will work best for you. There is no point in paying for a piece of hardware that won't do what you want.

As you investigate scanners, either online or at a computer store, you will find that the associated specifications are the clue to what you can hope to accomplish with a particular scanner. If necessary, take a copy of the glossary with you so that you completely understand what the specifications tell you.

IT'S ALL ABOUT RESOLUTION

Because genealogists are most interested in scanning photographs or documents, the most important issue is the resolution of the scanner. How high the resolution needs to be depends on what you want to do with the scanned image.

Reminder

The resolution determines how clear the image will be when you print it out or use it in a Web page. The final output will largely determine the resolution you need when scanning a photograph or document in the first place.

If the project requires it, take the maximum resolution that your scanner can run without interpolation (see page 155). Many of today's scanners will tell you that you can have a $1,200 \times 2,400$ dpi resolution (or maximum resolution) through the scanner's interpolation. There is no need to rely on the scanner's interpolation. The graphics software programs will do a much better job with this. The key when working with the scanner is to get the best scan resolution possible for the job needed.

Getting the Best Scan Possible

You may be mumbling about how you never get a good scanned image regardless of what you scan. Usually the quality of the scanned image is directly related to the amount of time spent learning the scanning and graphics software. In chapter eight I included a chart of some of the available graphics programs. Once you select a scanner and a graphics program, take a little time to learn how to get the most from them.

One way to get some hands-on experience with this software is to take an adult education course at a local vocational technical school or college. The training you will get in such an environment will far exceed what you could do at home on your own.

Another way to learn about the capabilities of your graphics program, which will be the deciding factor on the quality of your images, is to read books about it. **There are many how-to guides on the market that introduce you to a software package and show you how to maximize your use of that package.** You have probably seen these at your local bookstore and not realized they could offer you such assistance.

Printed Source

A search at Amazon.com <http://www.amazon.com> of books on Adobe

IMPORTANT TERMS

bit depth: Refers to the color depth of a pixel. A 1-bit scanner would scan only in black and white. Newer scanners scan at a level of 24 bits or higher, resulting in more than 16 million colors. Generally, the higher the bit depth, the more colors recognized by the scanner.

BMP: Bit map. A file format used for graphics such as wallpaper in Microsoft Windows.

dpi: Dots per inch. Indicates the resolution of the scanner, the printer, or the image itself. The higher the number, the sharper the image.

flatbed scanner: A scanner that offers a flat glass plate upon which to place an item for scanning. Flatbed scanners are especially useful when working with bound volumes.

gamma settings: The relationship between the input levels of the scanner and the output levels. Adjusting the gamma settings, when possible in your scanner software, is more precise than working with the brightness and contrast options when a scan appears darker or lighter than it should.

GIF: Graphics interchange format. A file format used at the World Wide Web. It supports data compression, which requires less space, making it desirable for use on the Internet.

handheld: A scanner that can be held in your hand. It allows you to make multiple passes of a page, which are then knit together using software specifically designed for that purpose. Generally this software must be used to scan an entire page of a book with a handheld scanner.

JPEG: Joint photographic expert group. Often used in discussing the .jpg file format that uses a compression technique to reduce the size of a graphics file. This is the preferred file format to put a photograph on a Web page.

native format: The preferred file type used by your graphics software.

OCR: Optical character recognition. Built into many scanning software programs, it allows you to scan a typed page and convert it to a text file that can be edited.

orientation: Refers to the position of the page. Page orientation can be portrait (vertical) or landscape (horizontal).

PPI: Pixels per inch. Used interchangeably with dots per inch (dpi) when referring to resolution.

resolution: Refers to the sharpness of an image. You will find it referenced when dealing with monitors, printers, and scanners. It is generally rated in dots per inch. The higher the dpi, the sharper the image.

continued

sheet feeder: A scanner that requires you to feed the pages through. It can scan only loose-leaf pages.

tif: File extension for TIFF files. TIFF is the acronym for tagged image file format. Like other graphics formats, it is one of the standard file formats for digitized images.

transparency capability: The ability of a scanner to backlight a transparent object, such as a photo negative or a 35mm slide, so that the object can be scanned and digitized.

TWAIN: Originally thought to mean "technology without an interesting name," the term actually gets its meaning from "ne'er the twain shall meet." This is because the data source manager sits between the driver and the application. This has become the standard interface in scanning. Many graphics programs and genealogy programs are TWAIN compatible.

RESOLUTION BY PROJECT	
Project	**Scan Resolution**
Web site or e-mail graphic	72–100 dpi (generally saved in either a JPEG or GIF format)
Print photo snapshot	200 or 300 dpi (best saved as a TIFF because you do not lose detail in the image, but also save some disk space)
Enlarging a snapshot	Maximum resolution of the scanner

Photoshop, one of the graphics programs mentioned in chapter eight, revealed the following books:

Adobe Photoshop 6.0 Classroom in a Book. Berkeley, Calif.: PeachPit Press, 2000.

Bouton, Gary David, Gary Kubicek, Mara Zebest Nathanson, and Barbara Mancuso Bouton. *Inside Adobe Photoshop 6*. Indianapolis, Ind.: New Riders/MTP, 2000.

Above all, the best way to become good at scanning is through practice, practice, practice. Did I mention you need to practice? Just as you will get more proficient with your genealogy database program over time, so too will you get more proficient with your scanner and graphics software over time.

Why Bother to Scan in the First Place?

Now that you have seen what is involved in scanning, you may think it isn't worth the trouble. You don't want to take that much time away from your

UNDERSTANDING INTERPOLATION

Today's scanners offer higher resolutions than ever before. While the information listed on a scanner displays the maximum scanner resolution, many now include an enhanced resolution. This enhanced resolution is higher and is achieved through interpolation.

Interpolation is where your scanner makes a scan of the document at maximum resolution, then enhances that resolution by inserting "estimate" pixels inbetween the existing pixels.

A scanned image file is simply a file of many dots, or pixels. Each pixel holds a duplicate of a piece of the original, usually a photograph. Enhanced resolutions squeeze additional pixels in between those received from the scan. This is done by guessing based on the surrounding pixels.

As you can imagine, these estimations are not always accurate. That is why relying on the interpolation options of a scanner is not always a good idea.

SCANNER MANUFACTURERS	
Canon	http://www.canon.com
Epson	http://www.epson.com
Fujitsu	http://www.fujitsu.com
Hewlett-Packard	http://www.hp.com
Microtek	http://www.microtek.com
UMAX	http://www.umax.com
Visioneer	http://www.visioneer.com

research. In some ways, scanning can help you with your research. When you scan documents and share them with your cousins, they may in turn find more information for you. **When you scan photographs you help to preserve them.**

You probably have some photographs that you don't want out of your hands. When you work with those photos, you would prefer to not have to touch the originals. After all, each time you touch an original photograph you expose it to the elements (humidity, pollution, fingerprints). If you scan the photo, you can use the digitized image over and over to share, both online and in print (these require different resolutions), with other researchers without disturbing the original.

When I got involved in genealogy, my grandfather went through his house from top to bottom. Any papers or photographs that he found he shipped down to me. I became the family archivist. Some of the photographs he sent I discovered I had duplicates of. Others were originals, with no negatives to

Important

Figure 10.1
The Luxembourg American Cemetery and Memorial, a once-in-a-lifetime trip. Such pictures deserve to be shared, but also preserved.

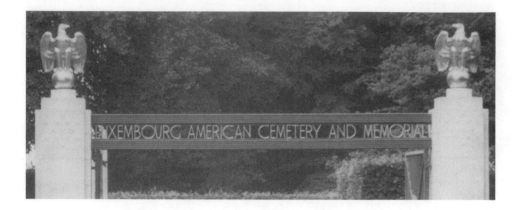

replace the original if it were damaged. I have a few tintypes, but most of the photos are on paper.

While many of these photos tug at my heartstrings, perhaps my favorite is the one of my grandmother and her twin sister when they were six months old. Berenice, the twin, died a short time after that photo was taken. I have not only that photograph, but I also somehow have the receipt for the little white coffin she was buried in. I have the start and finish to a very short but precious life.

Not Just for Photographs

To this point, we have talked primarily about scanning photographs. We have looked at how scanning them makes it easier to share them with other researchers or place them on the Web. You can use your scanner with documents and microfilm, too. We are all so caught up in thinking that a scanner is only good for photographs that we do not use it to its fullest. **One way to enhance your genealogy is to scan signatures of your ancestors.** Sharing these reminds others that these people were real. They experienced all the ups and downs that life had to offer them. The signature may be on a deed for property the family sold before striking out again to try and make a go. Perhaps your ancestor was the enumerator for the local census, and his signature is on a census record.

Idea Generator

Once in a while, we discover a special document—perhaps the homestead papers for our ancestor. Wouldn't it be nice to have a scan of these and make them available on your Web site for other relatives to access?

When scanning such a document to share it on the Web, make two files. One file should be a thumbnail. The other can be the full-size image. This allows those who are not interested to bypass the larger, more time-consuming download. In chapter three I included the Web-publishing standards according to the National Genealogical Society. Among other things, you are encouraged to keep graphics to a minimum for the casual visitor. The thumbnail is one way to do this.

Figure 10.2
The tombstone of George S. Patton Jr., buried in the Luxembourg American Cemetery, is a piece of history. Sharing a scanned image protects the original from excess handling.

A New Breed of Scanner

At the National Genealogical Society's annual Conference in the States in Providence, Rhode Island, in May 2000, one of the vendors offered a microfilm-to-computer scanner. Many were sorely tempted by this little gadget, but the price tag was a bit daunting. While this machine would certainly supply a top-quality scan from a microfilm reel, it may be possible to get a similar utility with a much lower price tag.

As I mentioned earlier in the chapter, I finally broke down and purchased a new scanner. My husband and I kept all of the numbers and specifications in mind as we set out on our shopping trek. I knew I wanted high resolution. He knew that some scanners can now scan slides and other transparent items, such as negatives. We settled on a new scanner that, in addition to meeting all of my requirements for resolution and bit depth, included a top-lit active transparency adapter. The adapter is basically a backlight. Light shines through the slide or negative so that the scanner can see the slide or negative.

As my husband unpacked this flatbed scanner, I looked at the extras that came with the scanner for use with its transparency adapter. I got to thinking that if it could scan a 35mm negative or a 35mm slide, it should be able to scan a 35mm microfilm.

Of course, I just happened to have some microfilm in my office. Off I went to pick one and see what the new scanner could do with it. When I finished I had a lovely scan of a Canadian census page. I sent that scan to my graphics program and worked with it more there. This takes a little experimentation to see what you can get away with, but it opens the door to so many possibilities for genealogists.

\di'fin\ *vb*

Definitions

Thumbnail: A miniature of a larger page or graphic. Used in Web sites as a graphic that can be clicked on to view the larger page. Allows those not interested in the image to bypass it without having to download the large graphic.

Figure 10.3
With transparency adapters, scanners can now be used to scan images from microfilms, like this census record from Prince Edward Island, Canada.

In fact, Ancestry.com at <http://www.ancestry.com> and Genealogy.com at <http://www.genealogy.com> both have begun the digitizing of census images for the United States. Instead of having to drive to the library and crank through a roll of microfilm, you can now visit a Web site and view the images online. Both companies, in addition to scanning the images, are seeking to enhance the quality of the images. At last it might be possible to read that extremely faded census page where you are certain your ancestor is listed.

Idea Generator

ENHANCE YOUR GENEALOGY

Many of the genealogy database programs offer features for working with digitized images. **Instead of just listing the date and place of burial, you can now add a picture of the tombstone.** The software packages listed in chapter three can all handle digitized images. In some instances, you can even launch your scanner while you are working in the genealogy software. While this is an option, I prefer to take advantage of the power of my graphics software. The limited capabilities built into the genealogy software packages are generally not up to the many tasks we have when working with photographs and documents. As you learned earlier, the strength is found in your graphics program.

OH MY! THAT'S A BIG FILE

Earlier you saw a chart that listed the sufficient dpi settings for some of the ways in which you might want to use digitized images. Now let's look at what each of those settings will cost you in hard disk space.

As you can see, you may need to invest in a larger hard drive before too long. If you have a CD-ROM burner as part of your computer package, you can save the final image file to a CD-ROM. This allows you to use the file as needed without tying up a lot of your hard disk space.

FILE SIZES OF SCANS			
Original Source	**Bit Depth**	**Resolution**	**File Size**
4″ × 6″ (10cm × 15cm) black-and-white photo	8 bits	300 dpi	2.2MB
4″ × 6″ (10cm × 15cm) color photo	24 bits	72 dpi	360KB
4″ × 6″ (10cm × 15cm) color photo	24 bits	300 dpi	6.5MB
4″ × 6″ (10cm × 15cm) color photo	24 bits	600 dpi	84.4MB

Another way to save these large files is on some sort of removable disk. If you go to any computer store, you will see products such a Zip disk or a Jaz drive. These are external drives that use a medium much like a floppy disk. Whereas a floppy disk can only hold 1.4MB of files, these slightly larger disks can hold much more. Some of them can hold up to 100MB while others can store one gigabyte of files.

SCANNING ENTHUSIAST BEWARE

We have already seen that scanned files can be cumbersome. One of the tricks is to know which file type is best for the job at hand. Some file types, due to their own internal compression properties, will take up less disk storage space.

Regardless of where and how you store your digitized images, they are not secure for eternity. **Electronic media like disks and CD-ROMs are not permanent.** Some say this media is stable for only about five years. Don't end up feeling sorry for yourself. Keep up on the images you have scanned. Periodically check the disks. As the technology improves, see if there is a better option for storing your files. Above all, keep a log of where your digitized images are stored and where the originals can be found. That way should something happen to the digitized file, you may be able to re-create it.

Remember that you can take advantage of some of the programs we looked

Definitions

CD-ROM burner: The official name is a CD-R drive (compact disc recordable drive). It allows a person to create a master CD of files from his or her computer. It is an excellent way to store digitized images.

Warning

DIGITIZED IMAGES LOG						
File Name	**Date of File**	**Description of File**	**Individuals Included**	**Document Number**	**Disk Location**	**Location of Original**
Oma1.gif	24 Jul 1999	Picture of my grandmother taken in 1982	Sylvia Bailey (Oma)	CD0001.01	Carousel #1	Bailey envelope in filing cabinet 2
Oma2.gif	24 Jul 1999	Picture of my grandmother as a small child ca. 1908	Sylvia Bailey (Oma)	CD0001.02	Carousel #1	Bailey envelope in filing cabinet 2
Oma3.gif	24 Jul 1999	Picture of my grandmother and her twin sister, 1902	Sylvia Bailey (Oma) and Berenice Bailey	CD0001.03	Carousel #1	Bailey envelope in filing cabinet 2

at in chapter eight to help you with the organization of your digitized files. Clooz, when kept up to date, will give you a catalog of your photographs and digitized images so you need never wonder what happened to them.

SHARE RESPONSIBLY

When you get bitten by the computer genealogy bug, and you will be if you haven't already, you will want to share everything on a Web site. You will scan photographs and place them online. You will share your lineage through a family history site. You will converse with others online. All of these are admirable pursuits, but as you share you must remember to protect the living. If you want to share with your parents photos of your children, do so responsibly: Take advantage of a private area, such as the ones discussed earlier in this chapter.

State Resources

We have talked a lot about how you should take advantage of any online resources. To get you started, here is a list of state vital records sites, state archives sites, and state library sites, where available. Please note that if a state's vital statistics are not accessible directly online, I have not included any offline alternatives.

Alabama
Alabama Department of Public Health http://www.alapubhealth.org/
Alabama Department of Archives & History
   http://www.archives.state.al.us/index.html

Alaska
Alaska Bureau of Vital Statistics
   http://health.hss.state.ak.us/dph/bvs/bvs_home.htm
Alaska Department of Education & Early Development, Division of Libraries,
   Archives, and Museums http://www.eed.state.ak.us/lam/
Alaska State Library http://www.library.state.ak.us/

Arizona
Arizona Bureau of Vital Records http://www.hs.state.az.us/vitalred/index.htm
Arizona State Library, Archives, and Public Records http://www.lib.az.us/

Arkansas
Arkansas Department of Health http://www.healthyarkansas.com/
Arkansas State Library http://www.asl.lib.ar.us/

California
California State Archives http://www.ss.ca.gov/archives/archives.htm
California State Library http://www.library.ca.gov/

Colorado
Colorado Department of Public Health & Environment
   http://www.cdphe.state.co.us/cdphehom.asp
Colorado State Archives http://www.archives.state.co.us/

Connecticut
Connecticut Department of Public Health http://www.state.ct.us/dph
Connecticut State Library http://www.cslib.org

Delaware

Delaware Public Archives http://www.archives.state.de.us

District of Columbia

State Center for Health Statistics http://www.dchealth.com/healthdata.htm

Florida

The Florida Department of Health http://www.doh.state.fl.us/

The Florida State Archives http://dlis.dos.state.fl.us/barm/fsa.html

State Library of Florida http://dlis.dos.state.fl.us/stlib/

Georgia

Georgia Division of Public Health (Vital Records)
    http://www.ph.dhr.state.ga.us/programs/vitalrecords/index.shtml

Georgia Archives and History Division http://www.sos.state.ga.us/archives/

Hawaii

Hawaii Department of Health http://www.hawaii.gov/doh/

Hawaii State Archives http://kumu.icsd.hawaii.gov/dags/archives/

Idaho

Idaho State Library http://www.lili.org/isl/index.htm

Illinois

Illinois Department of Public Health http://www.idph.state.il.us/

Illinois State Archives
    http://www.cyberdriveillinois.com/departments/archives/archives.html

Indiana

Indiana State Department of Health (Birth and Death Certificates)
    http://www.state.in.us/isdh/bdcertifs/birth_and_death_certificates.htm

Indiana State Archives http://www.ai.org/icpr/webfile/archives/homepage.html

Indiana State Library http://www.statelib.lib.in.us

Iowa

Iowa Department of Public Health http://idph.state.ia.us/pa/vr.htm

State Library of Iowa http://www.silo.lib.ia.us/

Kansas

Kansas Department of Health and Environment, Office of Vital Statistics
    http://www.kdhe.state.ks.us/vital/index.html

Kansas State Library http://skyways.lib.ks.us/kansas/KSL/

Kentucky
Kentucky Department for Libraries and Archives http://www.kdla.state.ky.us/

Louisiana
Louisiana State Archives
   http://www.sec.state.la.us/archives/archives/archives-index.htm
State Library of Louisiana http://www.state.lib.la.us/

Maine
Maine Department of Human Services (Frequently Asked Questions)
   http://www.state.me.us/dhs/main/faq.htm
Maine State Archives
   http://www.state.me.us/sos/arc/general/admin/mawww001.htm
Maine State Library http://www.state.me.us/msl/mslhome.htm

Maryland
Maryland State Archives http://www.mdarchives.state.md.us/

Massachusetts
Registry of Vital Records and Statistics
   http://www.state.ma.us/dph/bhsre/rvr/rvr.htm
Massachusetts Archives http://www.magnet.state.ma.us/sec/arc/arcidx.htm

Michigan
Division for Vital Records and Health Statistics
   http://www.mdch.state.mi.us/PHA/OSR/vitframe.htm
State Archives of Michigan
   http://www.sos.state.mi.us/history/archive/archive.html
Library of Michigan http://www.libofmich.lib.mi.us/index.html

Minnesota
Minnesota Department of Health http://www.health.state.mn.us/forms.html
Minnesota Historical Society http://www.mnhs.org/

Mississippi
Vital Records Information http://vitalrec.com/ms.html#state
Mississippi Department of Archives and History http://www.mdah.state.ms.us/

Missouri
Missouri Department of Health
   http://www.health.state.mo.us/BirthAndDeathRecords/
   BirthAndDeathRecords.html
Missouri State Archives http://mosl.sos.state.mo.us/rec-man/arch.html
Missouri State Library http://mosl.sos.state.mo.us/lib-ser/libser.html

Montana

Montana State Library http://msl.state.mt.us/

Nebraska

Nebraska State Historical Society http://www.nebraskahistory.org/index.htm

Nevada

Nevada State Library and Archives http://www.clan.lib.nv.us/

New Hampshire

New Hampshire Division of Records Management and Archives
http://www.state.nh.us/state/index.html
New Hampshire State Library http://webster.state.nh.us/nhsl/index.html

New Jersey

New Jersey Department of Health & Senior Services (Vital Statistics)
http://www.state.nj.us/health/vital/vital.htm
New Jersey State Archives http://www.state.nj.us/state/darm/archives.html
New Jersey State Library http://www.njstatelib.org

New Mexico

New Mexico Department of Health
http://www.health.state.nm.us/website.nsf/frames?ReadForm
New Mexico State Library http://www.stlib.state.nm.us/

New York

New York State Department of Health (Vital Records)
http://www.health.state.ny.us/nysdoh/consumer/vr.htm
New York State Archives http://www.archives.nysed.gov/
New York State Library http://www.nysl.nysed.gov/

North Carolina

North Carolina State Center for Health Statistics
http://www.schs.state.nc.us/SCHS/
North Carolina Division of Archives and History http://www.ah.dcr.state.nc.us/
State Library of North Carolina
http://statelibrary.dcr.state.nc.us/NCSLHOME.HTM

North Dakota

North Dakota Department of Health
http://www.ehs.health.state.nd.us/ndhd/admin/vital/

Ohio

Ohio Department of Health http://www.odh.state.oh.us
State Library of Ohio http://winslo.state.oh.us

Oklahoma

Oklahoma State Department of Health http://www.health.state.ok.us

Oklahoma Department of Libraries—State Archives and Records Management
http://www.odl.state.ok.us/oar/

Oregon

Oregon Health Division http://www.ohd.hr.state.or.us/chs/certif/certfaqs.htm

Oregon State Archives http://arcweb.sos.state.or.us/default.html

Oregon State Library http://www.osl.state.or.us/oslhome.html

Pennsylvania

Pennsylvania Department of Health http://www.health.state.pa.us/

Pennsylvania State Archives
http://www.state.pa.us/PA_Exec/Historical_Museum/DAM/psa.htm

State Library of Pennsylvania
http://www.statelibrary.state.pa.us/Libstate.htm

Rhode Island

Rhode Island State Library http://www.sec.state.ri.us/library/web.htm

South Carolina

South Carolina Health and Human Services http://www.state.sc.us/health/

South Carolina Archives & History Center http://www.state.sc.us/scdah/

South Carolina State Library http://www.state.sc.us/scsl/index.html

South Dakota

South Dakota Department of Health http://www.state.sd.us/state/executive/doh/

South Dakota State Archives http://www.sdhistory.org/archives.htm

South Dakota State Historical Society http://www.sdhistory.org/

Tennessee

Tennessee Department of Health http://www.state.tn.us/health/vr/

Tennessee State Library & Archive
http://www.state.tn.us/sos/statelib/tslahome.htm

Texas

Texas Department of Health http://www.tdh.state.tx.us/

Texas State Library and Archives Commission http://www.tsl.state.tx.us/

Utah

Utah Department of Health, Office of Vital Records and Statistics
http://www.health.state.ut.us/bvr/

Utah State Archives and Records Service http://www.archives.state.ut.us/

Utah State Library Division http://www.state.lib.ut.us/

Vermont
Vermont Agency of Human Services http://www.ahs.state.vt.us/
Vermont State Archives http://vermont-archives.org/

Virginia
Virginia Department of Health http://www.vdh.state.va.us/
The Library of Virginia http://www.lva.lib.va.us/

Washington
Washington State Department of Health http://www.doh.wa.gov/
Division of Archives and Records Management
   http://www.secstate.wa.gov/archives/default.htm
Washington State Library http://www.statelib.wa.gov/

West Virginia
West Virginia State Archives http://www.wvculture.org/history/wvsamenu.html
West Virginia Library Commission http://www.wvlc.wvnet.edu/

Wisconsin
Wisconsin Department of Health & Family Services http://www.dhfs.state.wi.us/
State Historical Society of Wisconsin, Archives
   http://www.shsw.wisc.edu/archives/index.html
State Historical Society of Wisconsin, Library http://www.shsw.wisc.edu/library/

Wyoming
Wyoming Department of Health, Vital Records Service
   http://wdhfs.state.wy.us/vital_records/index.htm
Wyoming State Archives http://commerce.state.wy.us/CR/Archives/
Wyoming State Library http://www-wsl.state.wy.us/Welcome.html

Country Resources

These sites for the countries of the world will get you started with your foreign research.

Australia

The Australasian Genealogy Web http://home.vicnet.net.au/~AGWeb/agweb.htm
Australia GenWeb http://www.rootsweb.com/~auswgw/

Austria

Austrian Genealogy, AustriaGenWeb http://www.rootsweb.com/~autwgw/

Belgium

Genealogy in Belgium (WorldGenWeb)
   http://users.skynet.be/sky60754/familiekunde/
Genealogy Benelux Home Page
   http://www.ufsia.ac.be/genealogy/genealog.htm

Canada

Canada Genealogy and History Links
   http://www.islandnet.com/~jveinot/cghl/cghl.html
Canada GenWeb Project http://www.rootsweb.com/~canwgw/index.html

Denmark

DIS, Computers in Genealogy Society of Denmark
   http://www.dis-danmark.dk/indexuk.htm
Genealogy Resource Index for Denmark http://www.genealogyindex.dkc/

England

EnglandGenWeb http://www.rootsweb.com/~engwgw/index.html

Finland

Family History Finland (WorldGenWeb)
   http://www.open.org/~rumcd/genweb/finn.html
Finnish Genealogy
   http://nordicnotes.com/Finland/Genealogy_Finland/genealogy_finland.html

France

FranceGenWeb http://francegenweb.org/

Germany

Genealogy.net, German Genealogy http://www.genealogy.net/gene/index.html
German GenWeb Project http://www.rootsweb.com/~wggerman/

Iceland

Icelandic Genealogy
  http://nordicnotes.com/Iceland/Genealogy_Iceland/genealogy_iceland.html
Icelandic GenWeb http://nyherji.is/~halfdan/aett/aettvef.htm

Ireland

Ireland Genealogical Projects http://www.rootsweb.com/~irlwgw
Irish Ancestors http://www.ireland.com/ancestor/

Italy

The Italian Genealogy Homepage http://www.italgen.com/
Italy WorldGenWeb http://www.rootsweb.com/~itawgw/

Netherlands

Dutch Research Corner http://www.ristenbatt.com/genealogy/dutch_rc.htm
Genealogy Links in the Netherlands WorldGenWeb
  http://members.tripod.com/~westland/index.htm

Norway

Norway Genealogy (WorldGenWeb)
  http://www.rootsweb.com/~wgnorway/index.html

Poland

PolandGenWeb http://www.rootsweb.com/~polwgw/polandgen.html
The Polish Genealogy Home Page
  http://hum.amu.edu.pl/~rafalp/GEN/plgenhp.htm

Scotland

The Gathering of the Clans http://www.tartans.com/
ScotlandGenWeb http://www.britishislesgenweb.org/scotland

South Africa

South African Genealogy http://home.global.co.za/~mercon/

Spain

Spain—Researching Your Spanish Roots
  http://members.aol.com/balboanet/spain/index.html

Sweden

Sweden Genealogy (WorldGenWeb) http://www.rootsweb.com/~wgsweden/
Swedish Resources http://www.montana.edu/sass/sweden.htm

Switzerland

Swiss Genealogy on the Internet http://www.eye.ch/swissgen/
Switzerland Family History (SwitzerlandGenWeb)
  http://www.rootsweb.com/~chewgw/

United Kingdom

GENUKI—UK & Ireland Genealogy http://www.genuki.org.uk

Library Resources Online

Λ few sites that have compiled links to online library catalogs were mentioned earlier. This set of links is included to give you a jump start.

Allen County Public Library   http://www.acpl.lib.in.us/
Cyndi's List—Libraries, Archives & Museums Index
   http://www.cyndislist.com/libes.htm
FamilySearch   http://www.familysearch.org/
Houston Public Library   http://www.hpl.lib.tx.us/
Library of Congress   http://lcweb.loc.gov/
Los Angeles Public Library   http://www.lapl.org/
National Archives and Records Administration, NARA Archival Information
   Locator http://www.nara.gov/nara/nail.html
National Society, Daughters of the American Revolution
   http://www.dar.org/library/default.html
The Newberry Library   http://www.newberry.org/nl/newberryhome.html
New England Historic Genealogical Society
   http://www.newenglandancestors.org
The New York Genealogical and Biographical Society   http://www.nygbs.org/
New York Public Library   http://www.nypl.org

Glossary of Genealogical and Technical Terms

Ahnentafel: German for "ancestor table" (a type of chart). The term also refers to a genealogical numbering system that makes it easy to identify the relationship between any individual listed on an Ahnentafel chart and the individual who is its primary subject.

ancestor tree: A type of chart that starts with an individual and moves back through the generations of his or her ancestors; also called a **pedigree chart**.

ancestors: The people from whom you descend, e.g., your parents, grandparents, and great-grandparents.

ancestral file: A lineage-linked database of families submitted by fellow genealogists. This database is available on CD at Family History Centers or online at the FamilySearch Web site.

annotated: Having explanatory or critical notes and commentary for text. One option sometimes included in bibliography reports found in genealogy software.

ASCII (pronounced as-key): American Standard Code for Information Interchange. The most widely used computer coding system in the world. Most word processing programs allow users to save and read documents in ASCII format.

banner ads: A form of advertising that appears at the top of your Web browser window.

bibliography: A report that shows the sources of information used in compiling a genealogy.

bit depth: Refers to the color depth of a pixel. A 1-bit scanner would scan only in black and white. Newer scanners scan at a level of 24 bits or higher, resulting in more than sixteen million colors. Generally, the higher the bit depth, the more colors recognized by the scanner.

BMP: Bit map. A file format used for graphics such as wallpaper in Microsoft Windows.

bookmark: In your browser software it records the necessary information for returning to a Web site. This way you don't have to follow the same links you did when you originally located the site. You just open a special section of your browser and select the site from a list.

Boolean search: A search based on the mathematics of inclusion and exclusion depending on which operator (AND, OR, NOT) you use.

browser: See **Web browser**.

bulletin boards: These are online message areas. The messages stay at the site where the bulletin board is located. When responding to a message, it is necessary to do so online.

CD-ROM: Compact disc with read-only memory. A CD can hold approximately 650MB of data, or approximately 300,000 pages of text, or what it would take about 450 1.44MB floppy disks to hold.

census: A recording of information that will be used by the government. It may be in tabular format with very few names or it may list the names of everyone in the household. There are different types of censuses: agricultural, population, and military. Each will offer you a different view of your ancestor.

citation: The formal notation of a source of information.

cite: To record or call attention to the proof or source of a piece of information.

clipboard: A memory feature that Microsoft Windows uses to store the last information that a user copied or cut (but did not delete). It is useful when transferring information within a document or between documents. However, it can hold only one item at a time.

collateral line: Persons with whom you share a common ancestor, but who are not on your direct line of descent.

copyright: Offers protection to authors, artists, musicians, and others to help encourage them in their creative endeavors. It does this by limiting what others may do with the works copyright holders have already completed and made available.

cutting: The act of highlighting specific text with your mouse (or other pointing device) and then pressing the Backspace or Delete key to remove it. If you want to move specific text, you need to cut using the Control-X key combination.

DAR: The abbreviation for Daughters of the American Revolution. This is a lineage society that admits individuals only when they have proven a family connection to a qualifying ancestor.

database: A searchable, compiled, and computerized list. It could be used to select items that include death records, or it could be used to research for certain names.

daughter out: Refers to a line that descends from a daughter. At that point the surname you would trace—her children's—changes from her maiden surname to the name of her spouse.

descendants: Those who descend from someone. You are a descendant of your grandparents.

digest (format of a mailing list): Puts together anywhere from five to thirty messages into a single e-mail message before sending it to you.

directories: Offer you a list of Web sites. Many times these lists are organized alphabetically or under subheadings to make it easier to find a particular page.

download: To receive a file sent from another computer via modem. *Download* is synonymous with *receive*, while *upload* is synonymous with *transmit.*

DPI: dots per inch. Indicates the resolution of the scanner, the printer, or the image itself. The higher the number, the sharper the image.

e-mail: An electronic form of writing a letter to someone. It gets sent directly to them and arrives much quicker than regular postal mail, and it never gets stamped "postage due." You will find yourself using it more and more as you get more involved in the Internet.

emoticons: A way of using characters on the keyboard to denote various emotions including happiness, anger, surprise, mischief, and more.

endnotes: Source citations and explanatory notes that appear at the end of a document. Similar to footnotes, only appearing at the end of the whole piece rather than at the bottom of each page.

export: To transfer data from one computer to another or from one application to another. See **import.**

e-zines: Electronic newsletters. They come out at set intervals and can be a number of different lengths. A couple of them are Missing Links (see http://www.rootsweb.com/~mlnews/) edited by Myra Vanderpool Gormley and Julia M. Case, and Family Tree Finders (see http://www.sodamail.com) which is written by Rhonda McClure.

family group sheet: A form that includes vital information on a father, mother, and children in a given family.

family history: The recording of a family's life and times.

Family History Center (FHC): A branch of the Family History Library, which is located in Salt Lake City, Utah. At an FHC, you can search their databases on CD and request microfilms from the Family History Library, which currently has some two million rolls of microfilmed records. FHCs are found in local Church of Jesus Christ of Latter-day Saints facilities and are usually listed in the phone book.

family traditions: The family stories that have been passed down through the years.

favorites: See **bookmarks.**

filters: A way of automatically placing your unopened incoming e-mail into specific folders based on specific preset criteria.

Five Civilized Tribes: Those tribes that were moved into the half of Oklahoma that was originally Indian territory. The tribes that made up this group included the Cherokee, Chickasaw, Choctaw, Creek, and Seminole.

flame war: An online argument that usually escalates to include many people in a matter of a few hours.

flatbed scanner: A scanner that offers a flat glass plate upon which to place an item for scanning. Flatbed scanners are especially useful when working with bound volumes.

frames: Offer a way of viewing multiple windows in a single browser. Each frame usually has a specific function. For instance, one frame may list the counties of a state. When you click on one of the counties, another frame may display the books for sale about that county.

gamma settings: The relationship between the input levels of the scanner and the output levels. Adjusting the gamma settings, when possible in your scanner software, is more precise than working with the brightness and contrast options when a scan appears darker or lighter than it should.

gazetteer: A dictionary for places. Instead of giving you a definition like a dictionary does, it gives you details about the place, including the county it is in.

GEDCOM: Stands for **GE**nealogical **D**ata **COM**munication. GEDCOM allows you to share your information with other genealogy programs without having to type it all in again. You can use the file created to generate a Web page.

genealogy: The recording of the descent of an individual from an ancestor.

GENUKI: The premier genealogy Web site for the United Kingdom and Ireland. It is a very fitting name for a site that brings you plenty of information for genealogists on the United Kingdom and Ireland.

GIF: Graphic interchange format. A bit-map color graphics file format that is widely used in HTML documents for images.

given name: First name (and middle name, where present) given to a child at birth or baptism. Also called a Christian name.

handheld: A scanner that can be held in your hand. It allows you to make multiple passes of a page, which are then knit together using software specifically designed for that purpose. Generally this software must be used to scan an entire page of a book with a handheld scanner.

home page: This is the first Web page on an Internet site where your information can be found. Your site will probably have many pages, but everything is accessed from the links on the home page.

hop: A hop represents a small jump from system to system taken behind the scenes to get you from one Web page to another.

horizontal rules: Dividers to help break up your text and make it more visually appealing. While you can ask the browser to insert a generic horizontal rule, very often themed graphics sets offer one or more horizontal rules in the color scheme of the theme.

HTML: Hypertext markup language. The standard language used for creating and formatting World Wide Web pages. HTML documents are essentially text documents (as you would create in a word processing program) that have embedded in them tags that contain coding for text formatting, graphics, and hyperlinks.

HTML editor: Allows you to work with the actual HTML codes. Does not necessarily show you what you are creating in graphics format.

hyperlink: Something in one file that automatically brings up another location for viewing if a user clicks the mouse on it. These links are graphics or different-colored text attached to HTML code that provides the actual connection to the other location. The other location may be part of the same file, another file on the same Web site, or a different Web site entirely.

icon: A small graphical representation of an object or idea. Used to represent a function on a program.

immigrant: Person who comes to a country from another to establish permanent residence.

immigrant ancestor: First member of a family line to arrive in the new country and establish a permanent residence there. Also called a gateway ancestor.

import: To bring a file created in one application or system into another application or system. See **export**.

inscription: Information that appears on a tombstone. It can be as simple as the individual's name and the year of death or as elaborate as a poem or other tribute by the surviving spouse or children.

International Genealogical Index (IGI): This was originally created as a means for Latter-day Saints to track religious ordinances done on behalf of their deceased family. Currently includes over 100 million names with a birth or marriage date and parents' or spouse's names included.

Internet: A noncommercial, self-governing network devoted mostly to communication and research, with millions of users worldwide. The Internet is not a service and has no real central hub. Rather, it is a collection of tens of thousands of networks, online services, and single-user components.

Internet service provider (ISP): A company or organization that offers a connection service by modem to the Internet for a fee.

JPEG: Joint photographic expert group. Often used in discussing the .jpg file format that uses a compression technique to reduce the size of a graphics file. This is the preferred file format to use when you want to put a photograph on a Web page.

kinship: In genealogy, refers to relationships to any and all of one's relatives.

land platting: Drawing a graphical representation of the land description found in a land deed or patent.

library type: Refers to the specialty of a particular library. Some library types include armed forces, college and university, government, law, public, and religious.

lineage-linked: Describes a database where the individuals are connected by family relationship. In Ancestral File this is displayed in the form of a pedigree or a family group view.

list (format of a mailing list): Sends each message posted to the list as a separate e-mail message.

list owner: Is responsible for keeping control on a mailing list. You sometimes have to subscribe or unsubscribe people. And sometimes you have to play "topic witch" to keep things on track.

lurker: Someone who has joined an e-mail group or bulletin board and simply reads the messages and does not join the conversations.

macro feature: In a camera, it allows the camera to get extremely close to a given document. The Sony Mavica digital camera that I have allows me to get within a half inch of a document without losing the clarity.

mailing list: A group of individuals that discuss a single idea, locality, surname or record type. The messages arrive in your e-mail box just as other e-mail does.

manuscripts: Generally consist of groups of papers. They can be a person's private papers, logbooks, or drafts. Usually a manuscript has a common theme and is created by or around an individual or family.

maternal ancestor: An ancestor on the mother's side of the family.

metasearch engine: A site where you type in your keywords and then the site generates searches in a number of different search engine sites.

Microsoft FrontPage extensions: Refers to specific capabilities found in Microsoft FrontPage, software for creating Web pages. If your Web server supports them, you can use Microsoft FrontPage to its fullest. If it doesn't you can still use Microsoft FrontPage but not all of its fancy extras.

MIDI: Musical instrument digital interface. A file format indicated by .mid, for digitally representing and transmitting sounds of electronic devices such as keyboards and sound cards. Provides a protocol for transforming music into data and vice versa.

modem: A device that allows your computer to convert its digital information to sound, which can then be sent over a normal phone line to another modem. The other modem converts it back to digital information.

native format: The preferred file type used by your graphics software.

network: A system of computers connected together so they can share files, printers, and sometimes resources. It allows you to have a file on one computer but access it with another.

newsgroups: Message areas where online discussions on a given topic take place. They require a newsgroup reader to view and respond to the messages. These readers are built into both Microsoft Internet Explorer and Netscape Navigator.

NGSQ style: A numbering scheme used in published genealogies, it assigns consecutive numbers to each individual and then adds a plus sign (+) next to those who have children.

notary records: Can trace their roots back to ancient Rome when a slave would keep notes and correspondence for his owner. They now record land transactions and other property (such as a car) transactions, loans, new businesses, and the collection of state taxes.

NUCMC: National Union Catalog of Manuscript Collections. Detailed descriptions of manuscript collections in public, private, and academic libraries are indexed and cross-referenced in this catalog, which has been published annually since 1962 by the Library of Congress.

oath of allegiance: Renunciated any claims by "pretenders" to the throne of England and denied the right of the Pope to outlaw Protestant monarchs. Generally these oaths were signed as the passengers disembarked from the ships once arriving in the colonies.

OCR: Optical character recognition. Built into many scanning software programs, it allows you to scan a typed page and convert it to a text file that can be edited.

online: Refers to the successful connection with another computer via a modem, cable line, or network.

online service: A service that provides news, information, and discussion forums for users with modem-equipped PCs and the access software provided by the service.

orientation: Refers to the position of the page. Page orientation can be portrait (vertical) or landscape (horizontal).

paternal ancestor: An ancestor on the father's side of the family.

PCX: A graphics file format.

pedigree chart: A road map showing your direct ancestral lineage.

PERSI: Periodical Source Index. This is an ongoing indexing project from the Allen County Public Library in Fort Wayne, Indiana. The genealogy department of the library began to index periodicals by surname, record type, and locality.

plug-ins: Add-on utilities that allow your browser to enter a chat room or do other things on the Internet.

pop-up ads: An ad that appears as a separate, self-launching window of your browser.

PPI: Pixels per inch. Used interchangeably with dots per inch (dpi) when referring to resolution.

presidential libraries: Are established to prevent the loss of papers when a president's term is finished. The records in the currently available libraries include over 250 million pages of textual materials; 5 million photographs; 13.5 million feet of motion picture film; 68,000 hours of sound and video recordings; and 280,000 museum objects. An impressive collection.

primary source: A source created by an eyewitness at the time of, or close to, the event.

public domain: Works are considered to be here when the copyright laws no longer cover them. Ask before assuming something is in the public domain.

Queries: Requests for help regarding a particular line that you are having problems with. Before computers, these were put into periodicals. Now they are still published in the genealogical periodicals, but they are also posted online on bulletin boards and other message areas.

RAM: Stands for random-access memory. Your computer puts information into RAM for easier and quicker access. This area can be written and rewritten to many times during a single session on the computer. This type of memory is easily expandable by adding chips to the motherboard. RAM is your computer's work space.

real audio: A way of listening to interviews, music, and other sound from the Internet on your system.

real estate: On the Internet, this is the space displayed in the browser window. This is where you put your graphics and text. You want to take advantage of the area displayed to grab the attention of someone surfing your Web site. Not everyone will think to use the scroll bar to see what else your Web page may hold.

Register style: A numbering scheme used in published genealogies. This system assigns consecutive numbers to those individuals who had issue (children).

release of dower: A wife's relinquishing of her one-third right to the property. Women were entitled to one-third of their husband's property at his death. So when he sold his land, the wife had to give her consent. I have never seen a case where a woman did not agree to the release of dower.

repository: Any building that houses records for safekeeping. It could be a state archive, a library, a museum, or a historical or genealogical society building.

research log: A page, sometimes preformatted, used to track research. Most of these forms have columns for important items such as date of search; call number, repository, and title of source; and results.

research outlines: Have been developed by the experts at the Family History Library. They detail the history of a given locality or record type and include information about the record availability, including addresses for repositories other than the Family History Library.

research planning sheets: Are designed to record pertinent information about a research problem. You include the name of the ancestor, the source information, the date of the search, the goal or problem you want to solve, and the results of the search. These are then filed along with any copies that might have been made from the source.

resolution: Refers to the sharpness of an image. You will find it referenced when dealing with monitors, printers, and scanners. It is generally rated in dots per inch. The higher the dpi, the sharper the image.

RTF: Rich text format. A cross-platform, cross-application text-document format. It includes some, but not all, of the formatting information that is included in many word processing documents.

SASE: Self-addressed, stamped envelope. Whenever you contact anyone to request information from them, include an SASE. You will be more likely to hear back from them.

search engine: A site that is designed to help you search for specific pages on the Internet. By evaluating certain keywords, the site displays a list of Web pages that it feels meet your search criteria.

secondary source: A source created later than an event and based upon hearsay.

shareware: Software that you can try before you pay. You are generally left on the honor system for registering and paying for the software. Unlike demos, shareware usually doesn't stop working after a set amount of time.

sheet feeder: A scanner that requires you to feed the pages through. It can scan only loose-leaf page.

siblings: Children of the same parents.

signature file: A closing to all your e-mail messages that is automatically inserted by your e-mail program. A signature file usually includes your name, e-mail address, and Web site address.

snail mail: Mail sent through the postal system rather than via e-mail. While it may be faster than in the days of the Pony Express, it crawls compared to the speed of e-mail.

Soundex: An index based on the phonics of surnames rather than on exact spelling. The Soundex code is a four-digit code comprised of the first letter of the surname followed by three numbers based on the next letters in the surname.

source: The book, record, or interview from which specific information was obtained. This information is necessary in order to properly document a genealogy.

spider: An automated, computerized search tool that reads the information on Web pages to categorize the information for a searchable directory.

spouse: The person to whom another person is married.

store front: The ability to handle purchasing and money transactions on your Web site. Such capabilities are good for societies and professional genealogists. However, your company must be set up to accept credit cards through a bank. The storefront software only handles the actual orders, not the processing of credit card charges.

surfing: When you go from a link on one page to a link on another page. From page to page you move about the Internet, going from one Web site to another.

surname: Family name or last name.

tag line: A one-line quote of some sort. You could consider them the bumper stickers of e-mail. There is an entire book of these quotes: *Everything's Relative,* compiled by Elizabeth Biggs Payne, was published by the New England Historic Genealogical Society.

textual holdings: Can be letters, census pages, passenger lists, homestead applications. Anything that has been written or typed on a piece of paper would be included in this group.

tif: File extension for TIFF files. TIFF is the acronym for tagged image file format. Like other graphics formats, it is one of the standard file formats for digitized images.

transparency capability: The ability of a scanner to backlight a transparent object, such as a photo negative or a 35mm slide, so that the object can be scanned and digitized.

TWAIN: Originally thought to mean "technology without an interesting name," the term actually gets its meaning from "ne'er the twain shall meet." This is because the data source manager sits between the driver and the application. This has become the standard interface in scanning. Many graphics programs and genealogy programs are TWAIN compatibile.

uniform resource locator (URL): The address of a page on the Internet. Just as you and I rely on addresses to find stores and restaurants, we rely on URLs to locate pages on the Internet. Without this important string of characters, you cannot get to a Web site.

upload: To transfer a file from a local computer to a remote host. *Upload* is synonymous with *transmit,* while *download* is synonymous with *receive.* See **download.**

user error: Something that we hate to admit. We will always blame the computer or program for a mishap before we admit that perhaps we didn't enter something quite right. *User error* generally means we didn't type something in correctly or accurately to tell the computer what we wanted in the first place.

USGenWeb: A project supported by volunteers. Volunteers manage state sites, and county coordinators maintain Web sites with information of all kinds pertinent to a county.

vital records: A term used to refer to those certificates recorded by civil authorities. Generally this includes birth records, marriage and divorce records, and death records.

WAV: Windows audio visual. Sound files that work with Microsoft Windows Media Player and Microsoft Windows Sound Recorder.

Web browser: A software application that allows you to maneuver around the Internet. Through the browser software's graphical interface you can click buttons, select links, or read text. The browser lets the user access sites on the Internet either by links within other pages or by typing in the URL of a Web page.

Web page: A document on the World Wide Web that is formatted with HTML, the standard format in which documents are exchanged on the Web. Web pages are found via addresses called URLs.

Web page editor: Allows you to create Web pages, usually without needing to know HTML coding.

Web site: A location managed by a single entity that provides information such as text, graphics, and audio files to users as well as connections (called hyperlinks or links) to other Web sites on the Internet. Every Web site has a home page, the initial document seen by users, which acts as a table of contents to the rest of the site.

Index

Explore your family history with Betterway Books!

Long-Distance Genealogy Gathering information from sources that can't be visited is a challenge for all genealogists. This book will teach you the basics of long-distance research. You'll learn what types of records and publications can be accessed from a distance, problems associated with the process, how to network, how to use computer resources, and special "last resort" options.
ISBN 1-55870-535-X, paperback, 272 pages, #70495-K

Your Guide to the Family History Library The Family History Library in Salt Lake City is the largest collection of genealogy and family history materials in the world. No other repository compares for both quantity and *quality* of research materials. Written for beginning and intermediate genealogists, *Your Guide to the Family History Library* will help you use the library's resources effectively, both on site and online.
ISBN 1-55870-578-3, paperback, 272 pages, #70513-K

The Weekend Genealogist Maximize your family research efficiency! With this guide, you can focus your efforts in searching for family documents while still gaining the best results. Organization and research techniques are presented in a clear, easy-to-follow format perfect for advanced researchers *and* beginners. You'll learn how to work more efficiently using family history facilities, the Internet—even the postal service!
ISBN 1-55870-546-5, paperback, 144 pages, #70496-K

Your Guide to the Federal Census This one-of-a-kind book examines the "nuts and bolts" of census records. You'll find out where to view the census and how to use it to find ancestors quickly and easily. Easy-to-follow instructions and case studies detail nearly every scenario for tracing family histories through census records. You'll also find invaluable appendixes, a glossary of census terms, and extraction forms.
ISBN 1-55870-588-0, paperback, 208 pages, #70525-K

These and other fine titles from Betterway Books are available from your local bookstore, online supplier, or by calling (800) 221-5831.